LEGISLATURES IN EVOLUTION /
LES LÉGISLATURES
EN TRANSFORMATION

LEGISLATURES IN EVOLUTION /
LES LÉGISLATURES
EN TRANSFORMATION

Edited by / Sous la direction de
Charles Feldman
Geneviève Tellier
David Groves

University of Ottawa Press / Les Presses de l'Université d'Ottawa
2022

University of Ottawa **Press**
Les **Presses** de l'Université d'Ottawa

The University of Ottawa Press (UOP) is proud to be the oldest of the francophone university presses in Canada and the oldest bilingual university publisher in North America. Since 1936, UOP has been enriching intellectual and cultural discourse by producing peer-reviewed and award-winning books in the humanities and social sciences, in French and in English.

www.press.uOttawa.ca

Library and Archives Canada Cataloguing in Publication

Titre: Legislatures in evolution / edited by Charles Feldman, Geneviève Tellier, David Groves = Les législatures en transformation / sous la direction de Charles Feldman, Geneviève Tellier, David Groves.
Autres titres : Législatures en transformation
Noms : Feldman, Charles, éditeur intellectuel. | Tellier, Geneviève, éditeur intellectuel. | Groves, David, 1987 – éditeur intellectuel.
Description : Mention de collection : Politics and public policy | Comprend des références bibliographiques. | Textes en anglais et en français.
Identifiants : Canadiana (livre imprimé) 20220163847F | Canadiana (livre numérique) 20220163596F |
ISBN 9780776637891 (couverture souple) | ISBN 9780776637907 (couverture rigide) | ISBN 9 780 776 637 914 (PDF) | ISBN 9780776637921 (EPUB)
Vedettes-matière : RVM : Parlements. | RVM : Parlements—Canada. | RVM : Procédure parlementaire—Canada.
Classification : LCC JF511.L44 2 022 | CDD 328—dc23

Legal Deposit: Third Quarter 2022
Library and Archives Canada

Production Team

Copy-editing	Trish O'Reilly-Brennan
Copy-editing	Pierrette Brousseau
Proofreading	Sabine Cerboni and Tanina Drvar
Typesetting	Nord Compo
Cover design	Lefrançois agence marketing B2B

Cover Image

Photo by / photo de Charles Feldman

The University of Ottawa Press gratefully acknowledges the support extended to its publishing list by the Government of Canada, the Canada Council for the Arts, the Ontario Arts Council, the Social Sciences and Humanities Research Council and the Canadian Federation for the Humanities and Social Sciences through the Awards to Scholarly Publications Program, and by the University of Ottawa.

ONTARIO ARTS COUNCIL
CONSEIL DES ARTS DE L'ONTARIO
an Ontario government agency
un organisme du gouvernement de l'Ontario

Canada Council   Conseil des arts
for the Arts   du Canada

Canadä

uOttawa

Table of Contents / Table des matières

List of Figures / Liste des figures

List of Tables / Liste des tableaux

Legislatures in Evolution

Charles Feldman and David Groves

Abstract

Understanding the evolution of parliamentary institutions is necessary in order to know our past, understand our present, and guide our future. This introduction outlines an analytical framework for examining evolution in legislative institutions—as well as providing examples from various legislatures at various times. Different themes in parliamentary evolution emerge as we introduce the various chapters of the book and connect them, demonstrating the depth, breadth, and importance of studying legislatures and their evolution. This introduction provides important contextual information to situate this work within the broader narrative of parliamentary evolution and reform.

Résumé

Pour connaître notre passé, expliquer notre présent et orienter notre avenir, il est nécessaire de comprendre l'évolution des institutions parlementaires. Ce chapitre propose un cadre d'analyse pour expliquer l'évolution des institutions législatives en plus de fournir des exemples tirés de diverses assemblées législatives à travers le temps. Ce chapitre présente aussi les divers thèmes abordés dans les différents chapitres de cet ouvrage afin de démontrer la profondeur, l'ampleur et l'importance des études traitant des assemblées législatives et notamment de leur transformation. Enfin, ce chapitre offre des informations contextuelles afin de situer cet ouvrage dans le cadre plus large des réformes parlementaires.

Although legislatures are grounded in traditions—some many centuries old—they are nonetheless evolving institutions. Studying their evolution is necessary to know our past, understand our present, and guide our future.

We can conceive of a legislature's evolution in two primary contexts: changes outside the legislature that permit it to evolve, and evolution wholly from within the legislature.

The first context is perhaps the most readily apparent. For example, technological innovation has allowed legislatures to evolve in terms of how they disseminate their proceedings, from written records to radio and television broadcasts, to streaming over the Internet in real time. Further, technological innovation—coupled most recently with the realities of the COVID-19 pandemic—has led some legislatures to adopt practices that were unimaginable just a few short decades ago, such as permitting electronic petitions, facilitating remote video participation in proceedings, and even, in some cases, allowing for voting by electronic means.

Considering technological innovation more broadly and historically, the impact of something like the advent of rail or air travel on the ability of a legislature to recall its members and have them quickly in attendance cannot be understated. This is to say nothing of the myriad modern conveniences that might be taken for granted but at one time were significant challenges for legislatures in managing their sittings, such as controlling the temperature in the chamber (Schoenefeldt 2018) and ensuring adequate lighting (Gillin 2017). Indeed, at the time of this writing, Canada's House of Commons meets in a temporary home in West Block with a state-of-the-art ceiling with mechanical louvers to control light (Coffey 2019)—a far cry from the time in history when members of the UK House of Commons complained of the legislature's wax candles dripping on them.

In the second context, evolution wholly within a legislature, procedural and practice innovation is likely the first thing that springs to mind. A 1966 article discussing recently implemented reforms to the House of Commons notes, for example, the elimination of lunch and dinner breaks to provide more time for debate as well as the removal of appeals from Speaker's decisions (Hockin 1966).

It is quite difficult to conceive of the House in its current form taking such breaks or allowing itself to depart from a decision of the Speaker.

Of course, procedural and practice evolution are not necessarily rapid. With the *Royal Assent Act*'s passage in 2002, Canada became the last Commonwealth country to modernize royal assent by allowing for a traditional ceremony to be dispensed with in favour of assent through written declaration (Richardson 2004). For decades prior, parliamentarians had complained about the delays and formalities that were occasioned by the traditional assent ceremony that required the Governor General to be present in person for a ceremony involving members of both Houses of Parliament to give assent to bills.

While that particular evolution may have been a long time in coming, it does not appear that parliamentarians are clamouring for a return to a bygone era. Indeed, in 2021, we see an example of the Senate adopting a bill received from the House of Commons without amendment just before 6:00 p.m. and returning from an adjournment at 7:00 p.m. to hear the Speaker announce that at 6:27 p.m. His Excellency the Administrator of the Government of Canada gave the legislation royal assent by written declaration (Senate 2021). Such an occurrence would have been simply unfathomable less than 20 years ago.

One challenge with institutions in evolution is that it is never possible to say with certainty that modifications made at one point in time represent the final state of affairs. In recent years, the Senate of Canada has seen significant changes (Furey 2017). For instance, for the first time in history, a majority of senators are not affiliated with any political party (Bridgman 2020). This has affected numerous facets of how the Senate functions, including how it reviews bills received from the House of Commons (Heard 2020).

In 2022, government legislation enshrined some of the recent changes to the Senate in statute. Further, the government's *Briefing Book for the President of the Queen's Privy Council for Canada* provides for that minister playing a "facilitating role in a number of non-legislative changes that could be introduced to reinforce the Senate's transition towards a less partisan chamber" (Privy Council Office 2020). Both current and future discussions about the Senate's role within Parliament cannot be properly contextualized without understanding the debates surrounding the Upper House throughout the course of Canadian history. Indeed, the Library of Parliament documents that discussions around Senate reform date to 1874, a mere seven years after Confederation (Barnes et al. 2009). Documenting and describing evolution in legislatures is essential if we are to understand how we have arrived where we are. Learning from what has happened allows us to prepare better for the future and to avoid repeating the mistakes of the past.

It should be considered that not every change made in a legislature is a lasting one. For example, several Canadian legislative assemblies have reduced the number of seats at various points in history and then, subsequently, increased them again (Marland 2019). In Ontario's Legislative Assembly, seats were rearranged into a semicircle (horseshoe) for a brief point in the 1930s before returning to the traditional Westminster style of government and opposition benches facing each other (Anthony and Ruderman 2018).

As well, a reform may not see immediate impact or may fall into disuse. As an example of the former, Bosc and Gagnon (2017) explain in *House of Commons Procedure and Practice* that reforms to the Standing Orders made in 1994 to allow bills to be referred to legislative committees were not taken advantage of, because the House simply reverted to its older practices. It has rarely used the new procedure since. As an example of the latter, a practice to allow debates in the Legislative Assembly of Manitoba to be sped up—initially introduced to help legislators who were farmers to return to their harvests—has not seen use in decades (Grafton 2011).

Pinpointing certain moments in the evolution of legislatures can be straightforward, particularly if the reforms find expression in a modification to the applicable Standing Orders, rules, or statutes. However, behind every moment in evolution is a broader narrative. Understanding the genesis and impact of these moments requires not only reflecting on the politics of the decision—but understanding the powers, forces, and players involved, some of which may find no expression in the formal parliamentary record.

Importantly, the conceptional distinction drawn above between internal and external evolution becomes simply impossible to maintain in many contexts. Indeed, it is not possible to discuss parliamentary evolution without wading into the often-circular discussion over whether Parliament changes society or whether society changes Parliament.

The evolution of salary and entitlements for parliamentarians provides a clear illustration of this phenomenon. In 1867, Members of

Parliament (MPs) received a sessional indemnity of $600 for the few weeks during which parliamentary business occurred and took them from their private occupations. As Canada rapidly grew and expanded after the Second World War, Parliament began to meet more frequently. Eventually, parliamentarian became a full-time occupation with associated remuneration (Commission to Review Allowances of Members of Parliament 1998, 38). While Parliament was shaping Canada, Canada was equally shaping Parliament.

With expanded access to the legislature—and changing societal norms—membership in Parliament came to include representation from groups that had previously been excluded from the political class. It is not surprising that during this time, Canada saw the election of its first visible minority MPs, and growing numbers of women became parliamentarians (Bird, Saalfeld, and Wust 2011). Eventually, legislative reforms including the *Canadian Charter of Rights and Freedoms* enshrined democratic rights, including a qualification right for membership in Parliament.

This evolution is by no means complete, as legislatures continue to address novel situations posed by their evolving membership. For example, Nova Scotia became the first Canadian legislature to have a person with quadriplegia, Kevin S. Murphy, serve as a presiding officer in 2013. Upon assuming the Speakership, Mr. Murphy did not wear the traditional Speaker's robe and the Speaker's riser was removed to accommodate his mobility device (Doucette 2013). As well, legislatures across Canada are addressing certain realities of legislators who are parents, for example, accommodating parental leave and permitting breastfeeding during proceedings (Lajoie 2019). Further, Canada's House of Commons has recently adopted new rules regarding the use of Indigenous languages in proceedings (Murphy and Goodwin 2021).

Changing societal currents also find expression in the evolution of legislatures. For example, the Senate's Standing Committee on Internal Economy, Budgets and Administration has in recent years moved to require anti-harassment training and unconscious bias training in the Senate workplace (Ryckewaert 2021). As well, the Senate has, on several recent occasions, considered its policies in relation to harassment (Chen 2021). Similarly, the Northwest Territories recently considered guaranteed seats for women to ensure their representation in the legislature. Ultimately, however, the guarantees were not needed. After the October 2019 provincial election, the territory went from having the lowest percentage of women legislators to the highest for any Canadian jurisdiction (Green 2019).

As the foregoing illustrates, there are numerous ways in which legislatures are evolving. It would be impossible, of course, for every possible point of evolution to be addressed comprehensively in one work. Accordingly, the editors of this collection have identified certain facets of legislatures in evolution that we felt warranted particular study and reflection. The authors of the various chapters then document and describe the evolution of specific practices and provide important insight on what conclusions, if any, can be drawn from that history. While every evolution is necessarily the product of its own unique context—including the individual legislature and its practices, the politics at the time, the personalities of key players involved, etc.— the experiences of one assembly inevitably provide important points of reference for others. Indeed, the lessons of an evolutionary process in one legislature may have universal resonance.

It is often said that Canadian parliamentary democracy features some of the strongest party discipline in the Westminster world. Academics, pundits, and even some legislators themselves lament what they perceive as a decline in independence, dissent, and cross-party voting among parliamentarians. It is often theorized that party discipline is imposed from "above"—by overbearing party leaders or prime ministers, eager to stifle any sign of internal caucus strife that could be read as weakness.

Cristine de Clercy and Alex Marland demonstrate in "Party Discipline in Canada: Former Members of Parliament Speak Up" that the sources of party discipline are far more complex than this narrative suggests. Drawing from the Samara Centre of Democracy's invaluable collection of exit interviews with retiring or departing MPs from the 38th to the 41st Parliaments, de Clercy and Marland examine and compare the perspectives of these legislators on various aspects of discipline within Parliament and, in so doing, find that discipline is not just top down. Rather, MPs impose discipline among themselves for many reasons, including loyalty to their caucus members, a team mentality, and even a sense that discipline may prevent the capacity of special interests to sway votes. So while members may fear or resent the party whip, they also understand the value of the position.

For any Canadian who looks fondly at the comparatively freer practices of the United Kingdom, de Clercy and Marland's findings must be carefully considered. Can Canadian legislatures promote a culture of looser discipline when members themselves see it, in some contexts, as a virtue?

The #MeToo era has forced institutions across Canadian society to take responsibility for violence, bullying, sexual harassment, and other harmful conduct that they have up until now ignored—and legislatures are no exception. But as Charles Feldman writes in "Aborder le harcèlement sexuel dans les législatures : description d'un lieu de travail 'unique'" (Addressing Sexual Harassment in Legislatures: Describing a "Unique" Workplace), the unique features of legislative workplaces mean that legislatures cannot necessarily rely on the same approaches or mechanisms that other institutions do to prevent, investigate, and remedy harmful behaviours.

Feldman observes several characteristics that make legislatures "unique" workplaces. They are the site of a multiplicity of employment relationships, each of which may carry its own contractual and legislative obligations around addressing harassment. Attempting to apply a uniform anti-harassment policy will always be a struggle when multiple sources of law cover various participants in an uneven and sometimes contradictory fashion. A given employer may have employees who operate under different regimes—for example, a legislator's staff at the legislature versus those who work at the constituency office. Feldman also describes in detail how legislatures are "shared spaces," which Canadians from every walk of life may enter thus multiplying the variety of contexts in which harassment or misconduct might occur, while having, at the same time, uncertain boundaries; that is, legislators do as much work outside the legislature—in their constituencies or elsewhere—as they do within it, and any one-size-fits-all policy will struggle to accommodate this reality. There is also the unique reality of legislators themselves, people who are not hired to their positions and thus have no employment "contract" under which they operate. As if this were not enough complication, questions also arise about parliamentary privilege and how an anti-harassment policy intersects with free speech and other legislative immunities.

Feldman's chapter reminds the reader that parliamentary evolution requires a delicate balance—adjusting with the times while acknowledging the particularities of the legislative world. Creating and maintaining a safe legislative workplace is imperative, but success can come only through acknowledging and accounting for its unique nature.

As the broader Canadian society works to re-examine and rede-
fine the relationship between Indigenous and non-Indigenous Peoples,
its legislatures are doing the same. Beyond ensuring necessary and
significant representation for Indigenous persons within the composition of those bodies, some Canadians are asking how Canada's duties
to Indigenous communities can be better incorporated into its legislative processes.

This question most notably arose in 2018, when the Supreme
Court of Canada was asked to consider the Crown's constitutional
duty to consult with Indigenous persons in the preparation of legislation. In *Mikisew Cree First Nation v. Canada (Governor General in Council)*,
the Court concluded that it could not enforce such a duty within the
parliamentary process. Steven Chaplin, former senior legal counsel at
the House of Commons and current adjunct professor at the University
of Ottawa, notes that this need not be the end of the conversation.

In "Parliament, the Duty to Consult, and Reconciliation," Chaplin
argues that while the duty to consult in the "development, introduction, and shepherding of legislation" cannot be enforced judicially, it
nonetheless exists. However, it is the responsibility of Parliament, as
the body that is tasked with the scrutiny and oversight of the Crown's
actions and legislative agenda, to ensure that this duty is appropriately
discharged.

Chaplin proposes two procedural changes that would enhance
Parliament's capacity to review the Crown's actions in light of its obligations to Indigenous people: First, the imposition of a requirement on
the government, when introducing legislation, to provide a written
statement on how it discharged its duty to consult during the development of the bill. Second, the appointment of an Indigenous Advisor,
who would serve Parliament in a similar fashion to the Parliamentary
Budget Officer in informing legislators about how the government's
agenda affects Indigenous communities in Canada. His argument—in
favour of a "made in Parliament" solution—reflects an attempt to
evolve the legislature to align with broader societal concerns, all while
recognizing Parliament's unique constitutional position.

Budgetary and financial scrutiny has always been a key function
of legislatures. How such scrutiny is conducted, however, is in con-
stant flux.

In "Les députés du contrôle budgétaire entre passion, intérêt et
désaffection" (Members Exercising Budgetary Control: Passion,
Interest and Disaffection), Anthony M. Weber takes a close look at

what drives legislators when examining government spending. Drawing on 32 interviews with legislators in Quebec, Luxembourg, and France, Weber posits that they come to this role with three distinct perspectives.

Some legislators, the *enquêteurs*, approach the task with intensity and dedication, animated by a sense that financial scrutiny is the central mission of all legislators. They remain engaged in the scrutiny of spending even after it has been approved.

Others, the *représentants*, see spending oversight in an instrumental fashion, seeking to ensure the spending decisions that best support their constituents. Their principal concern is being faithful to the wishes of their voters. As such, they are far more involved in *ex ante* oversight—reviewing proposed spending—to ensure that the interests of their constituents are represented in budget allocations.

Those whose parliamentary passions and pursuits lie elsewhere, are more than happy to leave the work of financial oversight to their colleagues. These *absents* are characterized by a lack of knowledge of, or interest in, budgetary processes. They tend to remain unengaged in financial oversight, deferring to their colleagues, in favour of pursuing other issues.

Weber's chapter reminds the reader that when examining the evolution of a particular legislative practice, the motivations of individual legislators cannot be ignored. It is true that legislators' behaviour is constrained by the practices under which they operate: An MP can only conduct as much scrutiny as the Standing Orders permit. But it is equally true that MPs, as masters of their own procedures, will act in the ways that they feel are appropriate. For those who feel that Canadian legislatures have, over the years, abandoned their rigorous review of spending, Weber's article poses the challenge: What procedural or structural reforms might motivate legislators to more aggressively guard the public purse?

Daily prayers, which serve to open sittings of legislatures across the country, offer a clear example of the parallel evolution of Canadian society and its deliberative bodies. Such prayers have been a consistent element of Canadian legislative schedules since Confederation, even as Canada has become more pluralistic, more diverse, and more secular. Teale Phelps Bondaroff, Katie Marshall, Ian Bushfield, Ranil Prasad, Noah Laurence, and Adriana Thom, the authors of "Change and Prayers: An Analysis of Prayers in the Legislative Assembly of British Columbia, 2003–2020," take a deep quantitative look at how the practice has evolved in the twenty-first century in the legislature of Canada's most ethnically diverse province.

The authors' research and analysis focuses on the effect of 2019 changes in the Legislative Assembly of British Columbia, which, among other things, expanded the practice of daily prayers to explicitly allow "reflections" as well. Working with transcripts of all prayers given in the legislature from 6 October 2003 to 14 August 2020, they coded these prayers into four categories, from not religious to explicitly sectarian in nature. Among their many findings, the authors observed that the 2019 changes led to a meaningful decline in the percentage of statements making reference to a deity, from 52.8 percent to 30.6 percent. However, they also suggest a possibly counterintuitive outcome: since 2019, those prayers that are sectarian in nature have become more explicit and more overt. As such, they suggest that the 2019 changes amount to only a "mild opening of this agenda item for non-religious content."

Beyond a detailed look at a seldom-discussed element of Canadian parliamentary practice, this chapter offers readers another key insight: changes in procedure drive changes in legislative behaviour. By reducing the explicitly theistic nature of the practice, the legislature opened the door for a variety of new types of "reflective" expressions by its members. However, the authors are undecided on whether the practice, even with this change, actually reflects modern Canadian society. It remains to be seen if, how, or when this practice may further evolve.

Time is Parliament's most precious commodity. For governments, the efficient use of the parliamentary schedule can mean the difference between enacting a legislative agenda and heading into an election with little to show for the time in power. For opposition parties, filibusters and dilatory motions are vital tools for various ends, whether it be to express concern about the government agenda or exert leverage when negotiating amendments and concessions.

Floyd McCormick's "Passive Time Management and the Erosion of Scrutiny of Government Bills in the Yukon Legislative Assembly," offers the reader a vivid example of how time management—one of the most important functions of legislative procedure—can affect the efficacy of a given legislature.

McCormick's account, which focuses on changes to the Standing Orders of the Legislative Assembly since 2000, shows that the assembly has, over time, abandoned active time-management procedures.

Instead, the Assembly has favoured passive time management—that is, pre-set rules about how the Assembly should meet, when, and for how long. These changes were brought about to bring predictability and consistency to the Assembly's schedule but, McCormick argues, they have had significant consequences on the capacity of the legislature to apply meaningful scrutiny to the bills before it.

McCormick draws particular attention to Standing Order 76, adopted on 19 November 2001, which allows the government to bypass stages of the legislative process for any of its bills if they remain on the Order Paper at the end of a sitting and have had a minimum of debate. While the intent of this rule is to ensure that the sitting ends as scheduled without unduly disrupting the capacity of the government to legislate, its effect is to cut short valuable debate. He notes that, of the 308 government bills passed between 2002 and 2019, 87 passed without third reading debate; of those, 17 never even received a review at committee.

Legislative time management requires a careful balancing of interests—ensuring a degree of predictability to encourage participation and transparency, while still guaranteeing that the legislature is capable of imposing genuine and meaningful scrutiny on the government's agenda. McCormick compellingly demonstrates that, without careful consideration, procedural changes around how a legislature organizes its time can have significant and unintended consequences.

* * *

The Canadian Study of Parliament Group is proud to present this collection as part of its mandate to enhance the understanding of parliamentary government and institutions by promoting research and dialogue on legislative systems in Canada. The project was conceived in 2019, far before the COVID-19 pandemic forced many legislatures to evolve quickly into new practices. The impact of COVID-19 on legislatures has been the subject of many works already and further discussion on this can be found in the Conclusion.

The study of legislatures and their evolution must not be merely an academic exercise. Empowering citizens to understand how their legislatures operate and see that they are changing is critical to ensuring engagement. If citizens view their legislatures as anachronisms frozen in time, it may breed a distrust and disregard that, in turn, undermines democratic principles and their associated institutions.

As well, legislators themselves need to understand the context in which they serve. For new parliamentarians, it would be impossible to expect expert mastery of current practices and procedures on day one, let alone knowledge of centuries of Westminster tradition. However, scholars elucidating the evolution of parliaments past can enable those presently in Parliament to chart a course for the betterment of Parliament in the future. Indeed, as the chapters in this book demonstrate, legislatures remain a work in progress.

The editors of this book recognize that it will someday be out of date—the case studies and examples in its chapters will eventually reflect practices no longer in play and even some of the vocabulary used might be seen as reflecting a bygone era. It is hoped, however, that future generations of scholars will continue to reflect critically on legislatures and their evolution. Indeed, we hope that legislatures themselves will continue their evolution and modernization to reflect the realities of a changing world.

The editors wish to thank the various contributors to this volume for sharing their insights and for their patience in the journey to bring this volume to press—one that was complicated by the COVID-19 pandemic. It is hoped that all readers will enjoy, learn, and be inspired by the words and work in the chapters that follow.

References

Anthony, Laura, and Nick Ruderman. 2018. "The Pink Palace and Parliamentary Green." *Canadian Parliamentary Review* 41 (3): 64–65.

Barnes, Andre, Michel Bédard, Caroline Hyslop, Célia Jutras, Jean-Rodrigue Paré, James Robertson, Sebastian Spano, and Hilary Jensen. 2009. *Reforming the Senate of Canada: Frequently Asked Questions.* PRB 09-02E, August 10, 2009. Ottawa: Library of Parliament.

Bird, Karen, Thomas Saalfeld, and Andreas M. Wust, eds. 2011. *The Political Representation of Immigrants and Minorities: Voters, Parties and Parliaments in Liberal Democracies.* London: Routledge.

Bosc, Marc, and André Gagnon, eds. 2017. "The Legislative Process: Historical Perspective." In *House of Commons Procedure and Practice,* 3rd ed. Cowansville: Yvon Blais.

Bridgman, Aengus. 2020. "A Nonpartisan Legislative Chamber: The Influence of the Canadian Senate." *Party Politics.* Published ahead of print, April 6, 2020. https://doi-org.proxy.bib.uottawa.ca/10.1177/1354068820911345

Chen, Alice. 2021. "Praise for New Senate Anti-Harassment Policy, but Concern Remains it Goes too Far—and Not Far Enough." *Hill Times*, March 17, 2021. https://www.hilltimes.com/2021/03/17/praise-for-new -senate-anti-harassment-policy-but-concern-remains-it-goes-too-far -and-not-far-enough/288906.

Coffey, Terry. 2019. "New (Temporary) Home of the House of Commons." *Sustainable Architecture & Building Magazine* (Spring).

Commission to Review Allowances of Members of Parliament. 1998. *Report of the Commission to Review Allowances of Members of Parliament*. Vol. 2. Ottawa: Minister of Public Works and Government Services.

Doucette, Keith. 2013. "Nova Scotia Legislature Elects First Paraplegic to Serve as Speaker." CTV News, October 24, 2013. https://www.ctvnews.ca/politics /nova-scotia-legislature-elects-first-paraplegic-to-serve-as-speaker -1.1511832.

Furey, George. 2017. "The New Senate: Still in Transition." *Canadian Parliamentary Review* 40 (1): 2–5.

Gillin, Edward J. 2017. *The Victorian Palace of Science: Scientific Knowledge and the Building of the Houses of Parliament (Science in History)*. Cambridge: Cambridge University Press.

Grafton, Emily Katherine. 2011. "The Manitoba Legislative Assembly." *Canadian Parliamentary Review* 34 (1): 35–43.

Green, Julie. 2019. "Women Achieve Parity in NWT Legislative Assembly without Guaranteed Seats." *Canadian Parliamentary Review* 42 (4): 4–6.

Heard, Andrew. 2020. "The Effect of Trudeau's New Senate Selection Process in Perspective: The Senate's Review of Commons Bills, 1997–2019." *Canadian Political Science Review* 13 (1): 108–145.

Hockin, Thomas A. 1966. "Reforming Canada's Parliament: The 1965 Reforms and Beyond." *University of Toronto Law Journal* 16 (2): 326–345.

Lajoie, Geneviève. 2019. "Des députés demandent l'allaitement à l'Assemblée nationale." *Le Journal de Québec*, June 3, 2019. https://www.journalde quebec.com/2019/06/03/allaiter-a-lassemblee-nationale.

Marland, Alex. 2019. "Fewer Politicians and Smaller Assemblies: How Party Elites Rationalise Reducing the Number of Seats in a Legislature— Lessons from Canada." *Journal of Legislative Studies* 25 (2): 149–168.

Murphy, Julian R., and Timothy B. Goodwin. 2021. "Indigenous Languages in Parliament: Comparing Canada and Australia." *Canadian Parliamentary Review* 43 (4): 16–21.

Privy Council Office. 2020. *Briefing Book for the President of the Queen's Privy Council for Canada*. https://www.canada.ca/en/democratic-institutions /corporate/transparency/briefing-document/president-queen-privy -council.html.

Richardson, Jessica J. 2004. "Modernisation of Royal Assent in Canada." *Canadian Parliamentary Review* 32 (2): 32–36.

Ryckewaert, Laura. 2021. "Unconscious Bias Training for Senators, Staff Coming to the Upper Chamber." *Hill Times*, February 17, 2021. https://www.hilltimes.com/2021/02/17/unconscious-bias-training-for-senators-staff-coming-to-the-upper-chamber/283592.

Schoenefeldt, Henrik. 2018. "The Historic Ventilation System of the House of Commons, 1840–52: Re-Visiting David Boswell Reid's Environmental Legacy." *Antiquaries Journal* 98 (September): 245–295.

Senate of Canada. 2021. *Debates of the Senate of Canada.* 43rd Parliament, 2nd Session, 152 (39), May 6, 2021, 1439–1440.

CHAPTER 1

Party Discipline in Canada: Former Members of Parliament Speak Up

Cristine de Clercy and Alex Marland[1]

Abstract

Canadian legislators routinely toe the party line when voting on bills and motions and making public remarks. This chapter examines transcripts from 131 in-depth interviews conducted by the Samara Centre for Democracy with Members of Parliament (MPs) who exited Parliament from 2004 to 2015. In examining seven propositions about how these former MPs perceive aspects of party discipline—such as the role of parties and their constitutions, election platforms, social media, team loyalty, and the benefits of formalized parliamentary groups— this chapter shows that many former parliamentarians accept party discipline as a necessary element of parliamentary life. We also find little evidence that the socializing effects of time in office correspond with a more positive view of party discipline.

Résumé

Les législateurs canadiens suivent régulièrement la ligne du parti lorsqu'ils votent sur des projets de loi, sur des motions et lorsqu'ils prononcent des allocutions publiques. Ce chapitre

1   The authors would like to thank David Dumouchel and Andrea Perrella for their comments on an earlier draft and especially the Samara Centre for Democracy for sharing their interview transcripts.

examine le contenu de 131 entrevues de fond, menées par le Centre Samara pour la démocratie, avec des députés qui ont quitté le Parlement entre 2004 et 2015. En examinant sept propositions cherchant à expliquer la façon dont ces anciens députés perçoivent la discipline de parti, comme le rôle des règles des partis, les plateformes électorales, les médias sociaux, la loyauté de l'équipe et la présence de groupes parlementaires formels, nous démontrons que beaucoup de ces anciens députés voient les groupes parlementaires obéissant à des règles et structures internes rigides comme un élément nécessaire de la vie parlementaire. Cependant, nous n'avons pas pu prouver que les effets de socialisation engendrés par la longueur des mandats se traduisent par une vision positive de la discipline de parti.

Canadian legislatures are reputed to have the strictest party discipline of any liberal democracy. For decades, critics have decried the constraints that party affiliation places on voting, how it turns backbenchers into so-called trained seals, and more recently how scripting turns them into party robots. In the House of Commons, members' statements are vetted by the leader's office, private members' motions and bills must navigate the constraints of party values, and Members of Parliament (MPs) have talking points thrust upon them to guide their speeches. Digital communications held the promise of providing an unfiltered forum for private members to speak their minds, represent constituencies, and generally communicate independent thinking; instead, the digital transformation has brought a clampdown on what MPs say. Inside and outside the legislature, private members are now alleged to parrot key messages, robotically recite scripted lines, and repeat the party leader's message of the day. Why do MPs put up with it?

This chapter documents the attitudes of some recently retired MPs towards party discipline. After reviewing what is known about discipline in Canadian party politics, we draw on a content analysis of transcripts of exit interviews with former MPs conducted by the Samara Centre for Democracy, a Toronto-based think tank, to explore how they perceive team loyalty, the role of the extra-parliamentary party, and the rise of social media. As well, we probe whether the socializing effects of time in office appear to deepen Members' commitment to preserving the role of party discipline in politics. We find that many MPs accept party discipline as a necessary facet of Canadian parliamentary life and that socialization does not appear related to how legislators view party discipline.

Review

Over time, party discipline has intensified in Canada (Godbout 2020). Its tightening grip on MPs is somewhat counterintuitive given the arrival of social media, which offers an unfiltered outlet for politicians to speak their minds.[2] Understanding why party discipline is so intense in Canadian parliamentary politics first requires establishing what it is and how it is measured, as well as the deeply rooted culture that sustains it.

There is no standard definition of party discipline. Typically, the term refers to cohesion among members of a parliamentary caucus when voting on bills and motions and the rewards and punishments that condition them to vote as a regimented group (e.g., Lecomte 2018). In reality, it is a much broader phenomenon that pervades the extra-parliamentary party, including the covert vetting of prospective election candidates, a requirement that they uphold party values articulated in the party constitution, and expectations that they publicly adhere to supplied messaging. During an election campaign, party candidates must staunchly defend election platform commitments that they likely played no role in formulating; those who are elected with the governing party have an extra obligation to cheerlead party policies that the cabinet may alter or abandon without consulting the caucus. Canadian political parties have become such monolithic brands that anyone affiliated with the organization must not publicly contravene its core tenets and must exercise extreme caution about causing an unauthorized communications disruption. MPs are acutely aware that tumult results from going off message, and therefore they self-censor what they say and do in public. Those farthest removed from the leader, such as candidates in unwinnable seats and rank-and-file members of electoral district associations, are easiest for party officials to expel from the party. A higher tolerance threshold exists for sitting MPs and members of the leader's inner circle.

Each parliamentary party leader has agents to whom aspects of party discipline are delegated. The House leader is responsible for

---

2   For a thoughtful discussion of the opportunities and limitations offered to parliamentarians by digital democracy see Bigelow (2009).

negotiating the parliamentary agenda, imparting the caucus position on issues, and readying MPs for Question Period. The party whip is a human resources manager who sorts out internal office and staffing matters, coordinates assignments, attempts to resolve disagreements, distributes vote sheets, and monitors attendance for quorum purposes. The government whip has a special obligation to deliver votes. The caucus chair hosts caucus meetings and, along with the whip, organizes social activities to keep morale up. Together, these House officers and their staff, particularly those in the leader's office, guide the actions of the parliamentary caucus.

Researchers' ability to measure party discipline is encumbered by its invisibility and the resolve of MPs not to discuss internal matters. In some parliamentary groups, voting is coordinated using the three-line whip system, whereby MPs are informed whether a vote is considered level one (free vote), level two (encouraged to vote with the leader), or level three (must vote the party line)—but typically the party's vote instructions are secret. Periodically there are bursts of media coverage about party representatives who incur the party leader's wrath for being disruptive. Media stories erupt about the leader's control over nominating election candidates, about the removal of an MP from a parliamentary committee after unsanctioned behaviour, and about the ability of the party whip to withhold speaking privileges in the House. Sometimes MPs rebuff the party line by voting differently than the rest of the caucus, although this normally occurs on matters of little consequence, such as a private member's bill or earlier stages of a government bill (Overby, Tatalovich, and Studlar 1998). MPs contradicting party policy is relatively rare, because most of them inherently support the party (Chartash et al. 2020) and because of internal disciplinary measures (Kam 2001). The Samara Centre has observed the frequency of MPs voting along party lines during the 42nd Parliament from 2015 to 2019:

> On average, an MP participated in close to 1,000 votes over the course of the 42nd Parliament. The data finds that the average MP voted with their parties an amazing 99.6% of the time. That loyalty rate may be modestly inflated, given Opposition-forced voting marathons which generated numerous recorded votes as a protest tactic. Nevertheless: Eighty percent of MPs cast five or fewer dissenting votes over the course of the Parliament. Forty-three MPs voted with their party a perfect 100% of the time. (Thomas, Petit-Vouriot, and Morden 2020, 13)

Another Samara Centre study, conducted in 2018, found that 51 percent of sitting MPs were dissatisfied with collaboration across party lines and 31 percent felt that control emanating from the leader's office was an obstacle to parliamentary work (Petit-Vouriot, Morden, and Anderson 2019, 8). Evidently, there are diverging opinions among MPs about whether party discipline is a pressing concern.

One driver of party discipline is the confidence convention. MPs on the government side of the House must vote with the cabinet on major bills and motions, such as a budget implementation bill, although confidence votes are expanded to encompass non-critical issues in order to require caucus solidarity (Heard 2007). At stake is the principle of responsible government—that is, that the cabinet must have the support of the legislature; if a confidence vote is lost, the prime minister is expected to recommend that the governor general dissolve Parliament so that a general election may be held. A government-side MP who votes differently than the government on a confidence vote is addressed in the harshest possible terms—eviction from the caucus—which potentially spells the end of their parliamentary career. Members of opposition caucuses face less pressure to vote the party line, particularly those in smaller parties, although shadow ministers in the Official Opposition might be expected to vote in unison to present an image of a government in waiting. The resulting strict party discipline on legislative voting is a "dark state of affairs" that causes some observers to believe that Parliament has become "a dead letter" (Brodie 2018, 77).

The hidden aspects of party discipline are so obscure that researchers may not even know what to look for, let alone how to measure it. MPs themselves are often unable to associate cause and effect between a defiant action and its consequence. In order to minimize negative publicity and avoid the disruption that would arise from establishing what appears to be a precedent, leaders and their House officers levy punishments in subtle ways. Non-compliant MPs can lose an appointment or be demoted during a general shuffle of roles. Their requests can be denied, and opportunities no longer offered. Disapproval is expressed by preventing an MP from delivering a member's statement, rescinding permission to go on an all-expenses paid trip, or withholding permission to speak in the House. They may find that the whip is more reluctant on administrative matters such as a request to fly home from Ottawa on a Thursday. Aggrieved caucus colleagues deliver some of the harshest punishment by giving a recalcitrant MP the cold shoulder or a tongue-lashing. And conversely, there are rewards for compliance, such as gaining a title that carries prestige and a salary increase or being invited to represent the party on a public affairs broadcast, as well as improved social standing in the group. Leaders must be careful when they dispense perks lest they spur jealously and resentment; equally, admonishment is a delicate matter because MPs who feel isolated and excluded are more likely to dissent (Garner and Letki 2005). However, most of these intra-party dimensions occur in private settings, often in an uneven manner that further complicates their analysis.

Scholars' preferred method for measuring party discipline—or, more specifically, cohesion—is to examine MPs' voting records. This is understandable given that the publicly available data may be the best available proxy. After all, how a legislator voted is a formal registration of whether or not they went along with the party line. For a century, parliamentary observers have commented on the prevalence of party cohesion in the House of Commons (Epstein 1964, 52), and a recent significant study of historical voting showed that changes to the Standing Orders gradually reduced MPs' individual agency (Godbout 2020). Still, analyzing roll call votes is problematic, because MPs who disagree with their party simply do not vote (Longley 2003) and, as the earlier Samara Centre passage identified, frequency counts are inflated by routine procedural votes including during a filibuster. The quantitative analysis also reduces party discipline to legislative voting, when in fact it encompasses a broader array of parliamentary privileges, as well as representation generally (Koop, Bastedo, and Blidook 2018).

A paradox of party discipline is its terrible reputation—despite its sustained widespread practice. Party discipline smacks of authoritarianism; thus, it can be perceived as anti-democratic. Few, on the other hand, defend its considerable benefits, which include making life easier for MPs by reducing the time needed to figure out how to vote or take a policy position and encouraging the caucus to achieve consensus on contentious issues. Perhaps the greatest reason for its persistence, though, is the electoral benefits that result from being able to present a united public image—compared with the turmoil that results from even a hint of division, including allegations of weak leadership. Political groups that have criticized the party establishment, such as the Progressives in the 1920s and Reformers in the 1990s, have done well on the campaign trail as "anti-parties" but have struggled to operate post-election in a system that rewards solidarity. From the moment they get involved in political life, party candidates are told about the perils of going off message and the benefits of party unity. Once in office, they are swamped with information; most are unable to process the deluge well enough to arrive at their own judgments or adequately hold the government to account (Boyer 2004). This creates an appetite for being spoon-fed messaging, and newly elected representatives quickly adjust to a level of cohesion that both simplifies their work and makes it easier for the leader to lead (Kilgour and Kirsner 1988, 10). Only a small number of MPs, usually those on the periphery of power, speak out publicly against message coordination and recoil at the party control that allegedly prevents them from representing their constituents.

The structures that condition toeing the party line are engrained within tales told by sitting and retired MPs. Upon assuming office, they can be astonished to see that there are intense rivalries within the party caucus that are never exposed to the public (Guay 2002). They are repeatedly informed that "Canadian politics is a team sport," meaning they should relinquish individualism for the good of the group, and in return the group will look out for them (Reid 1993, 2). They constantly experience "stresses and tensions" as they attempt to balance dilemmas of representation that pit the party's position against constituent opinions (Penner 1991, 22) and are faced with reconciling personal conviction with ambition (Brown 1994).

As MPs accumulate years of service in the party caucus, many of them become more loyal to the party leadership and, so, less likely to dissent (Kam 2009, 36). MPs view politics as a team endeavour. David Docherty observes that MPs are socially conditioned to accept party discipline as long as they are part of a parliamentary group:

> Time spent inside the legislative environment helps to warm members to the virtues of party discipline. Members of Parliament are far more willing than candidates to accept the constraints of party discipline, and careerist politicians seem more willing than most to defend the rationale behind strict adherence to caucus decisions. In fact, members indicate they find some virtue in party discipline, beyond the opportunity for personal promotion. (Docherty 1997, 164)

On the other hand, recent analysis of the historical canon of division votes in the House of Commons finds that veteran MPs have not always been more likely to toe the party line (Godbout 2020, 118). Regardless of how many years of experience they have, many MPs seem to accept that party discipline is necessary for parliamentary politics to work and to believe in the importance of being a team player. Others are resentful of party control and constantly express a desire for greater freedom to represent constituent interests or personal views.

The Samara Centre for Democracy routinely compiles insights from former and current MPs to inform recommendations that, if adopted, would empower the legislative branch. The think tank has repeatedly sounded the alarm about excessive party discipline. In *Tragedy in the Commons: Former Members of Parliament Speak Out About Canada's Failing Democracy*, Samara Centre researchers report former MPs holding diverging opinions about party discipline in the 38th to 40th Parliaments, with some ex-MPs embracing partisanship and others voicing discomfort (Loat and MacMillan 2015). For MPs exiting the 41st Parliament, the Samara Centre detected increased frustration with the polarization of partisanship. Researchers identified concern about extreme partisanship, an inability to hold party leaders to account, intense peer pressure to behave as a team player, the hollowing out of local electoral district associations, and the growing influence of the leader's staff (Morden, Hilderman, and Anderson 2018). The organization warns of "unhealthy partisanship," namely party uniformity that polarizes caucuses, vests more power in the leader and House officers, fuels polarization and partisan hostilities, and makes cross-party collaboration impractical (Thomas, Petit-Vouriot, and Morden 2020, 13).

MPs going along willingly with party discipline seems incompatible with representation ideals. Scholarly awareness of party control extending outside the legislature increased when the Conservative governments led by Stephen Harper from 2006 to 2015 began to be characterized by campaign-style communications. It is notable that this period was also marked by the rise of social media. A permanent campaigning approach to governance took hold, whereby the executive branch emphasized "communications control, carefully crafted messages, and message discipline" (Esselment 2014). And after a brief settling-in period, this communications emphasis persisted in the Liberal government headed by Justin Trudeau, who appears to give high priority to social media visuals (Remillard, Bertrand, and Fisher 2019). The marketing mindset of message repetition, spin, and talking points now permeates Canadian party politics to such an extent that MPs have added the role of brand ambassador to that of legislator and constituency caseworker in their repertoire (Marland 2020). The general public—unaware of the considerable internal and external pressures on a caucus to present a united public face—is baffled when their MP seems to "unflinchingly support" the party leader (de Clercy 2018, 151). The resulting perception that party leaders are perverting democracy is easier to grasp than the possibility that many MPs welcome vote sheets and message lines.

Hypotheses and Method

We explore seven hypotheses around the institutional structures that contribute to party discipline. Coursing through our propositions is an expectation that the more an MP gains experience in the House, thereby working with their caucus colleagues in a variety of circumstances, the more that MP will perceive party discipline and the tools of party discipline in a positive light. More experienced MPs should communicate a better opinion of the instruments and exercise of party discipline, including more support for loyalty to the party caucus and for the exercise of discipline over groups and individuals, than do their less experienced counterparts.

The first proposition we would like to test posits that MPs perceive party constitutions as a significant source of a leader's disciplinary power, which is essential for ensuring party cohesion (P1). Every major, competitive political party in Canada has a constitutional document that outlines political values, organizes the party's structure and internal processes, and serves a legal purpose (de Clercy 2018; Smith and Gauja 2010). The principles and tenets in the party constitution empower party leaders and ensure that they control the most prized rewards of political life, such as representing the party in a general election and financial resources. We anticipate that former MPs will view party constitutions as a source of a leader's disciplinary power that is essential for ensuring party cohesion.

In a similar vein, election platforms support the exercise of party discipline and cohesive messaging. Election promises are critical elements for attracting supporters and for guiding the party in the post-election period (Wesley and Nauta 2020). These commitments provide the prime minister, the cabinet, and House officers with the capacity to demand that parliamentary secretaries and backbenchers support the legislative manifestations of pledges that were validated by voters (Birch and Pétry 2019). A second proposition (P2) reflects our anticipation that former MPs, particularly those who spent time on the government side of the House, perceive leaders as gaining disciplinary power from the election platform and the confidence convention.

We are also interested in conflicting loyalties. Once elected, MPs become part of a team that functions in a specific political context. As parliamentary scholar C. E. S. Franks put it, the "essence of a good sports team is discipline, coherence and co-ordination" (Franks 1987, 109). Team loyalty in a competitive, high stakes context rests upon fealty to the needs of the group and the sublimation of individual self-interest. Belonging to a comparatively larger, extra-parliamentary party group, on the other hand, suggests a looser, less constraining loyalty that may allow or even encourage less disciplined behaviour. We propose that MPs value team loyalty in the parliamentary context (P3) and place less emphasis on the political value of loyalty to the extra-parliamentary party (P4). Furthermore, we anticipate that most MPs see team discipline as a positive when it is applied to the parliamentary group (P5) and a negative when it constitutes a personal constraint (P6). When a party leader sanctions a caucus member for rebuffing the party line, the rest of the caucus supports this sort of discipline, because it ensures the group's cohesion and loyalty to each other and to the leadership. On the other hand, we expect that the individual who is sanctioned will view discipline as a negative. As Franks notes, while MPs often find their parties to be a source of strength and support, they must submerge their identity within the party, which can prove to be quite difficult (Franks 1987, 115).

Finally, we are interested in how digital communications technologies have reinforced existing practices in Canadian politics despite their democratic promise (Small 2016). The proliferation of social media and the diminished role of legacy media have altered the relationship between parliamentary leaders, the party caucus, the broad party, and ordinary citizens. Today, MPs almost ubiquitously use popular social media platforms, with all MPs maintaining a Facebook account and 99 percent having a Twitter account in 2019 (Petit-Vouriot, Morden, and Anderson 2019, 16). Yet behind the scenes, caucus research bureaus provide social media content to MPs and their staff for sharing online and maintain repositories of message lines (Marland 2020, 204–220). In proposition 7 (P7), we propose that MPs do not view social media as a way to offset or escape the strictures of party discipline.

To investigate these seven propositions, we accessed transcripts of 131 in-depth interviews conducted by the Samara Centre with MPs who exited public office from the 38th to 41st parliaments (Table 1.1; Samara Centre for Democracy 2020).[3] Those exit points coincide with successive minority governments and much of Stephen Harper's time as prime minister, a period characterized by an intensification in top-down messaging. Owing to the voluntary nature of the exit interviews and variance of turnover at each election, the collection does not reflect the exact socio-demographic composition of the four parliaments. This is not a random sample of MPs and, therefore, we cannot assume that the views of respondents adequately represent the views of all those in office during the period under study. There are some obvious biases in the group of interviews. For example, most interviews were administered in English. As well, participants might have had different views at different stages of their parliamentary career, particularly if they served on the front benches. Nevertheless, the relatively large number of transcripts represents an impressive level of access and is a robust avenue through which to investigate our propositions.

TABLE 1.1.
Samara Centre Exit Interviews with Retiring or Defeated MPs

Parliament (Dates)	Type	Prime Minister	# Interviews
38th (Oct 2004 –Nov 2005)	Liberal minority	Paul Martin	24 English, 11 French
39th (Apr 2006 –Sept 2008)	Conservative minority	Stephen Harper	27 English, 3 French
40th (Nov 2008 –March 2011)	Conservative minority	Stephen Harper	11 English, 3 French
41st (June 2011 –Aug 2015)	Conservative majority	Stephen Harper	42 English, 10 French

Source: ATLAS.ti (2020) coding of Samara Centre interview transcripts; House of Commons (2020).

---

3   There were 130 transcripts for 131 former MPs because of an interview dyad with two former MPs.

The Samara Centre employed semi-structured interviews to allow the former MPs to express their thoughts within the structure of a common question battery about life as a parliamentarian. The interviews were conducted after a general election that the participants did not contest, or in which they were defeated, and therefore presents retrospective perspectives. Most of the interviews were at least two hours or more in length, with participants addressing many different topics and offering extensive commentary, including candid perspectives about the political process and party discipline. The transcript collection contains more than 1.2 million words.

We explored the seven propositions using ATLAS.ti to analyze unstructured information and non-numerical data. The software originates in grounded theory, which emphasizes the exploration of related concepts through specific means of coding, as well as nested relationships and networked ideas. For each hypothesized relationship, we search the transcript texts using open code groups. For example, when searching for the code group "party discipline," we assembled the following constituent words, terms or phrases: discipline, caucus discipline, cabinet solidarity, leader's power, le pouvoir du chef, le pouvoir du dirigeant politique, le pouvoir du leader politique, and la solidarité du cabinet. Other code groups included election platform, group, individual, loyalty, party, party constitution, social media, and team. Details about the coding are available in *Coding Appendix 1: Code Method and Code Lists* at the University of Western Ontario library repository.[4]

The unit of analysis is the word or phrase reflecting the overarching concept. A "hit" is an occurrence of the specific word or phrase within each of the main code groups. Each hit or code occurrence that the program found was reviewed by one of the authors to determine its veracity. Errors were removed from the final results, and meaningless results with respect to the core concepts under study were ignored. We used the ATLAS.ti program's search capacity to locate and tabulate occurrences of the key word codes. In the following pages, all quotes from former MPs are drawn from the applicable Samara Centre exit interview transcript.

---

4   See https://ir.lib.uwo.ca/politicalsciencepub/157.

Findings

Our search of the Samara Centre's exit interview corpus found more instances of participants discussing party discipline than election platforms or party constitutions.[5] The findings indicate that these institutions do help to structure a leader's power over the caucus. Yet retiring MPs who are intimately familiar with the legislative exercise of discipline apparently regard the party's constitution as a bit of an afterthought and as an unimportant disciplinary constraint. People who talked about election platforms universally mentioned the Liberal Party's 1993 Red Book document and did so in relation to specific policies, as opposed to in the context of party discipline. For example, Charles Hubbard, who sat as a Liberal MP from 1993 to 2008, mentioned the Red Book strictly in the context of the Liberal Party's plans for infrastructure spending. Overall, we found little relationship between the concept of party discipline and ex-MPs mentioning party constitutions or election platforms (P1 and P2).

As one might expect, the relative content of the interview data concerning the concepts of the team and political parties is substantial. The content analysis located several thousand individual mentions of party and team, as well as a smaller number of references to the concept of loyalty.[6] We found support for the third proposition: the concept of loyalty is often linked in the first case to the parliamentary team. Many MPs spoke strongly about their attachment to their colleagues and the party leader. Eleni Bakopanos, a Liberal MP from 1993 to 2006, explained that "whether you like it or not, you belong to a team. I think your loyalty to the values of that political entity [are important]." Bakopanos explained that loyalty to the party organization matters as well, but clarified that by "party" she meant "not the party entity, but the values and principles that the party has represented over decades." So, in her view loyalties are tied to a larger, more enduring kind of party than the formal, narrow extra-parliamentary organization. This view of loyalty is similar to that articulated by Claudette Bradshaw, the Liberal MP from 1997 to 2006,

---

5   Using 17 discrete codes, we found 86 instances of interview participants discussing party discipline, along with 40 references to election platforms and 23 references to party constitutions. Some participants may account for more than one hit.

6   We identified 5,155 mentions of "party," 3,356 of "team," and 344 instances of "loyalty."

who commented, "If you can't be a team player then stay away [from politics] [and if] you can't be loyal to your party then stay away." Raymond Côté, an NDP MP from 2011 to 2015, communicated the deep, personal nature of caucus ties and how the relationship within the party caucus is a familial one. He explained that "a caucus, at the base, is a big family. As in any family, you have brothers and sisters with whom you find yourself to be attached, it is the apple of your eye, there are others, well when you can avoid them you do not bother" (translated from French; all translations in this chapter are those of the authors).

The interview participants routinely presented loyalty to caucus colleagues as being of utmost importance, alongside loyalty to the party leader. We observed that another kind of loyalty was mentioned by a handful of politicians: loyalty to leadership rivals. Several former MPs remarked that the internal leadership tensions between Jean Chrétien and Paul Martin stressed their collegial loyalty. They felt pressured to pick sides within the caucus, which strained their desire to work with the Liberal team. Claude Drouin, a Liberal MP from 1997 to 2006, articulated the challenges he faced as a team player when the leadership rivals sought support from parliamentary caucus members. Initially, he refused to take sides, pointing out that members of a caucus are all friends and colleagues. However not picking a side was difficult; people did not believe him. Eventually he felt pressure to choose one of the leadership camps: "We decided that I was in a clan. I explained that I was a team guy, that when there was a leader in place, I respected the leader. And that when the leader leaves, I will be with the next one and be loyal and faithful" (translated from French). Drouin concluded that the tensions around the leadership turnover negatively affected him in the subsequent election in 2004. He tried to refuse appointment as Prime Minister Martin's parliamentary secretary, partly because he feared the reward would undercut his valued reputation as a team player. Clearly, some legislators were deeply affected by an acrimonious leadership contest that placed great stress on their sense of team solidarity.

We also found that many of these former MPs did not perceive much loyalty to the extra-parliamentary party organization (P4). Omar Alghabra, the Liberal MP from 2006 to 2008 who was later re-elected, put it this way: "There is no such thing as a party [it] is so vast and made up of different individuals." Terence Young, a Conservative MP from 2008 to 2015, remarked, "if you think that being loyal, as I did, to the party is going to pay off in some way to you, [that] the party is going to take care of you or something, forget it! The party is not going to take care of you." For other former parliamentarians such as Kyle Seeback, the Conservative MP from 2011 to 2015 who was subsequently re-elected, views of party loyalty changed with experience:

> Initially I believed in everything the party was doing. I thought we were right on basically every issue and my job was to support every single decision that the party of the prime minister made in Parliament or outside of Parliament. That was my absolute mindset for, I would say, at least the first year to year and a half. [Then] I had a whole series of events that sort of woke me up.

A few former MPs stated that their primary loyalty was not to their colleagues or to their leader but to their constituents. Derek Lee, a Liberal MP from 1988 to 2011, emphasized that he "was always ready to express loyalty to my constituents."

To explore whether the length of time as an MP influences their perspectives on this topic, we examined the interview transcripts of the 15 former MPs who most fully commented on the concept of loyalty, and then summarized their years of experience. As shown in Table 1.2, most of them commented on their deep attachment to their team of party colleagues in the House, and most did not mention loyalty to the extra-parliamentary party or indicated that they held no such loyalty. This was generally true regardless of how long they sat in the Commons. At the same time, two of the most experienced members articulated a view that centred on their enduring commitment to their constituents. From this we might infer that although most MPs perceive loyalty to the caucus team as very important and do not communicate much loyalty to the extra-parliamentary party, a subset possess a deep alliance with their constituents, which can endure across many years of parliamentary service. Even so, the primacy of partisan allegiance ultimately comes through when MPs must cast public votes in the House of Commons (Godbout 2020).

TABLE 1.2.

Former MPs' Loyalty to the Parliamentary and Extra-Parliamentary Parties

Name	Years Served	Party	Loyalty to Parliamentary Group (P3)	Loyalty to Extra-Parliamentary Party (P4)
Derek Lee	23	Liberal	No	No
Keith Martin	18	Reform/ Alliance; Liberal	No	No
Marlene Catterall	17	Liberal	Yes	No
Eleni Bakopanos	13	Liberal	Yes	No
Claudette Bradshaw	9	Liberal	Yes	No
Claude Drouin	9	Liberal	Yes	No
Meghan Leslie	7	NDP	Yes	No
Stephen Owen	7	Liberal	Yes	No
Terence Young	7	Conservative	Yes	No
Omar Alghabra[1]	6	Liberal	Yes	No
Raymond Côté	4	NDP	Yes	No
Kyle Seeback[1]	4	Conservative	Yes	Initially Yes, then No
Stella Ambler	4	Conservative	Yes	Yes
John Efford	4	Liberal	No	No
Guy Côté	2	Bloc Québécois	Yes	No

[1] Re-elected to the House of Commons after the exit interview.

Source: ATLAS.ti (2020) coding of Samara Centre interview transcripts; House of Commons (2020).

In this sub-sample, an outlier is Keith Martin, the former Canadian Alliance leadership contestant who briefly sat as an independent in 2004 when his party transformed into the Conservative Party of Canada and who was then re-elected as a Liberal. Upon announcing his intent to switch parties, Martin cited discomfort with macro policy, such as the war in Iraq, and concern about the community implications of social policies (Yourk 2004). In his exit interview, he expressed increasing discomfort sitting in a caucus with social conservatives and that he agitated on a number of votes when Harper was leader of the official Opposition. But Martin found that taking a stand has consequences:

> [Y]ou marginalize yourself from your party and destroy your future ability to move forward. [...] Right now in Parliament, power trumps public service, negativity trumps positivity, and in the House of Commons, the currency is to destroy the other side by being negative. Ideas are not a currency that is valued in Parliament. Control is paramount and that is exerted over both MPs and the public service. So, Parliament or the public service as an idea generator is of no value within the system; it has no currency.

He went on to say that the political system rewards those who support the leader and "play the game" as a means of self-interested advancement. In his opinion, MPs live a "bipolar existence" of wanting to serve to the best of their ability and yet being pressured to undermine their "sense of self by working as part of a team."

Our fifth proposition holds that MPs will see the exercise of discipline as positive when it is applied to the group, and this perception is stronger if an MP has more years in public office. As well, the sixth proposition suggests that MPs will perceive the exercise of discipline as negative when it is applied to them personally, but they will be more likely to embrace discipline as they gain experience holding public office. We created code groups reflecting the overarching concepts of party discipline, the group, and the individual, and then used ATLAS. ti to explore the document set.[7] The coding process identified 24 participants who discussed the concept at length. We reviewed the context of their remarks to ascertain whether the speaker communicated a clear position. If the speaker did not engage with the topic or provided an ambiguous comment, the cell entry was left blank. The results of this analysis appear in Table 1.3.

---

7   We identified 139 hits for "party discipline," 3,858 for the "group," and 6,220 for the "individual".

TABLE 1.3.

Former MPs' Views on Party Discipline and Social Media

Name	Years Served	Party	Discipline Is Good for the Group (P5)	Discipline Is Bad for Individual MPs (P6)	Social Media Extends Discipline and/or Is Just Another Tool (P7)
Bill Blaikie	29	NDP	Yes		
Libby Davies	18	NDP	Yes		Yes
David Anderson	17	Liberal	Yes		
Marlene Catterall	17	Liberal	Yes		
Jay Hill	17	Reform/CA/ Conservative	Yes		
Irwin Cotler	16	Liberal	Yes	Yes	
Art Hanger	15	Reform/CA/ Conservative	No	Yes	
Andrew Telegdi	15	Liberal	No		
Bill Graham	14	Liberal	Yes		
Reg Alcock	13	Liberal	Yes		
Roger Galloway	13	Liberal	No	Yes	Yes
Pat O'Brien	13	Conservative	No		
Judy Wasylycia-Leis	13	NDP	Yes	No	
Stéphane Bergeron	12	Bloc Québécois	Yes		
Paul De Villers	12	Liberal	Yes		
Bill Matthews	11	PC; Liberal	No		
Odina Desrochers	9	Bloc Québécois	No	Yes	Yes

Christian Paradis	9	Conservative	Yes	No	Yes
Bob Rae	9	NDP; Liberal	Yes	Yes	Yes
Olivia Chow	8	NDP	Yes		
Brian Fitzpatrick	8	CA/ Conservative	Yes		Yes
Ève Péclet	4	NDP	Yes		
Kyle Seeback[1]	4	Conservative	No		Yes
Jeremy Harrison	2	Conservative	Yes		

[1] Re-elected to the House of Commons after the exit interview.

Source: ATLAS.ti (2020) coding of Samara Centre interview transcripts; House of Commons (2020).

Sixteen of the 24 MPs who talked at length about party discipline clearly supported its application to the caucus (P5). Paul DeVillers, a Liberal MP from 1993 to 2006, commented that he was a "big defender" of party discipline, because it inhibits the ability of special interests and the wealthy to influence how individual legislators vote. Stéphane Bergeron, a Bloc Québécois MP from 1993 to 2005 who was later re-elected, stated that discipline is simply an entrenched feature of parliamentary politics.

Other respondents were critical. Odina Desrochers, a Bloc MP from 1997 to 2006, opined that the power of media clips and leaders "means that democracy cannot function and above all crushes the role of parliamentarians" (translated from French). Veteran MP Art Hanger, who served from 1993 to 2008 with the Reform Party, the Canadian Alliance, and then the Conservative Party of Canada, espoused the anti-discipline belief system that was initially promoted by the Western-based Reform founders. Hanger remarked that an MP should "have the freedom to express his viewpoints without repercussion" and was appalled at the internal mobilization that occurs to urge private members to toe the party line. He observed that the timing of bills and motions changed when caucus officers realized that he was likely to defy the leadership's position on a vote. Hanger reflected that "the manipulation that went on behind the scenes was disgraceful. They said okay, well okay, we'll put that [vote] off until next week then. And then, so we're preparing to travel, the last minute of maybe Thursday or early Friday, [the bill is] brought to the floor and voted on, and, end of story."

Few participants remarked that party discipline was good for the group but bad for them personally (P6). Bob Rae, who was a New Democrat MP from 1978 to 1982 and a Liberal MP from 2008 to 2013, including time as interim party leader, stated that as leader he needed discipline to keep the caucus together. He did not resort to harsh threats to force conformity; rather he articulated to the caucus that voting against the party line "won't help us, it won't help me. And I don't think it will help you in the end, either." Rae commented, though, that as he gained experience, he felt more compelled to speak up internally and say, "Well, I actually don't agree with this. And we should be more careful about letting people express their own points of view." Bill Matthews, who from 1993 to 1999 sat as a Progressive Conservative and then as a Liberal until 2008, had engaged in unspecified policy disagreements in PC caucus meetings, was shut down by leader Joe Clark, and then ceased attending until he switched parties. "I just had to move. I wasn't content. And then, of course," Matthews reasoned about his decision to cross the floor, "I had to think about where's the best place to land for the people that sent me up here." The length of parliamentary service did not seem to obviously relate to the respondents' views on discipline, at least for this set of former legislators.

The final way that we examined how MPs perceive the exercise of discipline concerns the role of social media. We created a social media coding category to code the 24 interview texts discussed above that contain substantive discussions of party discipline. We then reviewed each mention in the interview transcripts and summarized the results in Table 1.3.[8] Consistent with the aforementioned normalization proposition (P7)—that information technology is adapted to existing practices—we find that this set of former MPs did not view social media as a means to escape party discipline. None of them suggested that the technology is an opportunity to express individualism or representation that differs from the party line. A fair number who spoke substantively on the subject regarded social media as merely another tool that MPs can use to reach citizens, and also for citizens to reach politicians, although some participants sensed that change

---

8   The analysis produced 133 hits.

was afoot. Seeback expressed a conviction that "old media is dead," while Rae observed that the impact of social media was difficult to pinpoint because of an inability to ascertain who was paying attention to his Facebook and Twitter posts. Many of these ex-MPs were in office when social media was in its infancy, so their perceptions likely reflect an earlier period when the full implications for party message and party discipline were not yet realized. Some might not have had accounts or been active users. Furthermore, as mentioned, caucus research bureaus now play a considerable role in coordinating digital messaging.

Conclusion

Party discipline is more organic than sensationalist headlines suggest. In our analysis of personal interviews administered by the Samara Centre for Democracy, we found little direct reference to either party constitutions or election platforms as salient mechanisms with respect to the exercise of party discipline. As expected, we found much evidence suggesting that MPs highly value loyalty to and within their party caucus team. Some people expressed these types of bonds as familial ones, underscoring their personal and durable nature. We found little loyalty expressed towards the parliamentary party, along with a handful of respondents who said that they valued loyalty to their constituents above all other connections and did so under the constraints of party discipline.

A majority of respondents who spoke about party discipline thought it was a beneficial institution for the group while a minority commented that it was bad for the group. There is some potential for conflicting interests, in that while some respondents believe party discipline benefitted the broader group, they also held it was bad for them personally. Several offered thoughtful insights into its causes and consequences that call for more complex and sustained analysis than our brief study affords. Further research is likewise needed around whether rookies or veterans are more likely to subscribe to the benefits of party affiliation. We expected that the length of time an MP served in office, and hence in the party caucus, would strengthen their support of the institution of party discipline, and thus less experienced MPs would be more critical of it. However, we did not find any compelling evidence of such parliamentary socialization. We also explored whether the rise of digital communications technology has reinforced disciplinary structures in Canadian politics or offered an escape from them but found that the effects of digital media on party discipline were indeterminate. Some of the former MPs interviewed believed that communications technology simply provides alternate means for the same patterns of discipline to exist and to be enforced; however, many of them retired just as the political importance of social media was expanding. The role of Facebook, Twitter, and other platforms in weakening or strengthening party loyalty warrants further monitoring.

While our analysis suggests that Canadian MPs experience frustrations with conformity, on balance they put up with strict party discipline for a myriad of reasons, ultimately determining that it is advantageous to toe the party line. We anticipate this attitude towards party discipline will hold up in future analyses of the Samara Centre for Democracy's interviews with MPs who exited the House of Commons following the 42nd Parliament and beyond.

References

ATLAS.ti. 2020. "What is ATLAS.ti?" https://atlasti.com/product/what-is-atlas-ti/.

Bigelow, John. 2009. Review of *A Digital Trojan Horse: How a Maverick MP Blogged His Way Out of the Conservative Caucus*, by Garth Turner. *Literary Review of Canada* 17 (6): 5.

Birch, Lisa, and François Pétry, eds. 2019. *Assessing Justin Trudeau's Liberal Government: 353 Promises and a Mandate for Change*. Québec City: Presses de l'Université Laval.

Boyer, Patrick. 2004. "Can Parliamentarians Become Real Players?" *Canadian Parliamentary Review* 27 (3): 4–8.

Brodie, Ian. 2018. *At the Centre of Government: The Prime Minister and the Limits on Political Power*. Kingston and Montréal: McGill-Queen's University Press.

Brown, Bert. 1994. "Parliamentary Discipline: An Informal Survey of Opinion." *Canadian Parliamentary Review* 17 (2): 14–15.

Chartash, David, Nicholas J. Caruana, Markus Dickinson, and Laura B. Stephenson. 2020. "When the Team's Jersey Is What Matters: Network Analysis of Party Cohesion and Structure in the Canadian House of Commons." *Party Politics* 26 (5): 555–569.

de Clercy, Cristine. 2018. "Communications as the Workhorse of Governmental Politics: The Liberal Party Leader and the Liberal Caucus." In *Political Elites in Canada: Power and Influence in Instantaneous Times*, edited by Alex Marland, Thierry Giasson, and Andrea Lawlor, 151–167. Vancouver: University of British Columbia Press.

Docherty, David C. 1997. *Mr. Smith Goes to Ottawa: Life in the House of Commons*. Vancouver: University of British Columbia Press.

Epstein, Leon D. 1964. "A Comparative Study of Canadian Parties." *American Political Science Review* 58 (1): 46–59.

Esselment, Anna. 2014. "The Governing Party and the Permanent Campaign." In *Political Communication in Canada: Meet the Press and Tweet the Rest*, edited by Alex Marland, Thierry Giasson, and Tamara A. Small, 24–38. Vancouver: University of British Columbia Press.

Franks, C. E. S. 1987. *The Parliament of Canada.* Toronto: University of Toronto Press.

Garner, Christopher, and Natalia Letki. 2005. "Party Structure and Backbench Dissent in the Canadian and British Parliaments." *Canadian Journal of Political Science* 38 (2): 463–482.

Godbout, Jean-François. 2020. *Lost on Division: Party Unity in the Canadian Parliament*. Toronto: University of Toronto Press.

Guay, Monique. 2002. "Party Discipline, Representation of Voters and Personal Beliefs." *Canadian Parliamentary Review* 25 (1): 7–9.

Heard, Andrew. 2007. "Just What Is a Vote of Confidence? The Curious Case of May 10, 2005." *Canadian Journal of Political Science* 40 (2): 395–416.

House of Commons. 2020. "Members of Parliament." https://www.ourcommons .ca/members/en.

Kam, Christopher. 2001. "Do Ideological Preferences Explain Parliamentary Behaviour? Evidence from Great Britain and Canada." *Journal of Legislative Studies* 7 (4): 89–126.

———. 2009. *Party Discipline and Parliamentary Politics*. Vancouver: University of British Columbia Press.

Kilgour, David, and John Kirsner. 1988. "Party Discipline and Canadian Democracy." *Canadian Parliamentary Review* 11 (3): 10–11.

Koop, Royce, Heather Bastedo, and Kelly Blidook. 2018. *Representation in Action: Canadian MPs in the Constituencies*. Vancouver: University of British Columbia Press.

Lecomte, Lucie. 2018. *Party Discipline and Free Votes*. Library of Parliament publication 2018-26-E. Ottawa.

Loat, Alison, and Michael MacMillan. 2015. *Tragedy in the Commons: Former Members of Parliament Speak Out about Canada's Failing Democracy*. Toronto: Vintage Canada.

Longley, Neil. 2003. "Modeling the Legislator as an Agent for the Party: The Effects of Strict Party Discipline on Legislator Voting Behaviour." *Contemporary Economic Policy* 21 (4): 490–499.

Marland, Alex. 2020. *Whipped: Party Discipline in Canada*. Vancouver: University of British Columbia Press.

Morden, Michael, Jane Hilderman, and Kendall Anderson. 2018. *The Real House Lives: Strengthening the Role of MPs in an Age of Partisanship*. Toronto: The Samara Centre for Democracy.

Overby, L. Marvin, Raymond Tatalovich, and Donley T. Studlar. 1998. "Party and Free Votes in Canada: Abortion in the House of Commons." *Party Politics* 4 (3): 381–392.

Penner, Keith. 1991. "Parliament and the Private Member." *Canadian Parliamentary Review* 14 (2): 22–24.

Petit-Vouriot, Adelina, Michael Morden, and Kendall Anderson. 2019. *Democracy 360: The Third Report Card on How Canadians Communicate, Participate, and Lead in Politics.* Toronto: The Samara Centre for Democracy.

Reid, John. 1993. "The Case for Party Discipline." *Canadian Parliamentary Review* 16 (3): 2–4.

Remillard, Chaseten, Lindsey M. Bertrand, and Alina Fisher. 2019. "The Visually Viral Prime Minister: Justin Trudeau, Selfies, and Instagram." In *Power Shift? Political Leadership and Social Media,* edited by Richard Davis and David Taras, 63–75. New York: Routledge.

Samara Centre for Democracy. 2020. *MP Exit Interviews: Volume I.* https://www.samaracanada.com/research/political-leadership/mp-exit-interviews.

Small, Tamara. 2016. "Two Decades of Digital Party Politics in Canada: An Assessment." In *Canadian Parties in Transition,* 4th ed., edited by Alain-G. Gagnon and A. Brian Tanguay, 338–408. Toronto: University of Toronto Press.

Smith, Rodney, and Anika Gauja. 2010. "Understanding Party Constitutions as Responses to Specific Challenges." *Party Politics* 16 (6): 755–775.

Thomas, Paul E. J., Adelina Petit-Vouriot, and Michael Morden. 2020. *House Inspection: A Retrospective of the 42nd Parliament.* Toronto: The Samara Centre for Democracy.

Wesley, Jared, and Renze Nauta. 2020. "Party Platform Builders." In *Inside the Campaign: Managing Elections in Canada,* edited by Alex Marland and Thierry Giasson, 123–134. Vancouver: University of British Columbia Press.

Yourk, Darren. 2004. "Keith Martin Turns to Liberals." *Globe and Mail,* January 14, 2004. https://www.theglobeandmail.com/news/national/keith-martin-turns-to-liberals/article1126145.

CHAPTER 2

Aborder le harcèlement sexuel dans les législatures : description d'un lieu de travail « unique »

Charles Feldman

Résumé

Les assemblées législatives ne sont pas comme les autres lieux de travail. Ce chapitre examine ce qui en fait des institutions « uniques » et les raisons pour lesquelles ces caractéristiques peuvent poser des problèmes particuliers pour lutter contre le harcèlement, y compris le harcèlement sexuel. Les assemblées législatives se caractérisent par une multiplicité d'employeurs et une variété de contextes dans lesquels les obligations en matière d'emploi apparaissent. De plus, le privilège parlementaire crée des considérations qui ne sont tout simplement pas présentes dans d'autres lieux de travail, y compris dans les secteurs public et privé. Il est nécessaire de comprendre ces caractéristiques « uniques » et leurs répercussions sur la lutte contre le harcèlement afin d'élaborer des propositions de politiques à cet égard et de les évaluer.

Abstract

Legislatures are unlike other workplaces. This chapter explores what makes them "unique" institutions and why these features may pose particular challenges for addressing harassment, including sexual harassment. Legislative workplaces feature a multiplicity of employers and a variety of contexts in which employment obligations arise. Further, the presence of parliamentary privilege creates considerations that are simply not present in other workplaces, including those in the public and private sectors. Understanding these unique features and their impact on addressing harassment is essential to being able to develop and evaluate policy proposals in this regard.

Les législatures du monde entier font leur examen de conscience alors que le mouvement #Moiaussi continue de faire la lumière sur le harcèlement sexuel. Aux États-Unis, la Conférence nationale des législatures d'État fait état d'une activité « sans précédent » à cet égard : en 2018 et en 2019, plus de 100 textes législatifs relatifs au harcèlement sexuel ont été présentés dans les législatures des États (National Conference on State Legislatures, 2019). En 2020, les membres de la Chambre des communes britannique ont transféré à un groupe d'experts indépendants leur pouvoir de sanctionner les députés qui se sont rendus coupables de harcèlement – y compris de harcèlement sexuel – ou d'intimidation, ce qui représentait un changement majeur (BBC, 2020). En 2021, un nouveau règlement fédéral sur le harcèlement et la violence dans les milieux de travail est entré en vigueur au Canada et s'applique aux employeurs parlementaires (Emploi et Développement social Canada, 2020).

La présente collection intitulée *Les législatures en transformation* serait incomplète si elle ne mentionnait pas les initiatives concernant le harcèlement sexuel dans les législatures. Devant l'évolution rapide de cette problématique, les législatures et les organisations parlementaires internationales examinent les moyens de prévenir le harcèlement et de traiter les plaintes propres au contexte législatif. Pour résumer l'évolution de la situation, disons qu'en 2019 seulement, l'Union interparlementaire a publié ses *Lignes directrices pour l'élimination du sexisme, du harcèlement et de la violence à l'égard des femmes dans les parlements* (Union interparlementaire, 2019) ; la Nouvelle-Zélande a réalisé une étude externe indépendante sur l'intimidation et le harcèlement dans son milieu de travail parlementaire (Francis, 2019) ; et la Chambre d'assemblée de Terre-Neuve-et-Labrador, l'Assemblée législative du Yukon, l'Assemblée législative de la Colombie-Britannique et le Parlement écossais ont annoncé de nouvelles politiques en matière de harcèlement sexuel (Newfoundland and Labrador House of Assembly, 2019 ; Yukon Legislative Assembly,

2019 ; Legislative Assembly of British Columbia, 2019 ; Freeman, 2019).
De plus, d'innombrables inconduites sexuelles dans les assemblées
législatives ont été signalées, ce qui a souvent conduit à la démission
de certains législateurs (Lieb, 2019).

Les corps législatifs sont indubitablement en train de s'ajuster
pour répondre au harcèlement sexuel, mais il va sans dire que ce
changement est encore loin d'être acquis (Nadel, 2019). Cela dit, une
législature qui veut s'attaquer au harcèlement sexuel affrontera de
nombreux obstacles et défis, dont bon nombre découlent du fait que
les législatures sont considérées comme des milieux de travail
uniques[1].

Les analystes qui se penchent sur le harcèlement sexuel dans
les assemblées législatives, sur leurs méthodes pour le combattre, et
qui suggèrent ce que certaines législatures devraient faire sur des
points précis, semblent peu tenir compte de la spécificité du milieu
de travail législatif (Collier and Raney, 2018 ; Collier et coll., 2019 ;
McCluskey and Read, 2018). Le présent chapitre décrit les caractéristiques particulières des législatures – en particulier au Canada – et
leurs conséquences possibles sur l'élaboration de toute politique de
lutte contre le harcèlement au travail en s'appuyant sur des études
antérieures dans ce domaine (Gaudreault, 2016).

Ce qui précède et ce qui suit n'ont pas pour objet d'affirmer que
les caractéristiques d'une législature exemptent les législatures de
lutter contre le harcèlement sexuel ou que les législateurs qui déter-
minent comment répondre au harcèlement sexuel ne devraient pas
s'inspirer des pratiques exemplaires tirées d'autres cadres d'emploi.
On estime plutôt que les législatures sont confrontées à des défis
uniques dans la lutte contre le harcèlement sexuel au travail, défis
qui n'existent tout simplement pas – ou à un autre degré – dans
d'autres cadres d'emploi, comme le secteur privé. Essentiellement, la
conclusion de Dame Laura Cox, DBE, dans son rapport de 2018 intitulé *The Bullying and Harassment of House of Commons Staff*
(L'intimidation et le harcèlement des employés de la Chambre des
communes) est irréprochable : « Si certains contributeurs ont tenu à
démontrer que la Chambre est une "institution unique", elle demeure
en fin de compte un lieu de travail. Il est vrai qu'elle présente des

---

1   Le rapport de l'Union interparlementaire mentionné plus haut indique qu'à l'égard
     du harcèlement sexuel, « [l]a diversité des catégories de personnel et les spécificités
     du parlement ont abouti à des procédures parfois complexes » (51).

caractéristiques inhabituelles, mais c'est un lieu où plus de 2 000 personnes travaillent et envers lesquelles leurs employeurs ont un devoir de vigilance[2] » (Cox, 2018).

Première caractéristique unique : Origine des obligations liées à l'emploi – personnel politique

Le nombre de relations de travail de nature distincte, même entre deux postes nominalement similaires, représente une caractéristique unique des lieux de travail législatifs. Cette variété et cette complexité sont peut-être plus facilement illustrées dans le cadre de la relation entre un politicien et son personnel. Les politiciens ne sont pas toujours ceux qui emploient leur personnel. Dans de nombreux cas, la relation contractuelle avec le personnel politique n'est pas conclue entre celui-ci et le législateur pour qui il travaille.

Par exemple, la législation de Terre-Neuve-et-Labrador prévoit ceci : « Le contrat de travail d'un adjoint de circonscription doit être conclu entre l'adjoint de circonscription et Sa Majesté la Reine du chef de la province de Terre-Neuve-et-Labrador, représentée ici par l'honorable président de la Chambre d'assemblée[3] ».

La relation entre un législateur et son personnel peut être encore compliquée par la présence d'autres intermédiaires. Par exemple, l'alinéa 7(1)a) de la *Loi sur les employés du cabinet et les employés des groupes parlementaires* du Yukon (LRY, 2002, c 22) autorise la Commission des services aux députés de la Législature à « créer des postes à répartir entre les partis à l'intention des personnes employées pour aider les députés. » Pourtant, le pouvoir de nommer les titulaires de ces postes en vertu de la *Loi* est donné au chef de chaque parti (voir l'article 8 de la *Loi*), qui « peut établir le contrat de travail des personnes employées sous le régime de la présente partie et fixer leurs fonctions, leur rémunération, les avantages auxquels elles ont droit et leurs conditions de travail » (art. 9).

Une législature peut établir des clauses obligatoires – ainsi que des politiques en matière de harcèlement – qui doivent faire partie des contrats de travail pour que les salaires soient payés à même les deniers publics. Toutefois, en l'absence de clauses obligatoires, un

---

2 Traduction libre.

3 Traduction libre. *Members' Resources and Allowances Rules* under the *House of Assembly Accountability, Integrity and Administration Act* (SNL 2007 c H-10.1 Schedule).

employeur peut établir un contrat de travail qui ne compte pas de dispositions spécifiques au harcèlement ou qui contredit des dispositions figurant dans d'autres contrats de travail sur le même lieu de travail. Le respect d'une politique de harcèlement ne peut devenir une condition légale de l'emploi d'une personne sans que cette politique soit intégrée dans ses conditions d'emploi.

Il existe certainement des recours pour remédier à une inconduite en milieu de travail par le biais d'un régime autre qu'une politique de harcèlement, comme les régimes provinciaux ou fédéraux de plaintes en matière de droits de la personne. En outre, il pourrait y avoir d'autres moyens pour que certains comportements donnent une ouverture à une poursuite. Cependant, certains recours juridiques peuvent être directement touchés par l'entente contractuelle entre l'employeur et l'employé. Par exemple, le succès d'une réclamation pour rupture de contrat liée au harcèlement au travail pourrait dépendre des parties au contrat ainsi que des dispositions du contrat.

S'il existe des recours multiples, la politique de la législature peut être inapte à prescrire la voie à suivre si cela peut être fait sous le régime d'une autre loi. Toutefois, le législateur ne peut pas s'attendre à ce que quelqu'un invoque une politique si celle-ci ne lui est pas accessible en tant que plaignant ; et il est certain que le recours à une politique qui ne s'applique pas à une personne mise en cause n'a qu'une utilité limitée. En l'absence d'obligations mutuelles liant le plaignant et la personne mise en cause à la même politique, celle-ci peut être inefficace et même juridiquement non pertinente dans certains cas.

De nouvelles difficultés peuvent surgir si la relation entre un législateur et son personnel est aussi régie par une convention collective. Par exemple, il existe une convention collective entre le Syndicat des employés de la fonction publique de l'Ontario et le caucus du Nouveau Parti démocratique de l'Ontario[4]. Différents syndicats peuvent souhaiter que des politiques ou des processus différents soient appliqués en cas d'allégation de harcèlement sexuel, risquant ainsi de bloquer l'objectif potentiel du législateur d'uniformiser le traitement des questions relatives au personnel. En outre, les employés

---

4 L'unité de négociation du Syndicat canadien des employées et employés professionnels et de bureau est composée de membres du personnel des bureaux de circonscription des députés néodémocrates de l'Assemblée législative de l'Ontario (le personnel de Queen's Park appartient à un autre syndicat). Voir *Ontario New Democratic Party Caucus c. Canadian Office and Professional Employees Union, Local 343*.

syndiqués peuvent disposer de ressources supplémentaires en matière d'emploi – comme une procédure de règlement des griefs – auxquelles leurs collègues non syndiqués n'ont pas accès.

Il est important de noter que toutes les relations entre un législateur et son personnel ne peuvent pas être officialisées de la même manière. Par exemple, un bénévole ou un stagiaire peut n'avoir aucun contrat ou entente formelle. Dans d'autres cas, il se peut qu'un stagiaire soit placé dans le bureau d'un parlementaire par le biais d'un programme du corps législatif (par exemple, le programme de stage législatif de la Colombie-Britannique) ou par une organisation externe (comme le programme de stages parlementaires du Congrès ukrainien canadien). Dans ces cas, le contrat de travail qui s'applique au stagiaire n'est pas conclu entre le stagiaire et le législateur qu'il sert, et la durée et les conditions peuvent varier.

Il faut également tenir compte de la possibilité qu'un législateur soit servi par un personnel différent. Par exemple, selon le guide des ressources et des allocations des députés de la Chambre d'assemblée de Terre-Neuve-et-Labrador, certains députés qui ont besoin d'un soutien pendant leur séjour dans la capitale peuvent utiliser le service de « secrétariat partagé » obtenu par le président de leur caucus[5]. De la même façon, dans certains rôles, les législateurs peuvent avoir – en plus du personnel qu'ils reçoivent en tant que législateurs – du personnel fourni en vertu de rôles législatifs supplémentaires. Par exemple, un député qui est secrétaire parlementaire peut avoir un employé supplémentaire, bien que le ministre pour qui le secrétaire parlementaire travaille soit responsable de cet employé (Bureau du Conseil privé, 2015)[6].

---

5   Selon les directives publiées :
    « le droit au secrétariat partagé s'applique uniquement aux députés qui ont des bureaux de circonscription en dehors du bâtiment de la Confédération et qui n'ont pas de personnel de soutien affecté au bâtiment de la Confédération. C'est-à-dire qu'il n'inclut pas le premier ministre, le président, les ministres, les secrétaires parlementaires, l'adjoint parlementaire, le chef de l'Opposition officielle, le chef du troisième parti et le leader parlementaire de l'opposition » (traduction libre) (Newfoundland and Labrador House of Assembly 2005, 1).

6   « Les ministres qui ont des secrétaires parlementaires au sein de leur portefeuille sont autorisés à embaucher un employé exonéré qui sera affecté au secrétariat parlementaire. [...] Rappelons que les ministres demeurent de façon générale responsables et doivent rendre des comptes en ce qui a trait à la direction des fonctionnaires et à l'utilisation des ressources du ministère » (Bureau de Conseil privé, 2015, 11).

En bref, la relation entre un législateur et son personnel prend de nombreuses formes au Canada et, dans certaines situations, aucun contrat de travail officiel ne lie directement le législateur et son personnel. À cet égard, les conditions d'emploi peuvent non seulement être incohérentes, mais le législateur qui interagit avec le personnel peut en fait ne pas les connaître. Cela est bien sûr très différent du secteur privé où il y a probablement un seul employeur pour tous les employés et des conditions d'emploi assez standardisées.

Cette variété est problématique d'un point de vue conceptuel, étant donné que deux personnes dans une relation de travail sont censées avoir formalisé une entente sur leurs obligations respectives. S'il est évident qu'il existe des déséquilibres de pouvoir qu'il convient de rappeler dans ce contexte particulier, il peut être futile de tenter de surmonter les disparités dans le pouvoir de négociation si, au bout du compte, il est impossible de formaliser une relation de travail entre un législateur et son personnel.

Ainsi, une assemblée législative qui tente d'imposer ou de modifier une politique en matière de harcèlement sexuel devra d'abord établir qui est employé par qui et, en conséquence, modifier ce qui régit cette relation afin d'imposer une obligation d'emploi contraignante pour garantir la conformité à une politique en particulier. Certaines législatures peuvent avoir plus de possibilités que d'autres à cet égard ; par exemple, le contrat du personnel d'un sénateur est limité à un an et il faut donc tout au plus attendre le renouvellement du contrat (Comité permanent de la régie interne, des budgets et de l'administration, 2019). Toutefois, il se peut que la relation de travail entre un législateur et son personnel dans d'autres contextes ne soit même pas régie par un contrat signé, ce qui arrive souvent pour les stagiaires.

Deuxième caractéristique unique : de nombreux employés, un espace commun

En partant de ce qui précède, les sources potentielles de relations de travail au sein du corps législatif vont bien au-delà de celles qui existent entre un législateur et le personnel qui le sert, telles que décrites ci-dessus. Les interactions et les incursions qui concernent les différents types d'employés au sein du corps législatif méritent d'être prises en considération.

À titre d'exemple, prenons une ministre fédérale. Elle peut avoir du personnel de bureau dans sa circonscription – potentiellement dans plusieurs bureaux de circonscription – ainsi que du personnel de bureau à Ottawa qui la sert dans son rôle de députée. Dans ces cas, la députée est l'employeur (Chambre des communes, 2018). Cependant, son bureau ministériel compte du personnel dit « exonéré » qui est nommé par la ministre en cette qualité ainsi que des employés du ministère qui sont des fonctionnaires (Secrétariat du Conseil du trésor, 2011, art. 3,2). Certains membres du personnel peuvent être régis par des conditions obligatoires établies par la législature, tandis que d'autres (comme les personnes nommées par les ministères) ne le sont pas. Il convient de noter que si bon nombre de ces employés ministériels se trouvent à Ottawa, il est également possible que des employés travaillent dans des bureaux régionaux, de sorte que la ministre est responsable de plusieurs lieux de travail (Secrétariat du Conseil du trésor, 2011, art. 3.2.1.2).

Au-delà de l'interaction avec « son personnel », telle que décrite de manière assez générale ci-dessus, un ministre peut tenir des réunions régulières avec son sous-ministre et d'autres fonctionnaires du ministère, des réunions avec ses collègues du cabinet et du caucus, des interactions avec le personnel d'autres ministres et ministères – tout cela sans même nécessairement mettre les pieds à l'Assemblée législative.

Une fois à la Chambre des communes, tout député peut interagir avec une série de personnes – le personnel de sécurité qui n'est pas nécessairement employé par la législature, les employés de la législature tels que les greffiers à la procédure, le personnel du caucus, les employés de la fonction publique tels que les interprètes, les employés d'autres entités comme la Bibliothèque du Parlement, les journalistes, les pages, les autres parlementaires et leur personnel, et même les membres du public, y compris les électeurs et les lobbyistes.

Il est compliqué, voire impossible, d'avoir une politique uniforme de lutte contre le harcèlement en milieu de travail lorsqu'il y a tant d'employeurs distincts. Cette réalité d'« employeurs distincts » comporte plusieurs aspects qui peuvent compliquer l'élaboration d'une politique de lutte contre le harcèlement sexuel en milieu de travail.

Cette problématique mérite d'être examinée de plus près à la lumière du nouveau régime législatif fédéral visant à lutter contre le harcèlement et la violence sur les lieux de travail parlementaires. Le projet de loi C-65, *Loi modifiant le Code canadien du travail (harcèlement et violence),* la *Loi sur les relations de travail au Parlement,* la *Loi n° 1 d'exécution du budget de 2017,* et le *Règlement sur la prévention du harcèlement et de la violence dans le lieu de travail* unifient l'approche fédérale du harcèlement et de la violence applicable aux employeurs parlementaires. Toutefois, la loi ne fait que créer un cadre. Chaque employeur doit établir sa propre politique conforme à ce cadre. Généralement, une personne employée par une entité ne peut pas porter plainte en vertu de la politique d'une autre entité. De plus, la loi elle-même contient une exclusion en matière d'exercice du privilège parlementaire (un sujet abordé plus loin dans ce chapitre) :

> 88.6 Il est entendu que les dispositions de la présente partie n'ont pas pour effet de restreindre de quelque façon les pouvoirs, privilèges et immunités du Sénat, de la Chambre des communes, des sénateurs et des députés ou d'autoriser l'exercice de toute attribution conférée par application de ces dispositions qui porterait atteinte, directement ou indirectement, aux affaires du Sénat ou de la Chambre des communes.

Ce qui précède n'est pas une critique du projet de loi C-65, mais plutôt un rappel que même les interventions législatives doivent composer avec les défis que posent les lieux de travail parlementaires « uniques » et le problème des employeurs multiples. Même si de nouvelles politiques sur le harcèlement ont été adoptées par le Sénat et la Chambre des communes dans la foulée du nouveau régime fédéral, elles ne s'harmonisent pas et ne sont pas étendues. Par exemple, la politique de la Chambre des communes énonce ce qui suit :

> Le processus de résolution de la présente politique est accessible seulement lorsque le plaignant y consent et que l'avis d'incident concerne :
> • des employés du même député ;
> • un député et un de ses employés ;
> • un ancien employé et un employé actuel du même député, ou un député actuel qui est son ancien employeur.

En clair, cela signifie que le processus de résolution prévu par cette politique n'est pas ouvert à certaines plaintes au sein de la Chambre des communes, comme les plaintes entre les employés de deux différents députés. De plus, le processus est fermé aux sénateurs et aux employés du Sénat qui pourraient avoir fait l'objet de harcèlement par un employé de la Chambre des communes. La nouvelle politique du Sénat, pour sa part, permet à deux personnes de participer au processus de résolution, notamment en ce qui concerne les plaintes entre sénateurs, ainsi que les plaintes entre le personnel de différents sénateurs. Ainsi, s'il est exact de dire qu'il existe un nouveau régime fédéral de lutte contre le harcèlement et la violence sur les lieux de travail parlementaires, cela ne veut nullement dire que chaque travailleur parlementaire a un recours en vertu d'une politique dans tous les cas de harcèlement, même si ce harcèlement a lieu sur la colline du Parlement et implique le personnel d'un employeur parlementaire assujetti à la loi. Comme nous le verrons plus loin, on peut imaginer le cas particulier où un sénateur et un député désirent s'accuser mutuellement de harcèlement – quelle entité parlementaire pourrait établir une politique bicamérale et comment ?

Le mécanisme pour imposer de nouvelles obligations

Comme mentionné ci-dessus, on peut généralement obliger un employé à respecter une politique de lutte contre le harcèlement en faisant du respect de cette politique une condition d'emploi. La législature n'est pas en mesure d'établir des contrats de travail avec des non-employés, bien que les non-employés du législateur puissent toujours être soumis à des politiques connexes établies par leurs employeurs respectifs.

Dans le cas présent, par exemple, les fonctionnaires tels que les interprètes sont liés par les politiques du gouvernement, et les employés du Service de protection parlementaire seraient soumis à ses politiques. La législature peut, par le biais d'ententes de service ou autres, renvoyer aux obligations de sa politique en matière de harcèlement, mais il existe des limites naturelles. Par exemple, un employé de la Bibliothèque du Parlement assujetti à la politique de lutte contre le harcèlement de la Bibliothèque ne serait pas facilement assujetti en plus aux politiques du Sénat et de la Chambre des communes – pas plus que les parlementaires ne seraient assujettis aux politiques de la Bibliothèque.

L'influence que peut avoir une législature est ici limitée. Pour prendre un exemple extrême, à moins que le Sénat ou la Chambre des communes ne soient prêts à engager leurs propres interprètes, personnel de sécurité et personnel de bibliothèque – le tout à un coût considérable pour le contribuable – les deux sont quelque peu à la merci d'autres entités pour coopérer aux efforts de lutte contre le harcèlement en l'absence d'une intervention législative nécessitant une réponse uniforme. Une intervention législative a eu lieu au niveau fédéral et une nouvelle réglementation s'appliquant à tous les employeurs parlementaires en matière de harcèlement et de violence au travail a été adoptée et est entrée en vigueur en 2021 (*Règlement sur la Prévention du harcèlement et de la violence dans le lieu de travail*, DORS/2020-130, [*Code canadien du travail*]). Toutefois, chaque employé reste assujetti à la politique de son employeur et les politiques peuvent ne pas s'appliquer aux plaintes de personnes qui travaillent pour d'autres entités. Il s'agit d'un défi unique qui touche particulièrement les assemblées législatives dont les composantes sont des entités juridiques distinctes, comme une bibliothèque législative non gérée par la législature[7].

Il est important de noter que, après avoir été élus ou nommés, les législateurs eux-mêmes n'ont pas de contrat de travail au sens traditionnel du terme ; leurs conditions d'emploi sont généralement régies par la loi. Cela peut signifier que pour imposer la même obligation aux législateurs et au personnel de la législature, il faudrait appliquer des mesures supplémentaires ou différentes dans certains contextes.

Par exemple, on pourrait envisager d'imposer une formation obligatoire à la lutte contre le harcèlement. Pour l'employé d'une législature, cela pourrait être une condition de sa période d'essai. Si l'employé ne participe pas à la formation, il peut être licencié. Mais comment cela pourrait-il fonctionner pour un législateur qui n'a ni période d'essai ni contrat de travail ?

En théorie, une législature pourrait empêcher un nouveau législateur d'accéder à son budget ou d'engager du personnel tant qu'il n'a pas terminé cette formation, car ces éléments peuvent relever du seul contrôle de la législature s'ils ne sont pas prévus explicitement

---

7   À titre d'exemple, la *Loi sur la Bibliothèque de l'Assemblée législative* du Manitoba (CPLM c L120) prévoit que « [l]e ministre dirige la Bibliothèque de l'Assemblée législative et donne des directives à son bibliothécaire » (art. 4), le ministre étant nommé par le cabinet provincial. Cette situation est différente de celle où la bibliothèque de la législature est directement sous l'autorité du président de la législature, par exemple.

par la loi. Mais, supposons qu'un législateur refuse de suivre la formation. À l'extrême, la législature pourrait prendre la décision de suspendre ou d'expulser le député, mais il s'agirait d'une décision politique qui nécessiterait l'engagement d'une majorité d'autres législateurs, ce qui ne serait pas garanti. De plus, en attendant qu'une telle décision soit prise, rien n'empêcherait facilement le législateur d'exercer ses fonctions telles que participer aux sessions législatives, aux débats et aux votes. Pendant ce temps, le législateur percevrait également son salaire. En d'autres termes, un législateur n'est pas affecté par une exigence de formation « obligatoire » de la même manière qu'un employé le serait si cette formation était une condition requise pour sa période d'essai.

Pour donner un exemple quelque peu frappant, bien que l'Assemblée nationale du Québec ait mis en place une formation « obligatoire » sur le harcèlement pour ses membres, depuis des années, il a fallu trois ans pour que les 125 députés en fonction suivent cette formation de deux heures. Aucun des 19 retardataires signalés (soit 15 % de la législature) – dont le premier ministre – n'a été empêché d'exercer ses fonctions et son rôle. Selon le Tribunal administratif du travail, un député est « l'unique employeur » de son personnel, mais le député continuait de gérer son personnel comme employeur bien qu'il n'avait pourtant pas suivi cette formation obligatoire.

Il convient de noter que les législateurs ne sont pas les seuls acteurs non assujettis à des conditions précises d'emploi dans le contexte législatif. L'un des derniers ajouts à la liste est le poète officiel de l'Ontario qui, selon la loi, doit être un fonctionnaire de l'Assemblée (*Loi de 2019 sur le poète officiel de l'Ontario (à la mémoire de Gord Downie)* [LRO 2019, chap. 16]). La législation est muette sur les politiques en matière d'emploi qui peuvent s'appliquer à l'éventuelle personne nommée. Il s'agit peut-être d'une préoccupation unique pour les fonctionnaires et les agents des législatures. Bien qu'ils soient au service du corps législatif, les fonctionnaires et les agents ne sont pas nécessairement assujettis aux politiques du corps législatif par le biais de leurs conditions d'emploi – ce qui ne serait pas nécessairement approprié étant donné que ces fonctions doivent être indépendantes. Cependant, la source de leurs conditions d'emploi peut même ne pas être claire dans certains cas. Par exemple, la *Loi électorale du Canada (L.C. 2000, ch. 9)* énonce que le directeur général des élections est nommé « par résolution de la Chambre des communes » (art. 13), résolution qui ne contient pas de conditions d'emploi.

Il existe également une catégorie de personnes faisant partie intégrante du corps législatif, mais dont l'emploi est établi par le pouvoir exécutif. Dans de nombreux territoires et provinces au Canada, par exemple, le greffier de la législature est nommé par le cabinet (Deller, 2018). Bien que cette question soit examinée plus en détail dans une section ultérieure, il convient de considérer que, puisque le pouvoir législatif ne régit pas la relation juridique qu'il peut avoir avec une personne nommée par le cabinet, il peut dépendre du pouvoir exécutif pour prendre des mesures visant à intégrer la lutte contre le harcèlement dans les conditions d'emploi de cette personne.

En bref, la pluralité des personnes qui travaillent dans la sphère législative et la diversité des mécanismes par lesquels les obligations en matière d'emploi leur sont imposées peuvent créer des disparités et donner lieu à des lacunes difficiles à combler dans les politiques de lutte contre le harcèlement. Dans le cas des législateurs en particulier, l'établissement de certaines exigences peut nécessiter des modifications de la loi. En outre, pour établir des obligations d'emploi concernant les fonctionnaires et les agents des législatures, il faudrait une action du pouvoir exécutif, des modifications législatives, voire des décisions additionnelles du pouvoir législatif au moment de la nomination.

La plupart des législatures du Canada seraient libres d'adopter des politiques et de modifier les lois qui s'y appliquent comme elles l'entendent. Dans le contexte législatif bicaméral fédéral, cependant, la modification des lois nécessite l'accord du Sénat et de la Chambre des communes. De façon intéressante, cela signifie que le Sénat a son mot à dire sur ce qui s'applique aux députés et que les députés ont leur mot à dire sur ce qui s'applique aux sénateurs. En pratique, selon les principes de courtoisie, aucune des deux chambres n'imposerait sa volonté à l'autre sur une question se rapportant à cette chambre. Cependant, le fait est que rien (sauf peut-être la constitution et les lois connexes) ne limite les choix d'une législature canadienne en dehors du contexte fédéral et que ces choix ne sont pas examinés par une autre législature au cours de leur processus d'adoption.

Efficacité du mécanisme d'imposition des obligations

La manière dont une politique de harcèlement est intégrée dans une relation de travail peut remettre son efficacité en question. Prenons le cas d'une législature qui utilise un service contractuel pour le nettoyage de ses locaux. Le contrat de travail applicable est celui entre un nettoyeur individuel et l'entreprise qui l'a engagé ; le contrat de la législature avec l'entreprise découle d'un processus d'approvisionnement. L'entreprise peut avoir sa propre politique de lutte contre le harcèlement, mais celle-ci peut ne pas correspondre à ce que la législature souhaite. Par conséquent, la législature pourrait, en théorie, obliger l'entreprise à respecter sa politique de lutte contre le harcèlement par le biais du contrat de service résultant du processus d'approvisionnement, mais les résultats pourraient ne pas être satisfaisants.

Supposons que l'employé d'un député d'une assemblée législative harcèle un nettoyeur sous contrat. Supposons en outre que le contrat de service contient une clause concernant la politique de lutte contre le harcèlement de l'Assemblée législative et que la politique elle-même protège contre les représailles et prévoit que les parties à une plainte pour harcèlement doivent se voir accorder un congé pour participer à un processus de résolution de la plainte. En pratique, l'assemblée ne serait pas en mesure de protéger l'employé contre les représailles de l'entreprise de nettoyage (son employeur), et il n'est pas évident que l'entreprise de nettoyage accorderait à l'employé le temps nécessaire pour participer à un processus de résolution de conflit de la législature – pas plus que l'assemblée ne pourrait le garantir. Il se peut donc que la seule option viable pour l'assemblée de démontrer son engagement envers sa politique de lutte contre le harcèlement soit de résilier le contrat de service. Bien que cela puisse être un geste noble, en définitive c'est le nettoyeur individuel qui serait désavantagé économiquement en plus d'avoir été victime de harcèlement au départ. En outre, la résiliation d'un contrat pourrait entraîner des coûts supplémentaires et une autre entreprise pourrait facturer davantage, de sorte que la valeur d'un contrat pour les contribuables devient un facteur dans un processus qui n'est pas censé inclure un exercice comptable.

Rien de tout cela ne signifie qu'il ne faudrait pas intégrer les politiques en matière de harcèlement dans des instruments juridiques qui permettent à des personnes de travailler en milieu législatif ; il faut plutôt noter que, dans certains contextes, l'intégration peut s'avérer plus symbolique que réelle étant donné les limites à gérer la conduite des personnes par le biais d'ententes qui ne sont pas des contrats de travail.

Dans le même ordre d'idées, les titulaires d'une charge publique qui sont nommés au sein de la sphère législative pourraient ne pas être directement contraints par les décisions de la législature. En conséquence, si une personne nommée peut s'engager volontairement dans certaines actions – comme dans une formation obligatoire sur la lutte contre le harcèlement – le pouvoir de la législature peut être limité en cas de refus. En d'autres termes, si le pouvoir de nommer et de révoquer une personne qui travaille au sein de la législature appartient au pouvoir exécutif, la législature peut ne pas avoir d'autorité légale en ce qui concerne la relation de travail, mais elle peut certainement exercer une pression politique sur les acteurs qui en ont. En théorie, la législature pourrait prendre d'autres mesures pour manifester son mécontentement, par exemple en déclarant la personne coupable d'outrage. De telles actions nécessiteraient des décisions politiques de la législature, dont la capacité à dénoncer et à blâmer peut inciter au respect de ses souhaits.

Limites des processus

Même si chaque entité responsable des employés sur le lieu de travail parlementaire adoptait une solide politique de lutte contre le harcèlement, il pourrait quand même être difficile de garantir son efficacité dans certains contextes. Dans sa forme la plus simple, ce problème se pose dans le contexte de l'applicabilité de la politique évoquée ci-dessus. En effet, si de multiples politiques s'appliquent aux personnes dans un même espace – les politiques de chaque employeur s'appliquant à ses propres employés – elles ne s'appliquent pas toutes à tout le monde dans cet espace, et il ne serait ni possible ni nécessairement approprié que cela se produise.

Prenons une situation extrême où un membre de la Chambre des communes serait accusé d'avoir harcelé un membre du Sénat au restaurant parlementaire. Le Sénat et la Chambre des communes étant des entités constitutionnelles distinctes, il serait difficile de voir comment les membres de la Chambre pourraient être contraints par la politique du Sénat de telle sorte que ce dernier puisse intervenir. De même, il serait étrange de dire que les membres du personnel du

Sénat sont assujettis à une politique et à un processus de la Chambre des communes. Même si une politique de la Chambre lui permettait d'intervenir dans une telle plainte, le règlement du Sénat[8] pourrait empêcher le membre du personnel du Sénat de participer à certains processus, surtout si ce processus vise une comparution devant un comité de la Chambre des communes.

Outre la possible concurrence des entités parlementaires, certaines réalités du corps législatif peuvent limiter le processus de résolution des plaintes. Par exemple, un processus qui vise à faire enquête sur un caucus ou à donner à un whip le rôle d'accueillir des plaintes pourrait être contrecarré si un législateur n'est pas affilié à un parti ou s'il fait défection à un autre caucus pendant le traitement d'une plainte. Si un processus prend fin lorsqu'un plaignant ou une personne mise en cause cessent d'être associés à la législature, cette situation pourrait être déclenchée par des actions sur lesquelles cette personne n'a aucun contrôle, comme une élection entraînant la cessation automatique du personnel[9].

En outre, les éléments du processus peuvent s'aligner de manière inadéquate sur certaines pratiques procédurales ou d'autres actes. Si l'on confie à un comité le soin de déterminer certains recours, les législateurs qui sont parties à la plainte ou qui sont témoins sont-ils tenus de se récuser ? Dans l'affirmative, le comité fait-il état de sa composition et des substituts aux réunions individuelles ? Il se peut que si une politique vise à protéger la confidentialité de toutes les parties concernées, les pratiques parlementaires applicables révèlent

---

8   L'article 16-4(3) du règlement du Sénat indique que :

Lorsque la Chambre des communes demande, par message, qu'un membre du personnel du Sénat comparaisse devant elle ou l'un de ses comités, ou qu'il réponde à ses questions par écrit ou par l'entremise d'un avocat, ce membre est tenu de se conformer à la décision prise par le Sénat en réponse à cette demande. Aucun membre du personnel du Sénat ne doit, sans l'autorisation du Sénat, comparaître devant la Chambre des communes ou un comité de celle-ci.

L'article 16-4 (4), quant à lui, stipule que :

Le sénateur ou le membre du personnel du Sénat qui, sans autorisation, comparaît devant la Chambre des communes ou l'un de ses comités, ou fournit des réponses par écrit ou par l'entremise d'un avocat est passible d'une sanction sous forme de détention par l'huissier du bâton noir, ou d'emprisonnement selon le bon vouloir du Sénat. (Sénat du Canada, 2020).

9   Par exemple, les directives de dissolution de l'Assemblée législative de l'Alberta prévoient que « tous les contrats de travail avec le personnel prendront automatiquement fin le 14e jour suivant le jour du scrutin » (traduction libre). (Legislative Assembly of Alberta, 2019, 12).

ou laissent entendre involontairement des détails de la plainte. En outre, le fait que des personnes impliquées dans une plainte participent aux décisions peut être remis en question. Les règles de conflit d'intérêts pourraient-elles s'appliquer à leur conduite ? Le cas échéant, le régime de conflit d'intérêts applicable exige-t-il que les conflits soient déclarés ou rendus publics ? Là encore, cela peut nuire aux efforts visant à garantir la confidentialité du processus.

En fin de compte, le processus conçu pour une législature donnée peut ne pas fonctionner dans une autre législature simplement parce que leurs réalités sont différentes. Par exemple, imaginez une politique qui exige une réunion annuelle entre chaque législateur et chaque membre de son personnel pour examiner la politique de lutte contre le harcèlement. Bien que cela puisse fonctionner dans une petite législature où chaque législateur a un seul adjoint de circonscription, une telle exigence de rencontre individuelle serait impraticable au bureau du premier ministre qui compte à lui seul plus de 100 employés.

Limites des recours

La pluralité des cadres de travail législatifs signifie que la même inconduite face aux personnes en présence peut entraîner des sanctions considérablement différentes. Par exemple, un membre du public qui adopte un comportement inapproprié peut facilement être banni de la Colline parlementaire (The Canadian Press, 2019). Cette personne n'aurait aucune relation de travail avec la législature et il est entendu que l'accès aux alentours de la Chambre lui serait limité pour des raisons de sécurité.

Cependant, l'approche décrite ci-dessus peut présenter des difficultés particulières dans d'autres cas. Supposons, par exemple, qu'un journaliste soit accusé d'avoir harcelé un parlementaire. La limitation éventuelle de l'accès d'un journaliste à l'ensemble de l'enceinte législative peut porter atteinte à la liberté de la presse telle qu'elle est garantie par la *Charte canadienne des droits et libertés*, bien que les médias puissent être exclus des procédures parlementaires *(New Brunswick Broadcasting Co. c. Nouvelle-Écosse)*.

Si une législature peut disposer de moyens efficaces pour discipliner ses propres employés, elle n'est peut-être pas en mesure de traiter efficacement le comportement des autres, y compris celui des législateurs. Prenons enfin l'article 3 de la *Charte des droits et libertés* qui prévoit que « [t]out citoyen canadien a le droit de vote et est éligible aux élections législatives fédérales ou provinciales. » Même si la législature peut embaucher les employés qu'elle juge appropriés, les former à la politique et licencier ceux qui se livrent au harcèlement, elle ne peut contrôler qui peut être élu ou qui peut être nommé. Pour illustrer de façon sans doute extrême ce qui précède, considérons la première phrase d'un reportage de CNN datant de 2015 et relatant la réélection en prison d'un délégué de l'État : « Ce n'est pas tous les jours qu'un politicien portant un bracelet de cheville posé par une prison de comté et accusé d'avoir eu des relations sexuelles avec sa secrétaire de 17 ans fait campagne pour sa réélection et gagne[10] » (Diamond, 2015).

Même si une assemblée législative peut prendre des mesures pour limiter la participation d'un législateur problématique aux activités de l'assemblée ou réduire sa capacité d'interaction avec le personnel, elle ne peut pas nécessairement l'exclure de l'assemblée en raison d'une inconduite de la même manière qu'elle peut interdire à un individu d'occuper un emploi ou de travailler dans les locaux.

D'autres disparités dans les recours prévus par une politique de lutte contre le harcèlement peuvent également apparaître en fonction des différents contextes d'emploi. Par exemple, on peut envisager de diminuer le salaire d'un employé qui s'est livré au harcèlement, mais ce recours ne serait pas possible dans le cas d'un bénévole non rémunéré. Il ne serait pas non plus nécessairement possible de réduire la paie d'un législateur dont le salaire est fixé par la loi.

De même, un comportement qui pourrait entraîner le licenciement d'un employé par le biais des pratiques traditionnelles des ressources humaines peut très bien rester confidentiel. On est loin de ce qui se passerait si l'Assemblée législative décidait d'expulser un législateur, ce qui ne pourrait se faire que par une décision politique explicite de la législature. Cette décision serait probablement extrêmement politisée et largement médiatisée – et il est peu probable que l'Assemblée législative prenne sa décision à huis clos.

Enfin, la réalité des positions particulières au sein des institutions législatives peut aboutir à des résultats politiques insatisfaisants dans certaines situations. Par exemple, supposons qu'un législateur soit accusé de harcèlement par un employé qui travaille pour lui dans le cadre d'une fonction particulière qui donne droit, disons à titre de

---

10 Traduction libre.

président du caucus, à un employé supplémentaire. Si le président du caucus démissionne pendant une enquête ou à cause de celle-ci, il n'est pas garanti que l'employé conserve son emploi si celui-ci est strictement lié à une nomination par le titulaire du poste. Un nouveau titulaire de poste peut souhaiter faire appel à son propre personnel, ce qui peut mettre fin à l'emploi du plaignant.

Toutes ces réalités distinguent la législature de nombreux autres employeurs qui peuvent mettre en place des procédures en matière de harcèlement sexuel entièrement internes, celles-ci s'appliquant uniformément à leurs employés tout en assurant potentiellement la sécurité d'emploi d'un plaignant au cours d'une procédure de résolution de plainte, et dont les effets peuvent être durables pour un individu particulier, comme une interdiction de réemploi.

Où et quand se fait le travail

Un autre élément du lieu de travail législatif mérite d'être pris en compte : le lieu et le moment du travail. Si les fonctions des législateurs s'exercent principalement à la législature et dans ses bureaux lorsque celle-ci siège, les législateurs peuvent s'acquitter de leurs tâches n'importe où. En plus des déplacements pour les comités et du travail des associations et groupes parlementaires (entraînant éventuellement des déplacements internationaux), les législateurs peuvent assister à des événements dans des circonscriptions bien au-delà de la leur. Les politiques doivent tenir compte de cette réalité problématique.

Il est assez simple de penser qu'une politique en milieu de travail s'applique aux personnes lorsqu'elles sont sur leur lieu de travail ou lorsqu'elles travaillent autrement. Toutefois, les limites du lieu et du moment où le travail commence et se termine ne sont pas toujours claires. Prenons l'exemple d'un législateur et de son personnel qui vont manger dans un restaurant après avoir travaillé tard au bureau : la politique doit-elle s'appliquer à un incident survenu au cours du dîner ? Que se passe-t-il si un législateur et son personnel assistent à une réception tenue en dehors de l'enceinte législative – comme une réception des Fêtes – mais n'y assistent pas dans le cadre de leurs fonctions professionnelles ?

Il existe des scénarios connexes dans lesquels l'application d'une politique doit être soigneusement étudiée. Supposons qu'un incident se produise entre un législateur et le personnel d'un autre législateur alors qu'il assiste au congrès de son parti politique. S'agit-il d'une question à traiter dans le cadre de la politique de la législature ou du parti ? Si le parti n'a pas de politique, quels sont les recours ?

Les législatures se sont attaquées à ces questions et ont élaboré leurs propres approches. Par exemple, la politique de lutte contre le harcèlement de l'Assemblée législative du Manitoba reconnaît explicitement que « les interactions peuvent prendre place à l'extérieur du lieu de travail et en dehors des heures de travail » et, par conséquent, « [l]a politique s'applique aux comportements inappropriés en dehors du travail » (Assemblée législative du Manitoba, 2019). De même, la politique de l'Assemblée législative de la Colombie-Britannique prévoit que « cette politique couvre les brimades, le harcèlement, la discrimination et la violence liés à l'emploi sur le lieu de travail ou en dehors de celui-ci et pendant ou hors des heures de travail[11] » (Legislative Assembly of British Columbia, 2019).

Une notion connexe problématique est celle de l'espace contrôlé par la législature. On peut comprendre qu'une législature veuille se proclamer zone exempte de harcèlement. Cependant, si un législateur se conduit de manière inappropriée avec un électeur qui se rend dans son bureau de circonscription qui est sous le contrôle de la législature, l'électeur doit-il recourir à la politique de la législature ? Si la législature crée des sites Web ou des comptes de médias sociaux pour les législateurs, les commentaires ou les messages qui y sont publiés relèvent-ils de la politique de la législature ?

De même, si les ressources de la législature sont utilisées d'une manière ou d'une autre – comme un téléphone ou un ordinateur – le comportement est-il visé par une politique ? Des actes tels que les politiques d'utilisation acceptable peuvent être utilisés de manière que le même comportement puisse être traité par plusieurs acteurs au sein de la législature, chacun considérant la situation à travers son propre prisme et ses propres outils. Cela n'est pas problématique en soi, car certaines questions peuvent être dissociées ; cependant, plus les acteurs sont nombreux, plus il est probable que la confidentialité ne sera pas respectée. En effet, il peut être utile de disposer d'actes qui permettent à la législature de s'attaquer à la conduite inappropriée d'un législateur même si une politique de lutte contre le harcèlement ne s'applique pas à la fois au plaignant et à la personne

---

11 Traduction libre.

mise en cause ou si un plaignant ne souhaite pas déposer une plainte. C'est ce qui est survenu notamment avec les allégations d'inconduite sexuelle contre le sénateur Don Meredith qui a démissionné un jour avant la tenue d'un vote sur son expulsion du Sénat.

Troisième caractéristique unique : les sphères privilégiées

L'existence du privilège parlementaire ajoute une couche de complexité à l'élaboration et à la mise en œuvre des politiques de lutte contre le harcèlement en milieu de travail. Comme l'a récemment expliqué la Cour suprême du Canada :

> Au Canada, les organes législatifs disposent de privilèges parlementaires inhérents qui découlent de leur nature et de leur fonction au sein d'une démocratie parlementaire basée sur le modèle du Parlement de Westminster. En protégeant certains domaines d'activité législative d'une révision externe, le privilège parlementaire contribue à maintenir la séparation des pouvoirs. Il accorde à l'organe législatif du gouvernement l'autonomie dont il a besoin pour exercer ses fonctions constitutionnelles. Le privilège parlementaire joue aussi un rôle important dans notre tradition démocratique puisqu'il fait en sorte que les représentants élus peuvent débattre vigoureusement des lois et demander à l'exécutif de rendre des comptes. (*Chagnon c. Syndicat de la fonction publique et parapublique du Québec*, par. 1).

Le privilège parlementaire comporte de nombreux aspects, mais les droits d'un législateur individuel à la liberté d'expression dans les débats législatifs et les droits collectifs de la législature de discipliner ses membres et de régir ses affaires internes sont particulièrement importants dans cette discussion. Il convient de noter d'emblée que le privilège parlementaire est un domaine extrêmement nuancé et que les perspectives de deux législatures données, même au Canada, peuvent diverger.

Liberté d'expression

Le *Bill of Rights* (déclaration des droits) anglais de 1689 a accordé une protection aux discours faits au Parlement de telle sorte qu'ils ne peuvent pas être contestés devant les tribunaux. Depuis lors, il est reconnu que les législateurs jouissent de la liberté d'expression dans les assemblées législatives au titre du privilège parlementaire. Chaque assemblée législative peut établir ses propres limites aux discours législatifs, y compris l'interdiction d'utiliser des mots et des phrases spécifiques considérées comme non parlementaires. En ce qui concerne la politique de harcèlement, il y a quelques points à considérer.

Premièrement, étant donné qu'une législature peut instituer des procédures pour traiter les discours inappropriés – par exemple, par le biais de recours au Règlement – les recours peuvent se chevaucher lorsque les interventions parlementaires contiennent des commentaires qui relèvent d'une politique de harcèlement. Si l'on demande au président de séance de se prononcer immédiatement sur un comportement donné, il peut être inopportun de soumettre ce même comportement à une autre entité pour enquête. Par exemple, on pourrait créer une situation au sein de la structure parlementaire où un comité est essentiellement invité à examiner une question sur laquelle le président de la législature s'est déjà prononcé ; et dans certaines législatures, les décisions du président peuvent être portées en appel auprès de l'ensemble de la chambre, ce qui est le cas au Sénat en vertu de l'article 2–5(3) du *Règlement*[12].

Les recours dédoublés au sein de la législature peuvent se justifier dans la mesure où la décision de savoir si un comportement enfreint la coutume en matière de décorum parlementaire est différente de la décision de savoir si ce même comportement enfreint une politique de harcèlement. Toutefois, les législateurs peuvent estimer que le réexamen des décisions d'un président est un exercice visant à déterminer la confiance de la législature en son président. Si la décision faisait l'objet d'un appel devant l'ensemble de la chambre, le recours externe n'aurait pour conséquence que de faire rapport aux législateurs sur une question qu'ils ont déjà examinée.

Par conséquent, il n'est pas surprenant que les législatures distinguent les discours parlementaires de leurs politiques de lutte contre le harcèlement. Par exemple, la politique de l'Assemblée législative du Yukon prévoit que « [p]ar souci de clarté, la présente politique ne s'applique pas aux débats et aux travaux de l'Assemblée

---

12 « Tout sénateur peut faire appel d'une décision au moment où le Président la rend, sauf si elle porte sur l'expiration du temps de parole. Le Sénat se prononce immédiatement sur l'appel suivant la procédure ordinaire pour déterminer la durée de la sonnerie. »

législative, des comités permanents ou spéciaux, ni aux personnes qui ne sont plus membres de l'Assemblée législative[13] » (Yukon Legislative Assembly, 2019, 2). De même, le code de conduite anti-harcèlement de l'Assemblée législative de la Saskatchewan prévoit que « la présente politique ne s'applique pas aux propos tenus par un député à l'Assemblée législative ou à l'un de ses comités[14] » (Saskatchewan Legislative Assembly, 2017, art. 3).

Deuxièmement, on peut se demander comment la liberté d'expression concorde avec les exigences de confidentialité d'une procédure de plainte. Par exemple, en vertu de la politique de lutte contre le harcèlement de Terre-Neuve-et-Labrador, « les déclarations faites dans le cadre d'un débat sur une question liée à la politique doivent respecter la confidentialité des processus prévus par la politique, ainsi que la vie privée du plaignant et des témoins[15] » (House of Assembly of Newfoundland and Labrador, 2019, 18). De même, la politique de l'Assemblée législative de la Nouvelle-Écosse prévoit que « toutes les déclarations faites à l'Assemblée législative doivent respecter la confidentialité du processus de résolution et la vie privée des personnes concernées[16] » (Legislative Assembly of Nova Scotia, 2016, 27).

Plaintes en matière de procédure

Supposons qu'une personne en interrompe constamment une autre pendant les réunions ou qu'elle choisisse de l'ignorer. Dans certains contextes, ces comportements peuvent être considérés comme du harcèlement ou une mise à l'écart en milieu de travail. Toutefois, il peut s'agir de comportements qu'un président de séance est tenu d'adopter en vertu des règles de procédure applicables de l'Assemblée législative. Les règles de procédure peuvent accorder à certains législateurs un temps de parole plus long que d'autres ou déterminer qui doit être reconnu dans le débat. De même, les règles de procédure et les lois en vigueur peuvent déterminer qui bénéficie d'avantages supplémentaires de certaines fonctions, de sorte qu'il existe des disparités dans le traitement des personnes en milieu de travail.

---

13 Traduction libre.
14 Traduction libre.
15 Traduction libre.
16 Traduction libre.

Certes, une personne peut se sentir marginalisée en milieu de travail en raison de la réalité parlementaire, comme un législateur non affilié qui peut avoir moins de possibilités de participation ou de mandats en comité. Même s'il faut invoquer le Règlement sur une question d'application inappropriée ou incorrecte des procédures parlementaires à un cas particulier, c'est à l'organe responsable de ces règles, généralement un comité des règles, qu'il revient d'en examiner les conséquences.

Imaginez ce qui pourrait se passer si les plaintes de harcèlement pouvaient être utilisées pour n'importe quelle question au sein de la législature. Si un législateur était contrarié par le rejet de sa demande de remboursement de frais de déplacement et faisait appel devant le comité ou la commission responsable, la décision de rejet de la demande pourrait-elle faire l'objet d'une plainte pour harcèlement ?

Bien que les deux exemples précédents soient frivoles, ce problème peut se poser avec acuité dans le cas d'un législateur dont le projet de loi est bloqué par le président d'un comité qui refuse de programmer des réunions à ce sujet. Il s'agit d'une impasse politique qui peut en effet être liée à un différend personnel qui pourrait constituer du harcèlement. Toutefois, l'exercice du pouvoir du président du comité n'est pas nécessairement approprié pour un examen externe.

En fin de compte, il se peut que les législateurs occupant certains postes utilisent leurs pouvoirs pour harceler. Cela justifie-t-il l'établissement d'un recours à une politique de harcèlement s'il existe un autre recours, par exemple un recours politique ?

Le dilemme du huis clos

Tous les débats législatifs ne sont pas publics pour de très bonnes raisons ; par exemple, lorsqu'un comité de gestion débat de questions de sécurité dans la Cité parlementaire. La divulgation des débats à huis clos viole le privilège de l'entité qui les mène (comme un sous-comité) et peut constituer un outrage à la législature. En outre, les conditions d'emploi du personnel de la législature contiennent généralement des dispositions très précises pour garantir la confidentialité des discussions à huis clos.

Selon la structure d'une politique donnée, il peut ne pas y avoir de mécanisme viable pour permettre les plaintes relatives à un comportement qui s'est produit au cours d'une procédure à huis clos. Le personnel pourrait non seulement violer les conditions de son contrat de travail, mais aussi risquer une condamnation pour outrage. En outre, en fonction de la politique, les détails de la réunion pourraient être communiqués à un autre acteur qui ne partage pas nécessairement le privilège parlementaire en question. Autoriser les plaintes concernant les procédures à huis clos pourrait permettre à une personne de communiquer les travaux d'un comité à un autre acteur.

Discipline et présence

Le privilège donne au corps législatif le droit de discipliner ses membres ainsi que d'exercer un pouvoir sur leur présence. Le privilège sur la discipline exclut la possibilité pour d'autres acteurs d'imposer des sanctions à un législateur qui enfreint une politique, ce qui signifie que les législateurs décident de leur sort entre eux ; cependant, les politiciens ne sont pas des acteurs impartiaux. Ce problème pourrait être résolu, comme cela a été fait récemment au Royaume-Uni, en autorisant des sanctions de la part d'une entité extérieure.

De même, la mise en œuvre d'une politique peut avoir une incidence sur la présence des législateurs, soit parce qu'elle les oblige à participer à un processus à des moments qui sont en conflit avec les séances, soit parce qu'elle limite la manière dont un plaignant et une personne mise en cause peuvent intervenir pendant le processus de résolution, par exemple en exigeant une séparation physique.

Bien que ces questions puissent sembler quelque peu alambiquées, la vraie question ici est celle du privilège d'un législateur individuel par rapport à celui de l'assemblée collective. Si l'assemblée complète décide d'une politique, elle doit examiner toutes les conséquences des privilèges qui en découlent. En règle générale, une question de privilège individuel devrait être rejetée au regard des droits collectifs lors de l'adoption d'une politique. Toutefois, si une politique n'est pas adoptée par la législature dans son ensemble, mais par un sous-groupe, comme un comité de gestion, l'intersection des obligations découlant de la politique avec l'existence et la réalité du privilège pourrait ne pas être claire. En outre, la mesure dans laquelle il est possible de renoncer implicitement à un privilège, par opposition à une renonciation expresse, n'est pas claire.

Conclusion

Les législatures continueront à débattre pendant un certain temps de la question de savoir comment réagir au harcèlement en milieu de travail, et en particulier au harcèlement sexuel. Les législatures étant des lieux de travail atypiques, de nouvelles questions complexes continueront de se poser.

Les différences entre les législatures ont une incidence sur les choix politiques qui se reflètent dans toute approche de lutte contre le harcèlement. Les réponses des législatures aux questions de harcèlement sexuel peuvent diverger selon que ses membres sont partisans ou non, élus ou nommés, ou même si elles ont des éléments de représentation ; une sanction contre une personne donnée – comme une suspension ou une expulsion – peut faire en sorte qu'une région ou un groupe minoritaire particulier ne soient pas représentés.

En fin de compte, les fondements juridiques qui permettent à une législature d'agir ou de s'insérer dans une relation de travail sont variés, et l'existence d'un privilège crée des difficultés peu communes dans le contexte du secteur privé. Bien que ces défis ne soient pas insurmontables, ils exigeront des législatures – et par extension, des législateurs – qu'ils examinent attentivement les politiques qu'ils élaborent pour répondre aux réalités uniques des législatures.

Références

Assemblée législative du Manitoba (2019). *Politique relative au respect en milieu de travail : Contrer et prévenir le harcèlement sexuel, le harcèlement et l'intimidation*, Winnipeg, Assemblée législative du Manitoba. Consulté le 16 avril 2021. https://www.gov.mb.ca/legislature/resources/pdf/rwp_policy.fr.pdf

BBC News (2020). "MPs Support Formation of Independent Bullying Complaints Panel", June 23, 2020. https://www.bbc.com/news/uk-politics-53153004.

Bureau du conseil privé (2015). *Guide du secrétaire parlementaire*, Ottawa, Gouvernement du Canada. https://pm.gc.ca/sites/pm/files/inline-files/Guide_for_Parl_Sec_2015_FR.pdf.

Chambre des communes (2018). *Manuel des allocations et services aux députés*, Ottawa, Parlement du Canada. Consulté le 16 avril 2021. https://www.noscommunes.ca/Content/MAS/mas-f.pdf

Collier, Cheryl N. and Raney, Tracey (2018). "Understanding Sexism and Sexual Harassment in Politics: A Comparison of Westminster

Parliaments in Australia, the United Kingdom, and Canada", *Social Politics: International Studies in Gender, State, and Society*, 25(3), 432–455. https://doi.org/10.1093/sp/jxy024

Collier, Cheryl, Raney, Tracey and Coltman, Linda (2019). "Harassment, Sexual Harassment and Provincial Legislatures – A Comparison of Policy Approaches in Nova Scotia and Newfoundland and Labrador", Paper presented at the annual Conference of the Atlantic Provinces Political Science Association, Acadia University, Wolfville (NS), October 18–20.

Comité permanent de la régie interne, des budgets et de l'administration (2019). *Modernisation de la politique du Sénat contre le harcèlement : Ensemble pour un milieu de travail sain*, Rapport du sous-comité sur les ressources humaines, Sénat du Canada, 42ᵉ législature, 1ʳᵉ session, Ottawa, Parlement du Canada.

Cour suprême du Canada (2018). Chagnon c. Syndicat de la fonction publique et parapublique du Québec, 2018 CSC 39, [2018] 2 RCS 687.

Cox, Dame Laura DBE (2018). *The Bullying and Harassment of House of Commons Staff: Independent Inquiry Report*, United Kingdom, House of Commons. https://www.parliament.uk/globalassets/documents/conduct-in -parliament/dame-laura-cox-independent-inquiry-report.pdf.

Deller, Deborah (2018). « Sélection et nomination des greffiers des provinces et territoires au Canada », *Revue parlementaire canadienne*, 41(3) (automne), 3–5.

Diamond, Jeremy (2015). "Virginia Lawmaker Re-Elected Despite Jail Sentence", *CNN*, January 14, 2015. Consulté le 16 avril 2021. https://www.cnn.com/2015/01/14/politics/lawmaker-jailed-wins-reelection /index.html.

Emploi et Développement social Canada (2020). *Le gouvernement du Canada publie le nouveau règlement sur le harcèlement et la violence dans les milieux de travail sous réglementation fédérale*, Communiqué de presse, 24 juin 2020. https://www.canada.ca/fr/emploi-developpement-social/nouvelles/2020/06 /le-gouvernement-du-canada-invite-les-milieux-de-travail-canadiens-a -se-preparer-en-vue-du-nouveau-reglement-sur-le-harcelement-et-la -violence.html.

Francis, Debbie (2019). *Bullying and Harassment in the New Zealand Parliamentary Workplace. External Independent Review*, Wellington, Parliament of New Zealand.

Freeman, Tom (2019). "Scottish Parliament launches new 'zero tolerance' sexual harassment policy", *Holyrood*, March 21, 2019. Consulté le 16 avril 2021. https://www.holyrood.com/news/view,scottish-parliament-launches -new-zero-tolerance-sexual-harassment-policy_10054.htm.

Gaudreault, Maryse (2016). « Politique sur le harcèlement en milieu de travail dans un contexte parlementaire », *Revue parlementaire canadienne*, 39(2) (été).

Legislative Assembly of Alberta (2019). *Dissolution Guidelines,* Revised February 2019. Edmonton, Legislative Assembly of Alberta. https://www.assembly .ab.ca/docs/default-source/reference/assembly-documents/dissolution _guidelines.pdf.

Legislative Assembly of British Columbia (2019). *Respectful Workplace Policy,* Victoria, Legislative Assembly of British Columbia. https://www.leg.bc .ca/content/CommitteeDocuments/41st-parliament/LAMC/2019-07-03 /Respectful-Workplace-Policy.pdf.

Legislative Assembly of Saskatchewan (2017). *Anti-Harassment Code of Conduct,* Regina, Legislative Assembly of Saskatchewan. Consulté le 1er avril 2021. https://www.legassembly.sk.ca/mlas/codes-of-conduct /anti-harassment-code-of-conduct.

Lieb, David A. (2019). "#MeToo Movement Was Not 1-Year Phenomenon in State Capitols", *National Post,* February 2, 2019. Consulté le 16 avril 2021. https://nationalpost.com/pmn/news-pmn/a-new-year-in-legislatures -brings-same-story-on-harassment.

McCluskey, Kalin and Read, Michael (2018). "Parliamentary Privilege and #MeToo", *Policy Options,* April 16, 2018. Consulté le 16 avril 2021. https:// policyoptions.irpp.org/fr/magazines/april-2018/parliamentary -privilege-metoo/.

Ministère de la Justice (2020). *Cahier d'information à l'intention de la ministre de la Justice du Canada,* Ottawa, Gouvernement du Canada. Consulté le 16 avril 2021. https://www.justice.gc.ca/fra/trans/transition/2019/nov /tab3.html.

Nadel, Jennifer (2019). "I Reported on Misogyny in Parliament 29 Years Ago – Shockingly Little Has Changed", *The Guardian,* July 18, 2019. Consulté le 16 avril 2021. http://www.theguardian.com/commentisfree/2019/jul/18 /misogyny-parliament-westminster-bullying-harassment-sexism.

National Conference of State Legislatures (2019). *Legislation on Sexual Harassment in the Legislature,* February 11, 2019. Consulté le 16 avril 2021. https://www.ncsl.org/research/about-state-legislatures/2018-legislative -sexual-harassment-legislation.aspx.

New Brunswick Broadcasting Co. c. Nouvelle-Écosse (Président de l'Assemblée législative), 1993, CanLII 153 (CSC), [1993] 1 RCS 319.

Newfoundland and Labrador House of Assembly (2008). *Shared Secretarial Assistance,* St. John's, Newfoundland and Labrador House of Assembly. https://www.assembly.nl.ca/ManComm/PoliciesGuidelines/Guide linesSharedSecretarialAssistance.pdf

Newfoundland and Labrador House of Assembly (2019). *Harassment-Free Workplace Policy Applicable to Complaints against Members of the House of Assembly,* St. John's, Newfoundland and Labrador House of Assembly. https://www.assembly.nl.ca/pdfs/HFWPApplicableToComplaints AgainstMHAsConcurredDec2-2019EffectiveApr1-20.pdf

Nova Scotia House of Assembly (2016). *Nova Scotia House of Assembly Policy on the Prevention and Resolution of Harassment in the Workplace*, Halifax, Nova Scotia House of Assembly. https://nslegislature.ca/sites/default /files/pdfs/people/harassment-policy.pdf

Ontario New Democratic Party Caucus v. Canadian Office and Professional Employees Union, Local 343, 2018, CanLII 47833 (ON LA).

Secrétariat du Conseil du Trésor (2011). *Politiques à l'intention des cabinets des ministres*, 28 janvier 2011. Ottawa, Gouvernement du Canada. Consulté le 16 avril 2021. https://www.canada.ca/fr/secretariat-conseil-tresor /services/politiques-cabinets-ministres-janvier-2011.html.

Sénat du Canada (2020). *Règlement du Sénat canadien*, sept. 2017, mise à jour en octobre 2020, Ottawa, Parlement du Canada.

The Canadian Press (2019). "27 Youth Banned from Parliament Hill for a Month after Climate Sit-In", *CTV News*, October 28, 2019. Consulté le 16 avril 2021. https://www.ctvnews.ca/politics/27-youth-banned-from -parliament-hill-for-a-month-after-climate-sit-in-1.4658691.

Union interparlementaire (2019). *Lignes directrices pour l'élimination du sexisme, du harcèlement et de la violence à l'égard des femmes dans les parlements*, Genève, Union interparlementaire. https://www.ipu.org/fr/ressources/ publications/reference/2019-11/lignes-directrices-pour-lelimination- du-sexisme-du-harcelement-et-de-la-violence-legard-des-femmes- dans-les.

Yukon Legislative Assembly (2019). *Respectful Conduct Policy*, Whitehorse, Yukon Legislative Assembly. https://yukonassembly.ca/sites/default /files/inline-files/Respectful-Conduct-Policy.pdf.

CHAPTER 3

Parliament, the Duty to Consult, and Reconciliation

Steven Chaplin

Abstract

Until 2018, there was uncertainty about the Crown's duty to consult Indigenous people during the preparation of legislation that might affect their rights. In 2018, the Supreme Court determined that the duty could not be enforced in the courts, because the legislative process was the domain of Parliament. This chapter argues that the duty still exists in the legislative context, but it is enforced through Parliament. To meet this responsibility, Parliament should modify existing procedures and appoint an Indigenous Advisor to assist them in holding the government to account for its duty to consult. In addition, Parliament should be more aware of Indigenous issues when considering legislation. If it does so in a constructive manner, this could play a major role in reconciliation.

Résumé

Jusqu'en 2018, l'incertitude régnait quant à l'obligation de la Couronne de consulter les peuples autochtones lors de la préparation de mesures législatives susceptibles d'affecter leurs droits. En 2018, la Cour suprême a déterminé que cette obligation ne pouvait pas être appliquée par les tribunaux, car le processus législatif relevait du Parlement. Cette décision soutient que l'obligation existe toujours dans le contexte législatif, mais qu'elle doit être appliquée par le Parlement.

> Pour s'acquitter de cette responsabilité, le Parlement doit modifier les procédures existantes et nommer un conseiller autochtone pour l'aider à demander des comptes au gouvernement sur son obligation de consultation. En outre, le Parlement doit être plus conscient des questions autochtones lorsqu'il examine des mesures législatives. En le faisant de manière constructive, il pourra contribuer significativement à la réconciliation.

Crown[1] consultation with Indigenous people forms a significant pillar of support for Indigenous rights.[2] If carried out to its fullest, consultation can be a meaningful aspect of reconciliation. Where consultation is successful, an arrangement is reached that allows for the fulfillment of both a government objective and the aspirations and rights of the Indigenous people who might have been adversely affected by a unilateral government decision. Until the Supreme Court of Canada decision in *Mikisew Cree First Nation v. Canada (Governor General in Council)* (hereafter *Mikisew Cree*), it was unclear whether the Crown's legal duty to consult with Indigenous people applied to the development of legislation and the legislative process. In *Mikisew Cree*, the Court determined that no judicially enforceable duty existed for those activities and functions of the Crown. Legislation and its development are part of the parliamentary process, which is immune from judicial review. As a result, when developing, introducing, and shepherding legislation through Parliament,[3] the

---

1   The Crown has various meanings. In this chapter, unless indicated specifically, the Crown is essentially the ministers of the Crown acting with collective responsibility. These ministers carry out both executive functions and legislative ones. They are responsible to the House of Commons for their executive actions and for the introduction of most legislation. The Crown is supported by the public service, which, when carrying out their functions, are part of the Crown.

2   In this chapter, the term "Indigenous rights" is used wherever possible, however, the *Constitution Act, 1982* and various court decisions prefer the term "Aboriginal rights." When discussing particular forms of consultation, I will use "First Nations" to signify that the consultation is taking place at a collective level with self-recognized Indigenous nations.

3   Parliament is a collective institution composed of the Queen, the Senate, and the House of Commons acting together, with the outcome of their work being legislation. For this chapter, I use the term "Parliament" in a more vernacular sense to mean primarily the House of Commons. For provincial legislatures, which are composed of the Lieutenant Governor and the Legislative Assembly, I generally use "Parliament" in this chapter to mean the Legislative Assembly.

actions and decisions of the Crown and its servants are not subject to oversight and review by the courts. They are, however, responsible to Parliament.

For those who only see rights protection and promotion through a court-centric and judicially based accountability structure, this decision would suggest that the duty to consult is not applicable to the development, introduction, and adoption of legislation. The Crown is off the hook for these activities. There is therefore a large scope of "Crown" activity that is outside of the duty. So long as legislation is used, consultation is not required, and Indigenous rights could be compromised.

But all should not be considered lost for Indigenous rights and the duty to consult when it comes to legislation. In fact, the *Mikisew Cree* decision has opened an avenue that could result in better and more meaningful consultation, public debate, and fuller reconciliation. By declining jurisdiction, the Court has shifted responsibility from the courts to Parliament for the oversight of the Crown's duty to consult in the legislative process. This chapter outlines why this can provide greater scrutiny and accountability for the performance of the duty as well as further the objectives of reconciliation. Parliament has different, and in some cases better, tools and processes than courts to hold the Crown to account for its duty in the legislative context. Parliament also has the ability, and I suggest the responsibility, to strengthen legislation to recognize and promote Indigenous rights and interests.

The Duty to Consult and Reconciliation

The duty to consult arises when the Crown "contemplates executive action that may adversely affect s. 35 rights." (*Mikisew Cree*, para. 25).[4] The duty ensures that the Crown acts honourably by preventing it from acting unilaterally in ways that undermine these rights (*Mikisew Cree*, para. 26). The duty not only recognizes and promotes Indigenous

---

4 Section 35 of the *Constitution Act, 1982* provides:
>   (1) The existing aboriginal and treaty rights of the aboriginal peoples of Canada are hereby recognized and affirmed.
>   (2) In this Act, "aboriginal peoples of Canada" includes the Indian, Inuit and Métis peoples of Canada.
>   (3) For greater certainty, in subsection (1) "treaty rights" includes rights that now exist by way of land claims agreements or may be so acquired.

rights, it is also an important aspect of reconciliation (*Mikisew Cree*, para. 26 [majority]; para. 58, 61 [dissent]). Addressing and accommodating all interests and rights through meaningful consultation results in just settlements and is less costly, more efficient, and less acrimonious than litigation (*Mikisew Cree*, para. 26). In short, a major purpose of consultation in the constitutional context is reconciliation (Brideau 2019).

That consultation is a duty means that the "right" to be consulted is more procedural than substantive. Consultation requires meaningful discussion, consideration, and potential accommodation. It does not suggest or demand a particular outcome. All duties in law are about relationship. One person owes another a duty to behave in a certain way towards, or to protect, another person. The expectation is that the person that owes the duty is required to compromise the exercise of their own rights and powers and to act in the interest the person to whom the duty is owed. In some cases, such as relationships of trust, the compromise required can be almost totally in favour of the person to whom the duty is owed. In the case of Indigenous rights, the courts have found that the duty to consult does not extend quite that far.

The duty to consult is said to flow from the honour of the Crown and is fiduciary in nature. It requires good faith by the Crown in all its dealings with Indigenous people. The duty, along with other substantive Indigenous rights, has also been determined to be entrenched in the Constitution. As such, when consulting with Indigenous Peoples, the Crown must recognize that the purpose of consultation is figuring out how to incorporate and accommodate Indigenous rights. Since these rights are engaged when balancing various policy outcomes, it must be borne in mind that such rights generally supersede the interests of others. However, like most rights, Indigenous rights are not absolute, and the Crown must also work with Indigenous people to determine reasonable accommodations for non-Indigenous interests. Where rights seemingly "collide," there is generally no hierarchy of rights, and a means must be found to reconcile them to each other such that each is given effect (*Chamberlain v. Surrey School District No. 36*, para. 135).

The fact that a duty is imposed on the Crown has implications for the duty to consult. These include a centralization of the duty in a single entity, the Crown, such that a coherent "policy" for carrying out the duty needs to be formulated (see, e.g., Department of Aboriginal Affairs and Northern Development Canada 2011; Government of

Manitoba 2009; Government of Quebec 2008).[5] The Crown, as government at all levels in Canada, is ubiquitous; it touches all aspects of society, therefore it has a duty to govern in a manner that respects Indigenous rights in all aspects of Canadian life. And the Crown represents the state, giving it the capacity to bind future governments to certain actions and behaviours. Any resulting agreement can be enforced in the courts, either as agreements, or possibly as treaties that embody Indigenous rights.

To date, the Crown has not been inclined to fully embrace the responsibilities implicit in the duty to consult or to enter into agreements (or treaties) based on the duty. Many government policies are designed and implemented so as to meet the minimum legal requirements that will allow the Crown to move its agenda forward with the least amount of "interference," including any impediment based on Indigenous rights.[6] This reluctance can partially be explained by a continuing colonial attitude that places Crown sovereignty supported by confidence from a majority in Parliament at the centre of the constitutional framework. This concept of sovereignty places all authority in the Crown, with constitutional rights being recognized as limits on Crown sovereignty. Even then, the majority of rights are subject to reasonable limits and justifications that are determined in parliamentary institutions representing majoritarian views.[7]

Constitutional rights of Indigenous people, as collective rights, are different from individual rights set out in the *Canadian Charter of Rights and Freedoms*. Their rights flow from a distinct and continuing sovereignty over their lands and people. This sovereignty was not extinguished or displaced by Crown sovereignty. In order to reconcile Indigenous rights and sovereignties, the duty to consult has been recognized by the courts. The duty supports the theory of "nation to nation" relationships between the Crown Indigenous people, whose inherent, unextinguished rights were held collectively within their

---

5   For a discussion on the effectiveness of such policies and reconciliation see Ariss, MacCallum Fraser, and Somani (2017).

6   For example, the Quebec policy (dating from 2008), attributing the notion to the courts, states: "The Aboriginal communities must not frustrate the efforts made in good faith by the Crown. Nor should they defend unreasonable positions to prevent the Crown from acting in those cases where, despite a true consultation, the parties are unsuccessful in reaching agreement" (Government of Quebec 2008, 7).

7   For example, section 1 of the *Charter* provides that most of the rights and freedoms can be subject to such reasonable limits as are demonstrably justified in a democracy.

pre-contact "nations." Treaties and the exercise of authority by the Crown are therefore seen as a nation-to-nation relationship, with overlapping rights and sovereignty within a single geographic area. On this view, the rights of Indigenous people flow from a sovereignty that is parallel, not subservient, to Crown sovereignty. Given the shared geography and the multiplicity of Indigenous nations within the geographic territory of Canada, a more accurate view is one of nations within a nation, with varying sovereignties and rights that must be consulted on and reconciled.

By imposing a duty to consult, the courts require that the necessary dialogue take place at an early stage to allow the political and governmental leadership of both the Crown and Indigenous nations to reconcile the rights based on "competing sovereignties," thereby avoiding litigation. Otherwise, the result is a court-imposed ruling on what are predominantly questions based on relationships, something the courts are not best at resolving. This is why when there is a failure to consult, the remedy is usually to invalidate or suspend the decision of the Crown, with a direction from the court to start the decision-making process over, or at least to consult on those aspects of the decision that required consultation (*Tsleil-Waututh Nation v. Canada*; *Coldwater Indian Band v. Canada*). This remedy makes sense. The concept of consultation does not necessarily lead to a particular result. It is designed to ensure a process of discussion and accommodation with a hoped-for mutual understanding of a way forward for the Crown's initiative in a manner that protects and promotes Indigenous rights. Although the result may be that the renewed consultation is more focused and limited (*Tsleil-Waututh Nation v. Canada*; *Coldwater Indian Band v. Canada*), the point of the remedy is to compel discourse, which is the foundation of reconciliation.

Before the Supreme Court of Canada decision in *Mikisew Cree*, there was uncertainty over whether the duty to consult applied to legislative activity. Did the duty apply to the Crown's preparation of Bills for introduction into Parliament? And if not, did the duty to consult therefore apply to Parliament itself? The Court has determined that courts only have jurisdiction to supervise the duty to consult when the Crown is engaged in executive functions pursuant to the prerogative or statutory authority. The focus must therefore shift to Parliament when considering the duty in the legislative context. The Court rejected the notion that the Crown's duty to consult shifted to Parliament, thus creating a duty on Parliament. The duty remains with the Crown, but the fulfillment of the duty, in the legislative context, is subject to parliamentary not judicial oversight. As a result, parliamentary processes and practices will have to be adopted and adapted to fulfill this responsibility. Along with changes to practices, parliamentarians will be required to adopt a revised mindset that appreciates the constitutional need to hold the government to account and legislate in a manner that respects, promotes, and, where necessary, enforces a recognition of Indigenous rights within the context of a nation-to-nation, or at least shared, governance framework.

The *Mikisew Cree* Judgment: The Crown and Parliament

The principal issue in *Mikisew Cree* was whether the Crown owed a judicially enforceable duty to consult when preparing legislation for introduction into Parliament. Given that the Crown operates only with the confidence of the House of Commons, has a large role in setting the agenda of the House of Commons, and is responsible for introducing the vast majority of Bills that are enacted as legislation, it was argued that the duty to consult should also attach to these aspects of the Crown's activities (Davis 2016). In the same way that the Crown was required to consult before taking any executive action or when implementing any policy that could have an impact on Indigenous rights, the Crown should also have to consult on, at least, the development of legislation. This was the position taken by the Mikisew Cree, and supported by numerous Indigenous groups, before the Supreme Court. The Court did not accept this position. It based its opinion on the separation of powers between the Crown and Parliament and parliamentary privilege that ensures the independence of Parliament from judicial review (*Mikisew Cree*, paras. 2, 102, 148).

The separation of powers, an underlying principle of the constitution, recognizes that the state has three branches—the Crown (the executive), the judiciary, and the legislature—that operate somewhat independently of each other,[8] but with complex accountability relationships to each other. In *Mikisew Cree*, the Court had to first consider

---

8   In Canada, as in all Westminster systems of government, there is some overlapping, since the government Ministry is composed of Members of Parliament required to sit in one of the Houses (predominantly the House of Commons), is required to have the confidence of the House of Commons, is continually accountable to the House, and enjoys many advantages in introducing legislation and controlling the House agenda.

the relationship of the Crown to the legislature. The Crown acts in a different capacity in Parliament. Formally, Parliament consists of the Queen, the House of Commons, and the Senate (*Constitution Act, 1867*, s. 17),[9] with the entire structure referred to as the Queen in Parliament. In the case of Parliament, the Court confirmed that within Parliament the Queen (Crown) acts in a legislative capacity, not an executive one.[10]

The next question for the Court was whether the development of legislation, prior to its introduction, formed part of a parliamentary proceeding. The Mikisew Cree accepted that the drafting of a Bill for introduction into the House of Commons and the processes following introduction were legislative. However, they asked the Court to find that the policy development prior to drafting should be subject to the duty to consult (*Mikisew Cree*, para. 116). The Court rejected any dividing line, finding that the entire process of policy development through enactment formed part of the legislative process. The Court based its reasoning on precedents (*Reference re Canada Assistance Plan*) where policy development for legislation was considered part of the legislative process. In concurring reasons, some judges added excerpts from cabinet manuals and other material that showed the complex multi-step processes of developing policy into legislation. This created a seamless process, and allowing judicial review at any point would suggest that review might be available at every point (*Mikisew Cree*, paras. 160–165, 170 per Rowe J.). This could not be allowed, since to do so would be an impermissible interference by the courts in Parliament's business.

A group of concurring judges added that failing to respect the separation of powers by imposing a duty to consult on the Crown pre-legislation could result in an infringement of parliamentary sovereignty (*Mikisew Cree*, para. 135). Parliament might believe that it had little choice but to pass legislation in a particular form, based on the Crown's duty to consult having been met. It would be possible that the Bill, introduced by the Crown, resulted from the consultation and that if it were to be amended, the rights upon which the consultation took place would thereby be violated. Parliament's hand would have been forced by the Crown's actions, and the process would remove Parliament's ability to amend or reject legislation based on the Crown's

---

9 Similarly, the provincial legislatures are composed of the Lieutenant Governor and the Legislative Assembly (ss. 69 and 71).

10 The executive is defined separately in the *Constitution Act, 1867*, ss. 9–14, 58.

relationship to a third party. Parliamentary sovereignty requires that the ultimate responsibility for the content of legislation lies with Parliament, not the Crown.

The position of the Court that sees the preparation of legislation as part of the legislative process, protected by parliamentary privilege and therefore immune from judicial intervention, is consistent with other jurisprudence that finds that pre-parliamentary activity is part of a parliamentary proceeding. Bill preparation is inextricably connected to materials (such as reports, questions, and speeches) that are produced for the purpose of a proceeding (i.e., preparatory materials). Preparation of Bills intended to be enacted as legislation, which is the sole domain of the legislative branch, fits within privilege as found in the jurisprudence (*Reference re Canada Assistance Plan*).

Once it was determined that the actions of the Crown in the development, introduction, and support of a Bill were all part of the legislative process, the Court turned its mind to the application of parliamentary privilege. Parliament has two constitutional functions: it legislates and it deliberates, including the holding of government to account (*Vaid v. Canada (House of Commons)*, para. 41). For both functions, the Crown is accountable to the House of Commons, not the courts. Legislation, however introduced, becomes the responsibility of Parliament. It controls the timetable, the capacity to examine and amend and, ultimately, to pass or reject the proposed legislation. The procedures for the enactment of legislation are established by Parliament. This is where parliamentary privilege becomes important to the discussion. Parliamentary privilege protects the proceedings of Parliament from being reviewed, questioned, or impeached by the courts or by any body outside of Parliament (*Bill of Rights 1689*, Article 9). As a result, the internal workings and proceedings of Parliament, including the introduction and passage of legislation, are solely the responsibility of Parliament. Not only does Parliament control and manage the actions of the Crown with respect to legislation, the processes of Parliament and the requirements for proposed legislation for Parliament are not reviewable by the courts. Any request for judicial review of any aspect of the legislative process would invite the courts to interfere with the business of Parliament, which is precluded by privilege. In the end, it was determined that the work product of the Crown relating to proposed legislation was not executive but rather legislative in nature—and therefore not reviewable in the courts.

The effect of the *Mikisew Cree* decision is to place within Parliament the responsibility for how the constitutional rights of Indigenous people are considered and protected throughout the entire legislative process. The recognition, policing, and enforcement of the duty to consult in the legislative process is for Parliament to determine. The recognition of this locus of accountability does not change the constitutional nature of the rights at issue nor the significance of consultation in the rights determination discussion. The duty on the Crown remains. It is the forum and processes for ensuring that this duty is met in the legislative context that have now clearly been identified as the responsibility of Parliament.

The Role of Parliament and the Crown's Duty to Consult in the Legislative Process

The Supreme Court makes it clear that the duty to consult always rests with the Crown. The finding of the Court does not transfer the duty to Parliament (*Mikisew Cree*, para. 36, 124). In other words, there is no duty in Parliament to consult. It may choose to consult as part of its legislating process, but it is a choice not a duty.

Although the Supreme Court has determined that the Crown's duty to consult in relation to the development, introduction, and enactment of legislation cannot be enforced by the courts and that courts cannot impose a duty to consult on Parliament, this does not mean that the Crown's duty cannot be applied to legislating or that Parliament should not play its part in the oversight of such duty. All the Court has determined is that the courts do not have a role to play. What they did not, and could not, explore was the role that Parliament can and should play in ensuring that the Crown meets its duty to Indigenous people in the legislative process. For the Court to suggest how Parliament should proceed, it was recognized, would be an unconstitutional interference, by the courts, in the proceedings of Parliament (*Mikisew Cree*, para. 164 per Brown J.). The *Mikisew Cree* decision placed oversight and accountability of the Crown for fulfillment of its duty in the legislative process where it constitutionally belongs—that is, with Parliament.

In the Westminster system of government, there are two forms of constitutional accountability of Crown and executive functions. One is judicial review in the courts for legal matters, including the exercise of authority by the executive. The other is accountability of the executive to Parliament. This second form of accountability, often referred to as holding the government to account, is as legitimate as judicial accountability. It too is an aspect of public law in Canada (Chaplin 2016, 277). In many instances, the underlying duty and responsibility of the Crown remains the same. The difference is the locus of the accountability. In the case of the duty to consult, the courts have determined that they do not have the jurisdiction to hold the government to account for the exercise of the duty in the context of legislating. However, Parliament does. The nature of the duty in the legislative context and how the government is held accountable for the exercise of the duty when preparing and presenting legislation is to be determined and enforced through Parliament. The fact that the duty is not enforceable through the courts does not mean that the Crown does not have the duty in the legislative context. It is just a question of where the fulfillment of the duty will be considered.

The recognition of the role that Parliament plays in holding the Crown to account both for its actions and its legislation is a recognition of two important principles underlying the duty to consult and reconciliation. The first is that the duty remains with the Crown and does not shift to Parliament or anyone else. Although the accountability of the Crown is to Parliament and not the courts, the duty remains. Second, Parliament has a role in helping to enact legislation that promotes and protects Indigenous rights. Through its public processes of debate and committee work, Parliament provides a public forum for both Indigenous and non-Indigenous people to engage in debate and examination of the issues. Such a forum provides a public manifestation of discussion, compromise, and reconciliation.[11]

Leaving the duty with the Crown also allows for the relationship between the Crown and Indigenous Peoples to rest upon a nation-to-nation framework. The Crown has a duty to Indigenous nations and people, and the Crown within the Westminster system is accountable to Parliament. Considered in this way, the Westminster system of government remains intact, and there is a recognition of continued nationhood as opposed to any form of forced assimilation of

---

11 The importance of public participation and the symbolism of inclusiveness as part of the reconciliation process should not be underestimated. For an examination of the importance of such public recognition in protocol see Williams (2020).

Indigenous people that would result from their absorption into the colonial apparatus of the dominant society's political and democratic institutions. The question becomes how democratic institutions should ensure that Crown's and country's obligations are met when the Crown is engaging, on behalf of the dominant society, with Indigenous Peoples and their governments and institutions. How can Parliament orient itself so that it balances the responsibility of the Crown in meeting its duty to consult with the rights and interests of both Indigenous and non-Indigenous people? How can Parliament further reconciliation?

The ability of Parliament to carry out this responsibility is dependent on a recognition by both Parliament and the Crown of the fact that the duty and obligation that the Crown owes to Indigenous Peoples is also applicable to its role in the development, introduction, and shepherding of legislation through Parliament. The Crown must accept that the accountability framework is in Parliament and that Parliament has responsibility for oversight of the duty in the legislative context. In the same way that the Crown accepts that it must respond to the courts' oversight for the fulfillment of its duty in its executive functions, it has the same responsibility to Parliament in the legislative context. And, in the same way that courts have developed rules, procedures, and tests on judicial review, Parliament needs to develop its own practices, rules, and tests for parliamentary review of the exercise of the duty to consult.

The responsibility for the protection of this right and the importance of consultation in the legislative process lies with Parliament. If parliamentarians do not accept and act on this responsibility, a major component of the rights of Indigenous people in the legislative context is ephemeral. Putting in place the processes and mechanisms to ensure that the Crown fulfills its duty to consult in the legislative context is a responsibility that parliamentarians owe to Indigenous Peoples.

Procedural Not Structural Changes as the Best Response

There have been some suggestions for structural reform to Parliament, or the House of Commons in particular, that would allow for direct Indigenous participation in the institutions themselves. I would suggest that Parliament has the necessary tools and capacity without structural change. In fact, such structural changes risk entrenching colonial ideas and frustrating reconciliation. Proposals such as designating seats in the House of Commons for Indigenous people,[12] establishing an additional house of Parliament,[13] or the inclusion of a constitutionally recognized Indigenous advisory body (Morris 2015) risk such entrenchment and assimilation. While such structural changes may work and be appropriate in other countries, such proposals are not workable in Canada.

There are two primary reasons for this. The first is the concern of Indigenous Peoples that participation directly in institutions could be regarded as a form of assimilation into a dominant culture as opposed to nation-to-nation engagement. There is also a risk of "ghettoization" or "tokenism," where the interests and rights of Indigenous people are likely to be consistently overridden by the "majority" that would continue to dominate parliamentary institutions. Any later challenges could be met with arguments based on the "fact" that Indigenous people were participants in the decision and, therefore, should live with the majority decision of which they were a part. The second is the complexity of First Nations, Inuit, and Métis people in Canada. There are approximately 600 First Nations with 60 linguistic groups, with each first nation having a different relationship with the Crown based on treaties, treaty negotiations, and status under the *Indian Act*. In addition, the Inuit and Métis Peoples have a different relationship with the Crown, since the *Indian Act* is not applicable to them. In countries or states where there are reserved seats in Parliament or the suggestion of an Indigenous assembly as part of Parliament or as a defined advisory group, there is essentially a single or more homogenous Indigenous nation with whom the government has a relationship. In Canada, where there is great diversity among the Indigenous nations and population and where the relationship between the Crown and Indigenous groups is at different stages of development, it is best that the involvement of the Parliament be such that it holds the Crown to account for respecting these relationships in its legislative agenda.

By using and modifying its existing tools and developing new ones within its purview, Parliament will be better able to play a significant and meaningful role in ensuring reconciliation between the

---

12 As is the case in Finland and the state of Maine.

13 As was proposed in the *Report of the Royal Commission on Aboriginal Peoples*, recommendations 2.3.53 and 2.3.54 (Royal Commission on Aboriginal Peoples 1996, 297–363).

Crown and Indigenous people. Such enhancements will also ensure that legislation is consistent with, and promotes, Indigenous rights and self-determination.

Parliamentary Oversight

The development, introduction, and enactment of legislation form part of a parliamentary proceeding for which both Houses are responsible. They can establish any rule, process, and condition relating to any aspect of proceedings. This includes the establishment of preconditions for those aspects of Crown activities that were the subject of the *Mikisew Cree* litigation. Parliament can insist on the duty being fulfilled in the legislative process, can develop the standard that it expects the government to meet prior to and during the legislative process, and can test the government's consultation process through examination of the actions of government officials as well as by questioning those who were consulted. Parliament also has the capacity to conduct its own form of "consultation" by calling witnesses, including affected Indigenous groups, to ensure that resulting legislation meets the objective of reconciliation.

Parliament has the constitutional function of holding the government to account for both its actions and for any proposed legislation. It can establish procedures for inquiring into how the Crown exercises its duties towards Indigenous Peoples in the same way that courts can, but for parliamentary reasons. Either House can impose any requirements it likes relating to the legislative process. Parliament has the capacity to demand answers from the Crown about what Indigenous issues were identified when developing legislative policy, whether or not a decision was made about consultation and the scope of consultation, the names of those who were consulted, what issues were identified by both Indigenous people and policy advisors with respect to the proposed legislation, and what changes in direction or content the Crown considered prior to its proposed legislation. These questions may be considered outside the jurisdiction of the courts to ask, but they are not outside the jurisdiction of Parliament.

One of the easiest ways for Parliament to exercise this oversight would be to require a written statement from the appropriate minister on Indigenous consultations that preceded the introduction of any government legislation. The obligation could either be included in changes to the *Department of Justice Act*, in language similar to that which was recently introduced with respect to *Charter* compliant statements (*Department of Justice Act*, s. 4.2), or each House could include language in its Standing Orders that requires such a statement. Since the statement is for the purposes of parliamentary oversight, Parliament has the capacity to insist on such a statement as well to determine the content required of the statement. Parliament could thereby satisfy itself that the duty was fulfilled or decide to inquire further into the Indigenous issues that pertain to any proposed legislation.

In order to ensure that such statements are not considered merely pro forma, a provision could also be included in the Standing Orders that requires that any statement made and any related legislation be referred to a parliamentary committee[14] to examine the question of how the duty to consult was respected in the drafting of legislation. At any such committee, government officials could be called as witnesses, as could the minister responsible. In addition, Indigenous Peoples would be able to address concerns with the report and thereby engage with Parliament. In either case, they would have the capacity to contact the parliamentary committee and become witnesses to explain to the committee the consultation process, if such a process took place, or to demand that consultation take place. In either event, the parliamentary committee would have the capacity to advise the House that it ought not to proceed with the legislation until such consultation takes place (the same remedy that a court would order with respect to failure of the duty to consult when legally required) or to amend any proposed legislation to take into account the concerns raised by Indigenous Peoples during the committee hearings. This second approach is one that is available to Parliament but is not available to the courts.

Ensuring that Indigenous consultations have taken place in the legislative process and that public debate and discussion have been undertaken with Indigenous people, who wish to participate, would be a hallmark of reconciliation. In addition, the degree of debate and the parliamentary exposure of the consultation process could be used by the courts in any subsequent litigation over whether resulting legislation violates any section 35 rights. Where there has been an alleged violation, the courts could examine the parliamentary record relating

---

14 *Standing Orders of the House of Commons*, SO 108(3)(g).

to the sufficiency of the Crown's consultation in the preparation of the legislation and any parliamentary response. This could assist the courts in determining whether the alleged violation can be justified.[15] Although a lack consultation does not necessarily result in a violation of section 35, meaningful consultation can form the basis of a justification for such a violation.[16]

Parliamentarians are generally not well versed in Indigenous issues, as a result of historical gaps in the education system, the complexity of Indigenous issues in the modern world, and the fact that Indigenous nations and histories are diverse. Also, the rights at issue and the Indigenous groups affected by any individual Bill may be subject specific. As a result, it would be advisable for Parliament to establish an internal Indigenous Advisor akin to the Parliamentary Budget Officer, who would have the responsibility to examine legislation and proposed Bills and advise Parliament on Indigenous issues that they believe Parliament ought to be investigating. If there is a single committee, or joint committee, established to examine legislation for Indigenous issues, an employee in the Advisor's office could also be the Library of Parliament analyst, or responsible for the analyst assigned to the committee. The creation of a position within Parliament would ensure continuity. Also, by the creation of the office, Parliament could adequately resource an internal body that has the capacity and the funds that are often missing for Indigenous groups to be able to access the government, Parliament, and other federal institutions.[17] This Advisor could have both the necessary funding and staffing that allows Indigenous groups the ability to see that their interests are brought before Parliament. The creation of the office would also

---

15 For a discussion of the limited but significant role that parliamentary debate can play in a justification exercise see Chaplin (2020), in which the use of parliamentary materials in section 1 of the *Charter* analysis is examined in detail. Since the concepts of reasonable limits and justification are similar, and here we are also examining legislation that potentially limits rights, how parliamentary materials may be examined in one context can provide guidance in the other.

16 Although not in the context of legislation, the relationship between the duty to consult and justification is the basis of the decisions *Tsleil-Waututh Nation v. Canada* and *Coldwater Indian Band v. Canada*.

17 The question of funding for Indigenous groups and nations to be able to fully participate in consultations, litigation, and other forms of advocacy, particularly when their counterpart is the Crown, with seemingly endless resources, is endemic. For an outline of the challenges, including financing, faced by Indigenous groups in the consultation process, see Ariss, MacCallum Fraser, and Somani (2017).

provide a single access point, that Indigenous leaders and lobbyists would have access to in order to ensure that their issues are brought to parliamentarians' and the public's attention. The Indigenous Advisor, through whom and with whom Indigenous leaders and individuals could work, would have the capacity to bring issues to the attention of Parliament and assist Parliament in assessing Indigenous issues for consideration, including the sufficiency of any ministerial statement. If there were also to be a designated committee, whether specific to Indigenous issues or for all constitutional issues, with which the Advisor and Indigenous leaders could work, this would also demonstrate the seriousness of the commitment to Indigenous rights and reconciliation. The highlighting of issues would not necessarily depend on political decision makers, but rather an independent internal parliamentary officer would provide neutral public information. Whether and how parliamentarians choose to engage the issue would still be left to them.

The combination of an independent Indigenous Advisor and the requirement of a ministerial statement on how the duty to consult was engaged in the development of legislation, with an automatic referral to an identified committee, would contribute to the necessary parliamentary oversight to ensure that Indigenous issues are appropriately engaged with and addressed in the legislative process. Such a parliamentary office could also have a constructive and meaningful role in a public forum, with public engagement, that is necessary for reconciliation.

The structures and processes outlined here might not be perfect, but the effort is important. If Parliament fails in this responsibility, or takes it too lightly, there is always the ability of Indigenous people to raise the failure at election time. Further, if any resulting legislation is considered to violate the Indigenous rights guaranteed by the *Constitution Act, 1982*, that legislation will be subject to review by the courts. If Parliament takes up its responsibility and ensures that the Crown exercises its duty to consult in the legislative process or corrects any Crown failure in the legislative process, then reconciliation, both legally and politically, has a better chance of being achieved.

Parliament's Additional Obligations

While the *Mikisew Cree* decision focuses on the duty to consult, with the result that Parliament has the obligation to ensure that the Crown has consulted in the legislative process, as set out above, Parliament's role with respect to reconciliation can, and should be, broader. For full reconciliation, all legislation needs to be developed in such a way as to integrate with the various Indigenous legal and governance systems and be workable with any treaty or other constitutional rights that exist. In addition to normative provisions in legislation, legislation often includes processes and procedures, decision-making authority, and regulation-making authority. All these aspects of legislation must be examined by Parliament within the context of a constitution which recognizes pre-existing, continuing, Aboriginal rights.

In addition to ensuring that Indigenous Peoples have been consulted, Parliament has an obligation to consider substantive content to ensure that proposed legislation meets the objectives of protecting and enhancing Indigenous rights in a way that reconciles the Canadian legal norms with those of Indigenous Peoples. In other words, Parliament has an obligation not only to consider whether Indigenous people have been consulted, but also to examine the outcomes of any consultations. Historically, legislation at the federal level has needed to be calibrated so that it is capable of being integrated with various provincial regimes as well as common and civil law legal traditions. Laws have had to enjoy substantially the same meaning in both English and French. This compatible juralism practice provides a guide for how federal legislation can be adapted and adopted in the Indigenous legal context. Laws that engage Indigenous rights and interests should be drafted taking into account that they will form part of, and be susceptible of being applied in, the various legal regimes developed by Indigenous people through forms of self-government and in the modern treaty context. In considering such legislation, parliamentarians will need to be aware of the various manifestations of Indigenous legal and governance regimes. Laws will need to encourage and support these regimes, particularly in the areas of culture, language, and family law.[18] There may also need to be legislative changes to allow for

---

18 For an example of a tentative start in the type of legislation possible see the *Indigenous Languages Act*, S.C. 2019, c.23 and *An Act respecting First Nations, Inuit and Métis children, youth and families*, S.C. 2019, c.24. More challenging were the attempts

accommodation in the criminal law context—for example, with respect to procedures, sentencing provisions, and potential defences based on cultural factors. In addition, Parliament will need to carefully assess various processes for decision-making powers given to the Crown, including regulation-making powers, so that those processes provide for enhanced consultation, or at least do not include provisions which would impede consultation or minimize its importance. These factors, in addition to ensuring accountability of the Crown for consultation in the development of legislation, also fall within the mandate and responsibility of Parliament and parliamentarians. It is only when they accept and act in accordance with these responsibilities that true reconciliation with Indigenous Peoples can be achieved.

As representatives of the body politic across Canada, the Houses of Parliament are the best vehicles for an enlarged public policy discourse that brings all potential views and interests to the table. It is through these bodies, which are responsible for consideration of various views, legislation, Crown accountability, and public engagement, that a holistic discussion can take place. Only bodies that have the combined constitutional functions of legislating, deliberating, and of holding the government to account that can fully bring about reconciliation between the body politic of Canada and its Indigenous Peoples. A full and proper exercise of these functions can be the foundation of reconciliation within the existing parameters of the Canadian Constitution, while protecting, enhancing, and promoting Indigenous rights. It is up to Parliament to develop the necessary processes, tools, and perspective to meet the challenge of reconciliation.

References

An Act respecting First nations, Inuit and Métis children, youth and families, S.C. 2019, c. 24.

Ariss, Rachael, Clara MacCallum Fraser, and Diba Nazneen Somani. 2017. "Crown Policies on the Duty to Consult and Accommodate: Towards Reconciliation." *McGill Journal of Sustainable Development Law* 13 (1): 1–55.

Bill of Rights 1689, 1 Wm and M, c. 3, Article 9.

---

to adopt, and the ultimate adoption of legislation to implement the *United Nations Declaration on the Rights of Indigenous People* (United Nations 2018) and its overarching relationship principles. The *United Nations Declaration on the Rights of Indigenous Peoples Act,* S.C. 2021, c. 14, received royal assent on June 21, 2021.

Brideau, Isabelle. 2019. *The Duty to Consult Indigenous People.* LOP No. 2019-17-E. Ottawa: Library of Parliament.

Chamberlain v. Surrey School District No. 36 2002 S.C.C. 86, [2002] 4 S.C.R. 710.

Chaplin, Steven. 2016. "Political and Parliamentary Accountability Aspect of Public Law." *Journal of Parliamentary and Political Law* 10 (2): 277–304.

———. 2020. "Hey Court, It's Me, the Legislature, Speaking—Can You Hear Me? Towards a True Dialogue between Courts and Legislatures." *Journal of Parliamentary and Political Law* 13 (February): 225–276.

Coldwater Indian Band v. Canada (Attorney General) 2020 F.C.A. 34.

Constitution Act, 1867, 30 & 31, Victoria, c. 3.

Constitution Act, 1982, c. 11.

Davis, Zachary. 2016. "The Duty to Consult and Legislative Action." *Saskatchewan Law Review* 79 (1): 17–48.

Department of Aboriginal Affairs and Northern Development Canada. 2011. *Aboriginal Consultation and Accommodation Updated Guideline for Federal Officials to Fulfill the Duty to Consult March 2011.* Ottawa: Government of Canada. https://www.rcaanc-cirnac.gc.ca/eng/1100100014664/160942182 4729.

Department of Justice Act, R.S.C. 1985, c J-2.

Government of Manitoba. 2009. *Interim Provincial Policy for Crown Consultation with First Nations, Métis Communities and Other Aboriginal Communities.* Winnipeg: Government of Manitoba. https://www.gov.mb.ca/inr/resources /pubs/interim%20prov%20policy%20for%20crown%20consultation%20 -%202009.pdf.

Government of Quebec. 2008. *Interim Guide for Consulting the Aboriginal Communities.* Quebec: Government of Quebec. https://numerique.banq .qc.ca/patrimoine/details/52327/1945770

Indian Act, R.S.C. 1985 c. I-5.

Indigenous Languages Act, S.C. 2019, c. 23.

Mikisew Cree First Nation v. Canada (Governor General in Council), 2018 S.C.C. 40, [2018] 2 S.C.R. 765.

Morris, Shireen. 2015. "The Argument for a Constitutional Procedure for Parliament to Consult with Indigenous Peoples When Making Laws for Indigenous Affairs." *Public Law Review* 26 (3): 166–192.

Reference re Canada Assistance Plan [1981] 1 S.C.R. 753.

Royal Commission on Aboriginal Peoples. 1996. *Report of the Royal Commission on Aboriginal Peoples, Volume 2: Restructuring the Relationship.* Ottawa: Government of Canada.

Tsleil-Waututh Nation v. Canada (Attorney General) 2018 F.C.A. 153, [2019] 2 F.C.R. 3.

United Nations. 2018. *United Nations Declaration on the Rights of Indigenous People.* New York: United Nations. https://www.un.org/development/desa /indigenouspeoples/declaration-on-the-rights-of-indigenous-peoples

.html.https://www.un.org/development/desa/indigenouspeoples/wp
-content/uploads/sites/19/2018/11/UNDRIP_E_web.pdf

United Nations Declaration on the Rights of Indigenous Peoples Act, SC 2021, c 14.

Vaid v. Canada (House of Commons) 2005 S.C.C. 30.

Williams, David V. 2020. "Rituals of Crown and State in the Realm of New Zealand: Incorporating Indigenous Protocols." *Journal of Parliamentary and Political Law* 14 (June): 43–53.

CHAPTER 4

Les députés du contrôle budgétaire entre passion, intérêt et désaffection

Anthony M. Weber

Résumé

Depuis les deux dernières décennies, l'exigence d'efficacité et de rendement des politiques publiques a su regagner l'attention des organisations internationales et des politologues sur le rôle des parlements dans le contrôle des finances publiques. Cependant, la littérature existante étant essentiellement consacrée à la capacité des parlements à contrôler, peu de recherches nous éclairent sur ce qui motive les principaux intéressés à s'impliquer dans leur fonction de contrôle budgétaire. Ce chapitre tente donc de mieux comprendre comment les députés perçoivent et exercent cette fonction, en empruntant l'approche motivationnelle du rôle de Donald Searing (1994), à travers les exemples du Québec, de la France et du Luxembourg. Trois rôles de contrôleur du budget émergent et se distinguent de notre analyse : l'enquêteur, le représentant et l'absent.

Abstract

Over the past two decades, the requirement that public policies be efficient and effective has refocused the attention of international organizations and political scientists on the role of legislatures in controlling public finances. However, the existing literature is largely devoted to parliaments' control capacity, and little research has been done on what motivates the principal parliamentary actors to become involved in budgetary control. This chapter aims to better understand how parliamentarians perceive and exercise their budgetary and fiscal oversight role by taking the motivational role approach of Donald Searing (1994) and analyzing the cases of Quebec, France, and Luxembourg. The analysis reveals three roles in parliamentary budgetary control: the investigator, the representative, and the absentee.

L'émergence des Parlements est intimement liée à leur pouvoir budgétaire. En Angleterre, la *Magna Carta* (1215) oblige l'exécutif au consentement à l'impôt et donne naissance par cet acte au parlementarisme britannique. Plus tard, les colons américains et les révolutionnaires français, affligés par le système fiscal confiscatoire de l'Ancien Régime, s'approprient à leur tour le principe de *No taxation without representation* et placent au centre de leurs revendications cette même exigence de consentement à l'impôt, qui permettra aux Parlements de connaître leur essor (Rousseau, 2019 [1755] ; Jefferson, 1943 [1774] ; Hamilton, 2010 [1774] ; Paine, 1776 ; Monjou, 2007). Depuis cette époque, difficile d'imaginer comment un système démocratique pourrait en être un sans l'existence de mécanismes de contrôle qui puissent faire respecter les principes de transparence et de responsabilité auxquels le pouvoir exécutif est censé se conformer (White, 2015 ; West, et Cooper, 1989 ; Thiers, 2010).

Pourtant, la fonction de contrôle budgétaire fait aujourd'hui face à de vrais défis qui peuvent complexifier sa perception et son exercice, au point de se demander quel rôle les députés ont encore à y jouer. Depuis les deux dernières décennies, on constate que l'exigence d'efficacité et de performance des politiques publiques a su regagner l'attention des organisations internationales et des politologues sur le rôle des Parlements dans le contrôle des finances publiques. Cependant, la littérature existante étant essentiellement consacrée à la *capacité* des Parlements à contrôler, peu de recherches nous éclairent sur ce qui motive les principaux intéressés à s'impliquer dans cette fonction. Ce chapitre tente alors de mieux comprendre comment les députés perçoivent et exercent cette fonction, en empruntant l'approche motivationnelle du rôle parlementaire de Donald Searing (1994), à travers les exemples du Québec, de la France et du Luxembourg. Comme nous le verrons, trois rôles de contrôleur du budget émergent et se distinguent de notre analyse : l'enquêteur, le représentant et l'absent.

Cadre conceptuel

Le contrôle budgétaire

Alors que l'élaboration du budget est exclusive au pouvoir exécutif et que son adoption demeure une activité proprement législative, le contrôle budgétaire peut se définir comme le fait de « contrôler et d'autoriser les recettes et les dépenses et de veiller à ce que le budget national soit correctement exécuté » (Stapenhurst *et al.*, 2008, 51). Ces deux formes de contrôle ont à la fois des moyens et des objectifs différents. Au moment de l'examen du projet budgétaire, la préoccupation du député est de connaître les prévisions du gouvernement notamment en ce qui concerne le volume et l'utilisation financière des deniers publics : « Qu'est-il prévu d'acquérir avec notre argent ? Le gouvernement s'emploie-t-il à accomplir les bonnes choses ? » (Fölscher *et al.*, 2008). Les députés peuvent ainsi tenter d'*orienter* les intentions gouvernementales en les soutenant ou en tentant de les modifier par l'utilisation des questions écrites et orales, des motions, ou encore par leurs interventions lors des travaux en séance ou en commission. Quant au contrôle de l'exécution budgétaire, la préoccupation du député est plutôt de *vérifier* si les prévisions gouvernementales ont bien été appliquées : « Qu'est-ce que l'argent du contribuable a servi à acquérir ? Le gouvernement a-t-il accompli ce qu'il avait promis ? Quels sont les effets de l'utilisation de l'argent du contribuable ? » (Fölscher *et al.*, 2008). Questionner oralement ou par écrit l'exécution des crédits budgétaires, rédiger un rapport d'information, auditionner des ministres ou des responsables d'organismes publics, ou intervenir lors des débats en séance plénière ou en commission sont les principaux outils de contrôle d'exécution pouvant être utilisés par les députés (NDI, 2000 ; Yamamoto, 2007 ; Chang, 2001). Une large littérature s'est penchée sur l'existence de ces outils et cela souvent dans une perspective comparée. Cet intérêt est principalement dû à la dernière vague de démocratisation et au contexte généralisé d'endettement et de déficit public qui a su motiver plusieurs chercheurs à étudier et à évaluer la *force institutionnelle* des Parlements et leur *potentiel de contrôle* (NDI, 2000 ; International Monetary Fund, 2001 ; OECD, 2002 ; Yamamoto, 2007 ; Pelizzo, Stapenhurst, et Olson, 2006 ; Wildavsky, 1975 ; Wehner, 2006 ; Krafchik et Wehner, 1998 ; Stapenhurst et Pelizzo, 2002 ; Stapenhurst, Olson et Trapp, 2008 ; Stapenhurst, 2004 ; Pelizzo et Stapenhurst, 2004). Tantôt perçu comme un remède à la corruption et aux mauvaises pratiques de gouvernance, tantôt comme une solution aux problèmes de mauvaise gestion publique, le contrôle budgétaire est aujourd'hui un objet surtout connu sous l'angle de ses moyens et de ses capacités. Mais cette littérature ne nous donne que trop peu d'indications quant à l'implication et aux motivations réelles des principaux intéressés : les parlementaires. Pourtant, l'existence d'outils de contrôle, aussi nombreux qu'ils soient, ne garantit pas leur utilisation. La question du *contrôle effectif* après celle du *contrôle potentiel* doit être posée, et tout particulièrement dans le domaine budgétaire où l'activisme des députés peut être mis en question.

L'implication des députés mise en question

Le contrôle budgétaire fait aujourd'hui face à trois défis qui nous interrogent sur l'implication réelle des députés. Premièrement, la marge de manœuvre des élus est connue pour être très limitée dans le domaine des finances publiques. L'initiative budgétaire est générale-ment réservée au pouvoir exécutif, et rares sont les constitutions et règlements qui permettent aux législateurs de modifier le projet de budget initial du gouvernement (Döring, 1995a, 1995b et Tsebelis, 2009). Deuxièmement, le fait majoritaire ou le fait que le gouverne-ment soit issu du pouvoir législatif dans les systèmes parlementaires crée l'ambiguïté dans la relation entre « contrôleur » et « contrôlé ». L'interdépendance entre le gouvernement et la majorité parlementaire a pour effet de rendre extrêmement prévisibles les discussions et l'adoption des lois (Griglio, 2012 ; Wehner, 2004). Troisièmement, la complexification des politiques publiques qui a accompagné l'avène-ment de l'État-Providence et les nouvelles normes de gestion pose un problème de traitement de l'information. La culture de l'information et de transparence des activités gouvernementales induites notam-ment par le Nouveau Management Public a provoqué une production disproportionnée d'information budgétaire rendant difficile la capa-cité des parlementaires à la traiter, même dans un contexte où le pouvoir de contrôle d'information des Parlements s'est vu valorisé et renforcé (Auel *et al.*, 2015, 7 ; Sinnassamy, 2008, 125 ; Türk, 2011, 16 ; Lauvaux, 2010, 23 ; OECD, 2002). Ces trois constats nous amènent à nous demander comment les députés perçoivent et exercent leur fonc-tion de contrôle budgétaire, et c'est à travers la notion de rôle que nous tenterons ici de répondre à cette question.

Cadre méthodologique

L'approche motivationnelle du rôle parlementaire

La prédominance des travaux portant sur la *capacité* des députés à contrôler peut en partie s'expliquer par la domination de l'approche stratégique dans les études législatives, qui place traditionnellement au centre de l'analyse les règles qui permettent ou empêche l'action intéressée des élus (Döring, 1995 ; Fish et Kroenig, 2009 ; Sieberer, 2011). Avec l'approche stratégique, la popularité de l'école du choix rationnel touche aussi la littérature des rôles parlementaires. Si celle-ci offre un apport indéniable à la compréhension du comportement parlementaire par ses recherches systématiques (Tsebelis, 2002 ; Shepsle, 2002 ; Loewenberg, 2011 ; Jenny et Müller, 2012 ; Strom, 2012 ; Zittel, 2012 ; Zittel et Gschwend, 2008), l'approche stratégique a pourtant une vision très réductrice des préférences individuelles. Vues comme « des stratégies cohérentes induites par la poursuite de différents objectifs, contraintes par l'environnement institutionnel dans lequel ils évoluent » (Strom, 1997, 163), cette conception des préférences néglige l'importance des considérations normatives, le respect de normes ou les valeurs des acteurs (Boudon, 2004 ; Brack, 2014). Pourtant, les préférences peuvent être endogènes aux interactions sociales et aux règles institutionnelles, puisque l'action résulte d'une composante complexe où s'entremêlent intérêt égoïste, principes et normes, et influence des règles formelles et informelles de l'institution dans laquelle l'action a lieu (Aspinwall et Schneider, 2009 ; March et Olsen, 1984).

En plaçant la subjectivité de l'acteur au cœur de son analyse, l'approche motivationnelle du rôle (Searing, 1994) partage cette conception plus élargie des préférences individuelles en ajoutant aux intérêts stratégiques des motivations plus larges. Défini comme « la configuration d'objectifs, d'attitudes et de comportements caractéristiques d'un acteur qui occupe une position sociale particulière » (Searing, 1994, 18), le rôle parlementaire est le résultat des interactions entre les règles et les motivations personnelles des acteurs (Brack, 2014, 86). Utilisée à plusieurs reprises dans les recherches législatives, l'approche motivationnelle a cet avantage de lier pratiques et motivations dans la compréhension du comportement parlementaire (Navarro, 2009 ; Wood et Yoon, 1998 ; Rozenberg, 2005). Cependant, celle-ci a généralement été entreprise dans des analyses de cas unique. En outre, la littérature du rôle parlementaire étant largement focalisé sur la fonction représentative, cette recherche pourra élargir le champ de ces études en se focalisant cette fois sur la fonction du contrôle parlementaire (Rozenberg and Blomgren, 2012 ; Andeweg, 2016 ; Kerrouche, 2004).

Comparaison du Québec, de la France, et du Luxembourg

Nous appliquerons l'approche motivationnelle à cette recherche en décrivant le rôle du *point de vue des députés*, c'est-à-dire en relevant pour chacun d'eux les objectifs (motivations), attitudes (perceptions) et comportements qui entourent leur fonction de contrôle budgétaire. De cette manière, nous tenterons d'en savoir plus sur la façon dont les députés perçoivent leur rôle et sur les raisons qui les poussent à contrôler d'une manière plutôt qu'une autre. Mais notre objectif est aussi de montrer que ces mêmes rôles résistent à la variation des systèmes politiques. Notre analyse se penche alors sur trois cas d'étude aux caractéristiques suffisamment différentes (système politique et taille du Parlement), mais aussi suffisamment similaires (notamment en ce qui concerne leur processus budgétaire) pour pouvoir les comparer. Il s'agit du Québec et du Luxembourg qui détiennent tous deux un système parlementaire, et de la France qui détient un système de type semi-présidentiel. Les premiers sont connus pour détenir davantage d'outils de contrôle et de potentiel de contrôle que les systèmes présidentiels et semi-présidentiels (Pelizzo et Stapenhurst, 2004, 7-11). Ensuite, le Luxembourg a ceci de particulier de posséder un petit parlement qui compte seulement 60 députés, en comparaison au Québec qui en comptabilise 125 et la France 577. Cette différence de taille peut avoir une incidence sur la répartition du travail en commission : dans un petit parlement, les députés peuvent être contraints de siéger à trois ou quatre commissions à la fois voire davantage, ce qui peut influencer le temps disponible à contrôler, mais aussi les priorités du mandat. Enfin, l'organisation du contrôle parlementaire du budget n'est pas identique dans les trois parlements étudiés. L'Assemblée nationale française dispose d'une unique Commission des finances dont les membres ont pour double mission d'examiner les projets de loi de finances et d'en contrôler la bonne exécution. A contrario, nous retrouvons au Québec et au Luxembourg une commission distincte exclusivement dédiée au contrôle de l'exécution budgétaire. Pour terminer, c'est au sein des *Commissions des finances publiques* que l'examen du projet budgétaire s'effectue dans les trois parlements, même si dans le cas du Québec cette activité n'est pas exclusive à cette commission puisque chaque commission permanente se voit confier comme mandat l'examen des crédits budgétaires qui lui sont rattachés (Bonsaint, 2012, 451). Malgré ces divergences, une similitude fondamentale rend possible la comparaison de nos trois cas : le contrôle traverse les mêmes étapes et offre aux députés des moyens équivalents : droit d'interroger et d'interpeller le gouvernement ou encore d'intervenir durant les travaux en séance et en commission (Pelizzo et Stapenhurst, 2004, 8).

Échantillonnage des députés du contrôle budgétaire

Cette recherche se base sur un corpus de 32 entretiens semi-directifs effectués avec 12 élus français, 11 élus québécois et 9 élus luxembourgeois, siégeant dans au moins une commission ayant pour mandat de contrôler le budget de l'État. Il peut donc s'agir aléatoirement de députés siégeant en commissions des finances, en commissions du contrôle de l'exécution budgétaire, les deux à la fois, ou encore au sein d'autres commissions ayant pour mandat de contrôler le budget de l'État comme dans le cas du Québec. Puisque nous recherchons l'échantillon le plus représentatif possible, nous avons procédé à une sélection de députés d'après une multitude de caractéristiques à la fois politiques, sociales et personnelles (voir annexe). Les 32 entretiens ont eu lieu entre le 12 avril 2017 et le 22 mars 2018. La période de notre analyse couvre la dernière législature de chacun de nos trois cas d'études, soit la 14e législature française (20 juin 2012 – 20 juin 2017), la 23e législature luxembourgeoise (20 octobre 2013 – 13 octobre 2018), et la 41e législature québécoise (7 avril 2014 – 30 novembre 2018).

Opérationnalisation du concept de rôle

Pour identifier les rôles joués par les députés du contrôle budgétaire, il nous faut connaître les trois éléments indispensables du rôle selon l'approche motivationnelle, à savoir : les objectifs, les attitudes et les comportements de chaque député. À cette fin, nous procédons par méthode inductive et interprétative à partir de deux types de données : les données d'entretien et les données d'activités de contrôle. La première étape a été de définir les objectifs et attitudes des députés à l'aide des données d'entretien. La grille d'entretien a été structurée sur la base de deux dimensions qui ont été au centre de notre attention : celle des motivations et celle des perceptions des députés entourant la fonction du contrôle budgétaire. Les réponses des élus servent d'indicateurs des attitudes et des objectifs. Pour les motivations, nous interrogeons chaque député sur les objectifs qu'il désire atteindre à travers le contrôle budgétaire, sur les principes et valeurs qui sous-tendent son action, et enfin sur le processus de sa nomination en commission, afin de savoir si elle a été désirée ou plutôt subie. Pour les perceptions, nous interrogeons chaque député sur la manière dont il priorise cette activité de contrôle parmi ses autres fonctions, sur la manière dont il perçoit lui-même le contrôle budgétaire et le rôle qu'il occupe en commission, et enfin s'il considère détenir suffisamment de moyens pour contrôler.

Selon l'approche motivationnelle, les objectifs, attitudes et comportements forment un tout cohérent. C'est pourquoi notre deuxième étape est d'analyser les activités de contrôle pour élaborer notre typologie. Basés sur les données accessibles par les sites officiels des Assemblées, nous nous concentrons sur l'examen du projet budgétaire (contrôle *ex ante*) et le contrôle d'exécution (contrôle *ex post*). Nous relevons, lors de ces étapes, le nombre d'interventions de chaque député en séance publique et en commission. Pour la France il s'agit principalement des interventions effectuées lors de l'examen du PLF *(ex ante)*, de l'examen du projet de loi de règlement et lors des auditions organisées par la Commission des finances, sans oublier les rapports écrits et/ou co-écrits *(ex post)*[1]. Pour le Québec, il s'agit des interventions effectuées dès le débat qui suit le discours sur le budget jusqu'à l'étude des crédits *(ex ante)*, ainsi que les interventions au moment des auditions organisées dans le cadre de reddition de comptes. Pour le Luxembourg, où les travaux en commission ne sont pas rendus publics, nous comptabilisons les interventions lors du débat sur l'état de la nation, de l'approbation du rapport de la Commission des finances, et lors de l'examen du projet de loi sur le budget *(ex ante)* et enfin, le nombre d'interventions au moment de l'examen du projet de loi portant sur les comptes généraux de l'État *(ex post)*.

---

1   Les rapports au Québec et au Luxembourg ne sont pas comptabilisés, car ils ne sont pas individuels.

Au total, 22 325 interventions ont été comptabilisées pour nos trois cas, 3 906 pour la France, 16 961 pour le Québec et 1 458 pour le Luxembourg. La moyenne des interventions de chaque élu a été calculée sur une année.

Résultats

Approcher les députés du contrôle budgétaire par la notion de rôle nous a permis d'identifier trois idéaux types : l'enquêteur, le représentant et l'absent.

L'enquêteur

L'enquêteur se caractérise par trois éléments principaux. Premièrement, la volonté de rendre des comptes aux citoyens en s'assurant de la bonne application du budget. Deuxièmement, la tendance à s'identifier personnellement à la fonction du contrôle budgétaire perçue comme une fin en soi. Troisièmement, l'analyse du comportement de l'enquêteur montre qu'il s'implique davantage dans le contrôle *ex post* même si cette implication n'empêche pas l'exercice d'un contrôle *ex ante*.

Une éthique des finances publiques

Le député enquêteur se voit confier dans le contrôle budgétaire une mission de haute importance envers les citoyens. Sa préoccupation est de s'assurer que l'État fasse une bonne gestion de l'argent public et qu'il respecte ses engagements. Dans son discours, cette préoccupation est marquée par un sentiment de devoir où la fonction de contrôle de l'exécution budgétaire est perçue comme l'activité qui donne le plus de sens au mandat parlementaire :

> Parce que fondamentalement c'est toute la notion de *l'efficacité* avec laquelle on dépense les deniers publics, j'vous dirais c'est un haut niveau de conscience tel que cet argent là qu'on dépense qui a d'abord et avant tout été gagné par des gens qui se sont levés tôt le matin pour aller donner une prestation de service efficace pour laquelle il n'y a pas de compromis. Parce que le compromis avec l'inefficacité pour ces gens-là c'est le congédiement. Ils ont des rêves, ils ont des aspirations, et puis à la fin de l'année ils remplissent une déclaration d'impôts dans laquelle on leur apprend que tout palier d'administration municipale et de

gouvernement confondus va leur chercher entre 50 et 70 % de l'argent qu'ils ont gagné, à la sueur de leur front. Fait que moi comme député j'me dis le « minimum » qu'on peut faire c'est de ne pas les remplir de n'importe quoi, et de s'assurer qu'effectivement ces sous qu'on leur a enlevé de leur portefeuille, de s'assurer de notre côté de remplir ces promesses-là. Il *faut* le voir comme ça, il *faut* le voir comme ça [...] parce que sinon c'est tellement injuste. (Entretien avec un député québécois – Q5).

Le contrôle budgétaire comme fin en soi : la politique au service des finances publiques

Lorsqu'on lui évoque le thème du contrôle budgétaire, l'enquêteur évoque systématiquement celui du contrôle de l'exécution. Il perçoit alors le contrôle budgétaire comme étant avant tout de nature *ex post,* et l'on découvre que cette fonction lui est indissociable. Le député décrit cette activité comme une fin en soi, c'est-à-dire un but à atteindre, et un but très valorisant, parfois même plus valorisant que le contrôle *ex ante* :

> Le contrôle de l'exécution du budget est un moment important, car c'est plus concret, on y apprend beaucoup de choses, des fonctionnements, comment les décisions s'appliquent [...] c'est à ce moment que le député doit jouer son rôle de contrôleur. (Entretien avec un député luxembourgeois – L2).

> Moi je pense que le contrôle budgétaire – la mission d'évaluation et de contrôle – je pense que c'est quelque chose d'essentiel. Aujourd'hui c'est peut-être la chose – sous réserve qu'on choisisse bien les sujets – la chose que le parlementaire doit le mieux savoir faire. (Entretien avec un député français – F3).

En outre, l'enquêteur évoque dans ses propos les obstacles pouvant nuire à son contrôle, comme le manque de ressources. Cependant, il évoque les outils et les ressources déjà existantes comme des occasions de s'impliquer, et partage des idées d'amélioration pour offrir encore davantage de moyens pour contrôler. Les obstacles évoqués sont minimisés et considérés comme surmontables. En conséquence, l'implication des députés dans cette fonction de contrôle *ex post* ne serait pas une affaire de *ressources* mais plutôt une affaire de *motivation personnelle.* À la question « Considérez-vous avoir suffisamment de ressources pour remplir votre travail de contrôle budgétaire ? » l'enquêteur répond :

> Je dirais que oui. Parce que c'est pas nous-mêmes ou la chambre, c'est parce qu'on a la Cour des comptes. Elle peut nous déposer un dossier, on fait ensuite une étude pour savoir pourquoi il y a un dépassement, et alors le ministre sera convoqué à la réunion, il devra nous expliquer pourquoi il y a eu un dépassement, et c'est la commission qui prend la décision sur la suite. Donc même avec le concours de la Cour des comptes je pense qu'on a assez de possibilités oui. (Entretien avec un député luxembourgeois – L4).

> On dit « on ne peut pas le faire [le contrôle *ex post*] parce qu'effectivement au sein de l'Assemblée il n'y a pas assez de ressources » – mais si le contrôle devient prioritaire, les administrateurs passeront moins de temps sur de l'amendement et davantage sur du contrôle dans l'autre sens. Je pense que si on réorganise ses ressources on doit pouvoir les trouver. (Entretien avec un député français – F5).

Parmi nos 32 députés interrogés, 14 ont été identifiés comme « enquêteur » dont 6 députés français, 6 députés québécois, et 2 députés luxembourgeois.

Une forte implication dans le contrôle ex post

Comme le montre le tableau 4.1, les enquêteurs sont particulièrement actifs au moment du contrôle de l'exécution budgétaire. Cependant, on note une activité soutenue de ces députés lors du contrôle *ex post,* mais aussi lors du contrôle *ex ante,* et ce tout au long de la législature[2].

---

2 L'enquêteur se caractérise par l'attention soutenue qu'il porte aux informations émanant des Institutions supérieures de contrôle (ISC). Cependant, il faut noter que la présence d'un vérificateur général ou d'une Cour des comptes n'affecte que d'une manière limitée l'émergence des rôles de contrôleur. Bien que l'ISC soit un organe central à l'atteinte de l'efficience du contrôle budgétaire, les informations émanant de cet organe ne représentent qu'une source d'informations supplémentaire mise à disposition des élus. Que cette information se traduise par des rapports annuels, spéciaux ou même par des échanges lors d'auditions en commission parlementaire, rien n'oblige les députés à étudier ou à utiliser cette information. Si l'enquêteur l'utilise pour évaluer la qualité de sa reddition de

TABLEAU 4.1.

Moyenne par année des interventions des enquêteurs

a) France

	Ex ante		Ex post		
	Séance	Commission	Séance	Commission	Rapports
F1	143,8	126,8	0,8	95	1
F3	6,2	1,2	0	35,4	1,4
F4	107,4	25	12,8	6,4	1
F5	2,2	2	1,4	10,2	1,6
F10	29,6	15,8	0,6	34,6	1,4
F12	106,5	30	7	27	0,5

b) Québec

	Ex ante		Ex post		
	Séance	Commission	Séance	Commission	Rapports
Q2	0,2	62		35,6	
Q5	8,8	131		85,4	
Q6	0,5	33,5		74,5	
Q8	0	58		32,4	
Q10	0,4	1675,4		96,8	
Q11	4	129,2		439,2	

compte, le représentant l'utilise, quant à lui, comme un moyen d'appuyer son propos lors des débats budgétaires ; quant à l'absent, cette information ne lui est tout simplement d'aucune utilité. Encore là, l'importance de l'ISC dans le processus budgétaire dépendra de la manière dont l'élu perçoit et exerce son contrôle budgétaire.

c) Luxembourg

	Ex ante		Ex post		
	Séance	Commission	Séance	Commission	Rapports
L4	74		4,8		
L2	13,2		2,8		

Source : *Anthony M. Weber*

Notes : Au Québec, l'étude des crédits se fait exclusivement en commission, donc aucune intervention en séance n'est comptabilisée. Par ailleurs, aucun rapport individuel ne peut être soumis par un député.

Au Luxembourg, les travaux en commission n'étant pas publics, seules les interventions en séance ont été comptabilisées. Par ailleurs, aucun rapport individuel ne peut être soumis par un député.

Le représentant

L'idéal type du représentant se caractérise par trois éléments principaux. Premièrement, par sa volonté que le projet de budget du gouvernement soit le plus fidèle possible aux attentes des électeurs, que cela se traduise pour lui par un effort de modification ou de soutien indéfectible au projet de budget initial. Deuxièmement, le contrôle *ex ante* est pour lui perçu comme un bon moyen de représentation, alors que le contrôle *ex post* est davantage jugé comme une fonction trop éloignée de la mission principale d'un député, mission qui serait avant tout celle de défendre une vision politique. Troisièmement, le représentant s'implique dans le contrôle *ex ante* tout en exerçant peu ou pas de contrôle *ex post*.

La priorité donnée à la représentation des intérêts budgétaires des électeurs

Le contrôle budgétaire est une occasion d'entrer dans le jeu politique, avec pour mission de représenter les intérêts des électeurs. La préoccupation du représentant est alors de s'assurer que le projet budgétaire est bel et bien fidèle à leurs attentes : « J'vous dirais que c'est sûr qu'on est là pour les citoyens en premier, le contrôle budgétaire autant du gouvernement que de mon bureau c'est important, mais en premier lieu j'suis là pour les citoyens » (entretien avec un député québécois – Q7).

C'est pourquoi le discours du représentant est marqué par le sentiment que la préparation du budget et l'examen du projet budgétaire sont des moments incontournables de la vie politique. S'il est de l'opposition, le représentant tentera de modifier le projet de loi de finances initial, s'il est de la majorité, il tentera de l'influencer au moment de sa préparation et le soutiendra au moment de son examen :

> On passe beaucoup de temps sur la LFI [loi de finances initiale], parce que c'est passionnant, parce qu'on propose des amendements, parce que c'est l'occasion pour le gouvernement de faire des effets d'annonce, de montrer ses muscles, de dire « vous allez voir ce que vous allez voir ! ». [...] Le contrôle est réussi quand il met le gouvernement dans l'embarras. Parce que, le contrôle budgétaire, par qui il doit être réalisé ? Est-ce qu'un membre de la majorité a intérêt à mettre le gouvernement en mauvaise posture ? (Entretien avec un député français de l'opposition – F2)

> J'ai été longtemps membre de la majorité, je dirais que l'on peut effectivement peser sur l'élaboration d'un projet de budget. Si moi, j'ai maintenant une idée précise sur un poste budgétaire précis je vais voir le ministre des Finances et faire un peu de lobbying auprès de lui pour qu'il accepte mes revendications. Je ne dis pas que ça marche toujours ! Que ça fonctionne toujours ! Mais quelques fois le ministre est d'accord pour faire une ouverture. (Entretien avec un député luxembourgeois de l'opposition – L7)

Le contrôle budgétaire vu comme un moyen : les finances publiques au service de la politique

Le représentant revendique le fait d'utiliser les finances publiques au service de sa vision politique. Il valorise alors dans son discours le contrôle *ex ante* qu'il perçoit comme un moyen important de faire valoir sa position et celle de ses électeurs, et décrit au contraire le contrôle *ex post* comme une activité moins attirante en raison de sa nature éloignée des préoccupations quotidiennes des citoyens :

> Pour moi, c'est le point de vue politique du contrôle budgétaire qui est surtout important, c'est ce qui fait sans doute la différence entre Charles De Courson [autre député] et moi. Charles De Courson, sa passion, c'est la complexité du domaine budgétaire

et c'est le budget pour le budget, voilà, moi c'est vraiment pas le sujet qui me passionne, ce qui me passionne, c'est les moyens qu'on a ou qu'on n'a pas pour les grandes politiques publiques. Pour un c'était la fin, pour l'autre c'était le moyen. (Entretien avec un député français – F7).

Le représentant perçoit le contrôle de l'exécution budgétaire davantage comme un travail de « comptable » éloigné des préoccupations réelles du député. Il soulève d'ailleurs le manque d'intérêt du public et des médias pour cette activité et y trouve une justification supplémentaire à s'impliquer davantage au moment de l'examen du projet budgétaire qu'au moment du contrôle de son exécution :

J'ai l'impression de peser plus, politiquement, en tant que membre de la commission des finances plutôt que membre de la commission de l'exécution budgétaire. Eux [les membres de la commission de l'exécution budgétaire] c'est plutôt [...] et c'est pas en termes péjoratifs, mais je trouve que c'est plutôt un travail de « comptable ». (Entretien avec un député luxembourgeois – L7).

Pour s'impliquer maintenant dans un suivi budgétaire, je pense qu'on est dépassé, là on est dépassé [...] puisque [...] primo c'est pas « sexy » [...] Qui s'intéresse à une évolution budgétaire si ce n'est pas un dépassement ? Si ce n'est pas un scandale ? (Entretien avec un député luxembourgeois – L5).

Enfin, le représentant évoque le manque de pouvoir coercitif du contrôle *ex post* comme facteur important de démotivation : « J'ai rarement vu des recommandations de missions d'évaluation et de contrôle qui soient suivies d'effet. C'est comme pour la Cour des comptes, les rapports sont excellents sauf que le gouvernement n'en tient jamais compte ! » (Entretien avec un député français – F2).

Parmi nos 32 députés interrogés, 11 ont été identifiés comme « représentants » dont 3 députés français, 4 députés québécois et 4 députés luxembourgeois.

Une plus forte implication dans le contrôle ex ante

L'activité du représentant se distingue par son implication quasi-exclusive au contrôle budgétaire de type *ex ante*. Comme le montre le tableau 4.2, les débats organisés lors de l'examen du projet de budget représentent le moment phare de leur implication au cours du processus budgétaire, alors que la vérification de la bonne application du budget, que ce soit lors des discussions en chambre ou en commissions, ne fait pas l'objet d'une attention égale.

TABLEAU 4.2.
Moyenne par année des interventions des représentants
a) France

	Ex ante		Ex post		
	Séance	Commission	Séance	Commission	Rapports
F2	15	6,2	0	6	1
F7	12,6	5,4	1	3,4	1
F11	28,5	7,5	4,5	4	1

b) Québec

	Ex ante		Ex post		
	Séance	Commission	Séance	Commission	Rapports
Q1	2	111		17	
Q4	3	121,4		11	
Q7	2,2	206,2		3,8	
Q9	2,4	71		0	

c) Luxembourg

	Ex ante		Ex post		
	Séance	Commission	Séance	Commission	Rapports
L3	55,8		0		
L5	12,8		0		
L7	31,8		0		
L9	87,6		0		

Source : *Anthony M. Weber.*

L'absent

L'idéal type de l'absent se caractérise par trois éléments principaux. D'abord, par la volonté de déléguer la charge du contrôle budgétaire à un autre député qui serait potentiellement plus intéressé ou plus spécialisé dans ce domaine. Ensuite, le contrôle budgétaire est perçu par l'absent comme une fonction totalement étrangère et pour laquelle il a un avis peu informé ou négatif. Enfin, l'absent n'exerce que peu ou pas de contrôle budgétaire, que celui-ci soit de nature *ex ante* ou *ex post.*

Faire de la politique autrement qu'à travers les finances publiques

Contrairement à l'enquêteur et au représentant, la nomination de l'absent à une commission des finances est subie et non souhaitée. D'après l'absent, cette nomination par défaut est expliquée par les circonstances électorales et le besoin de combler des places en commissions :

> C'est la fraction [groupe politique] qui fait la répartition et c'est une question de résultat d'élection, mais aussi d'ancienneté. Moi je suis dans le cas spécifique que je n'ai pas été élu tout de suite, donc je suis rentrée dans la chambre un an après les élections donc, vous savez, on prend ce qu'on veut bien vous donner [...] (Entretien avec une députée luxembourgeoise – L8).

> Moi je me suis toujours intéressée aux questions de santé et d'environnement. Je siège à la commission de l'environnement et ça me plaît beaucoup, mais pour la commission du contrôle de l'exécution on m'a juste dit « c'est toi qui y va », c'est comme ça que j'y suis entrée je n'ai pas vraiment eu le choix. (Entretien avec une députée luxembourgeoise – L6).

Cet aveu d'une nomination non désirée est accompagné dans le discours de l'absent par une volonté de déléguer à d'autres députés la fonction de contrôle budgétaire : « Je n'en sais rien [...] je ne pourrais pas vous dire en pour cent ou en fréquence de temps, quand c'est un dossier qui m'intéresse je le sais, mais ça il faut le demander à Mme Adhem notre présidente [de la commission du contrôle de l'exécution budgétaire], parce que c'est elle qui maîtrise le mieux l'information » (entretien avec une députée luxembourgeoise – L8).

Le contrôle budgétaire et l'absent : entre indifférence et désillusion

L'absent manifeste peu d'intérêt pour le contrôle budgétaire, mais ce désintérêt peut provenir de deux sources distinctes. Premièrement, l'absent peut simplement percevoir la fonction de contrôle budgétaire comme trop fastidieuse et finalement secondaire par rapport à d'autres fonctions et domaines pour lesquels il se sent davantage concerné. Dans ce cas, l'absent justifie sa faible implication dans le contrôle budgétaire par son activité qui serait plus concentrée dans d'autres domaines. À ce propos, l'absent évoque un intérêt plus grand pour des sujets davantage sociétaux comme ceux de l'environnement, de la santé ou de l'éducation, – même si en réalité ces domaines n'empêchent pas de les aborder dans une perspective budgétaire. Ce désengagement relève donc à la fois un manque d'intérêt pour le domaine des finances publiques et une priorisation d'autres domaines durant le mandat :

> Comme je ne suis pas trop dans la matière, il se peut qu'il y ait d'autres députés qui y voient plus d'importance, mais pour moi-même [...] moi ce qui me motive le plus c'est les domaines où je suis impliquée dans ma commission du développement durable puisque je connais mieux ces projets-là que d'autres. (Entretien avec une députée luxembourgeoise – L6).

> Pour moi, personnellement, ça [le contrôle budgétaire] ne m'intéresse pas beaucoup. [...] Ce qui me *passionne* c'est des questions d'éthiques, des questions [...] c'est une question de caractère, je pense que c'est [le contrôle budgétaire] très important mais je ne suis pas la plus forte là-dedans il y a d'autres domaines où je suis meilleure. (Entretien avec une députée luxembourgeoise – L8).

Deuxièmement, l'absent peut percevoir le contrôle budgétaire comme une activité très décevante qu'il a décidé d'abandonner. L'insuffisance des moyens et la faible portée du travail de contrôle font partie des justifications de sa faible implication. Ce désengagement *a posteriori* ne relève donc pas d'un manque d'intérêt pour le domaine des finances publiques, mais survient plutôt à la suite d'une déception qui amène le député à se désintéresser de cette fonction spécifique :

> Quand j'entends comme hier à la télé les macronistes qui disent « on va faire changer ! on va faire changer ! » ils ne vont rien

changer du tout ! Moi quand je suis arrivé à l'Assemblée nationale j'ai dit « il faut brûler Bercy[3] », tout le monde s'est marré,
mais c'est moi qui avais raison. Ce sont les hauts fonctionnaires
qui commandent en France, faut pas rêver. » (Entretien avec un
député français – F9).

J'en ai fait une des MEC [mission d'évaluation et de contrôle]
ouais, vous faites « un constat » […] c'est tout ce que vous pouvez
faire ! les débits et les crédits sont déjà passés, vous faites un
constat vous pouvez dire « ça va pas bien » si vous voulez, mais
vous n'avez pas le pouvoir. Le pouvoir je le répète c'est « Bercy »
qui l'a. (Entretien avec un député français – F9).

Parmi nos 32 députés interrogés, 7 ont été identifiés comme
« absent » dont 3 députés français, 1 député québécois, 3 députés
luxembourgeois.

Une implication quasi inexistante

L'activité de contrôle budgétaire de l'absent se caractérise par une
implication quasi nulle, tant au moment du contrôle *ex ante* qu'au
moment du contrôle *ex post*. Comme le tableau 4.3 le démontre, peu
d'interventions sont effectuées que ce soit lors de l'examen du projet
budgétaire ou lors du contrôle de son exécution.

TABLEAU 4.3.
Moyenne par année des interventions des absents
a) France

	Ex ante		Ex post		
	Séance	Commission	Séance	Commission	Rapports
F6	3	6	0	3	0
F8	6	0	0	0	0
F9	0	1,2	0	8	0

---

3   « Bercy » est le surnom du ministère des Finances français.

b) Québec

	Ex ante		Ex post		
	Séance	Commission	Séance	Commission	Rapports
Q3	0,8	29,6		9	

c) Luxembourg

	Ex ante		Ex post		
	Séance	Commission	Séance	Commission	Rapports
L1	0,4		0		
L6	7,8		0,6		
L8	0		0		

Source : *Anthony M. Weber.*

Discussion

Mis en perspective des recherches effectuées jusqu'à ce jour sur les rôles parlementaires, nos résultats semblent retrouver, à travers l'exemple du contrôle budgétaire, certains profils types déjà identifiés dans les études législatives, notamment ceux du *trustee* et du *delegate* (Wahlke *et al.*, 1962). L'enquêteur par son travail de vérification se rapproche du *trustee* du fait qu'il soit souvent un député ayant une longue expérience politique avec une forte influence en commission (rapporteur, porte-parole de groupe, ancienneté au sein de la commission). Il possède généralement une spécialisation dans le domaine budgétaire rendue possible par une expérience professionnelle pré-parlementaire en lien avec les finances (magistrat de la Cour des comptes, comptable, entrepreneur [...]). Ces expériences sont favorables au développement de normes et de principes qui motivent une telle implication dans le contrôle *ex post*. Pour sa part, le représentant se rapproche davantage du profil du *delegate* en priorisant la représentation de ses électeurs. Il a généralement moins de responsabilités au sein de l'assemblée et a moins d'influence sur les travaux en commissions.

Le budget de l'État n'est donc sous le contrôle que de certains types de députés, qui exercent d'ailleurs cette fonction de manières différentes et pour des raisons différentes. Notre objectif a été de rendre ce phénomène plus intelligible grâce à l'élaboration d'une typologie descriptive qui nous amène à identifier trois idéaux types de députés bien distincts, qui se retrouvent dans les trois parlements français, québécois et luxembourgeois, malgré les différences inhérentes aux systèmes politiques auxquels ils appartiennent.

Le premier constat que nous pouvons faire de cette recherche est que notre typologie semble être structurée selon la nature du contrôle budgétaire. En effet, qu'il soit davantage défini comme l'examen du projet de budget ou comme le contrôle de l'exécution, la manière qu'ont les députés à définir le contrôle budgétaire semble avoir une incidence importante sur leur façon de se comporter et d'approcher cette fonction. Par exemple, de fait de son implication plus importante au moment du contrôle *ex ante,* le représentant se montre « proactif » et justifie ce choix par sa perception à la fois utilitariste et stratégique du contrôle budgétaire. Utilitariste puisque le moment de l'examen du projet de budget représente pour lui le *timing* politique parfait lui permettant d'exercer une représentation qui saura bénéficier de toute l'attention des médias et des électeurs. Le contrôle *ex ante* est pour lui un moyen de révéler les visions politiques qui se cachent derrière les chiffres du projet budgétaire, ce qui aide à vulgariser la matière financière et à attirer l'attention des citoyens sur des débats de fonds. La capacité d'influencer et de peser sur les décisions gouvernementales à l'aide des outils disponibles procure au représentant une réelle satisfaction dans son travail de contrôle *ex ante,* là où il est selon lui encore possible d'apporter des modifications ou un soutien supplémentaire au projet du budget du gouvernement. Ensuite, le représentant se montre stratégique en préférant le contrôle *ex ante.* Selon lui, le contrôle *ex post* s'effectue lors d'un *timing* politique moins intéressant étant donné la très faible visibilité publique d'un tel travail : le contrôle de l'exécution se réalise « après coup », des mois, des années après l'adoption du budget, à un moment où les préoccupations des électeurs et des médias sont assez éloignées des sujets soulevés, sauf dans les rares cas où ce type de contrôle met au jour de graves dysfonctionnements ou des scandales financiers. De plus, comme le représentant le rappelle, le contrôle *ex post* peut déboucher sur des recommandations pertinentes pour l'amélioration de la gestion des deniers publics, mais aucune d'entre elles n'est de nature contraignante pour le gouvernement.

De son côté, l'enquêteur est à ce titre surprenant par son profil plus « rétroactif » malgré ces constats défavorables au contrôle *ex post.*

En effet, les réalités du contrôle *ex post* qui dissuadent l'implication du représentant ne semblent pas affecter celle de l'enquêteur. Mû par les normes d'une bonne gestion, l'enquêteur voit dans le contrôle *ex post* non pas un moyen, mais bien la finalité du mandat parlementaire : celui de rendre des comptes aux « citoyens-contribuables ». Au-delà du manque de ressources, au-delà du faible impact politique que peut avoir cette action, vérifier si le gouvernement a tenu ses engagements financiers est pour l'enquêteur un *devoir* qui semble être davantage une affaire de motivation personnelle qu'une affaire de moyens ou de stratégie électorale.

Enfin l'absent, quant à lui, ne perçoit dans le contrôle budgétaire ni d'intérêt stratégique au moment du contrôle *ex ante* ni d'intérêt personnel pour le contrôle *ex post*. Plutôt « inactif » dans son contrôle budgétaire, il est généralement nommé malgré lui au sein des commissions des finances, ne se sent pas concerné par le domaine budgétaire et préfère concentrer son attention dans des activités lui procurant davantage de satisfaction. Nous avons également pu constater que ce désintérêt pour le contrôle budgétaire peut aussi bien trouver sa source dans un manque d'affinité pour le domaine budgétaire que dans un sentiment de déception ou de désillusion après expérimentation. Mais dans les deux cas, l'absent est un idéal type peu investi dans sa fonction de contrôle du budget.

Conclusion

Notre typologie des députés du contrôle budgétaire révèle un trait intéressant du comportement parlementaire. En intégrant dans l'analyse les motivations larges des députés, l'approche motivationnelle du rôle permet de démontrer que malgré les défis inhérents à la fonction de contrôle budgétaire, les députés s'y impliquent, pour différentes raisons. Nous observons avec l'idéal type de l'enquêteur que le comportement parlementaire peut être influencé par des considérations éthiques et des principes dont l'importance dépasse le calcul strictement stratégique, comme c'est davantage le cas pour le représentant. Du côté de l'absent, on remarque que ce n'est pas l'existence de moyens de contrôle qui motive nécessairement le député à agir. C'est pourquoi même si les règles institutionnelles permettent au député d'orienter ou de vérifier les politiques budgétaires du gouvernement, c'est davantage la manière dont le député « perçoit » le domaine d'action qui motive son implication.

Annexe

TABLEAU 4.4. Caractéristiques des trente-deux députés rencontrés

Caractéristiques	Détail	France	Luxembourg	Québec	Total
Appartenance politique	Nombre de députés de la majorité	5	5	5	15
	Nombre de députés de l'opposition	7	4	6	17
Fonction	Nombre de députés président des commissions des finances ou du contrôle de l'exécution, rapporteur ou porte-parole de groupe	8	5	7	20
	Nombre de députés membre de la commission	4	4	4	12
Commissions	Nombre de commissions dont le député est membre au moment de l'entretien	1	Entre 3 et 8	Entre 1 et 4	Entre 1 et 8
Ancienneté	Ancienneté en nombre d'années au moment de l'entretien	Entre 3 et 24	Entre 6 et 28	Entre 2 et 20	Entre 2 et 28
Cumul de mandats	Nombre de députés ayant un cumul de mandats (mandat national et local)	10	2	0	12
	Nombre de députés sans cumul de mandat	2	7	11	20
Expérience politique pré-parlementaire*	Expérience politique pré-parlementaire en nombre d'années	Entre 2 et 26	Entre 0 et 13	Entre 0 et 17	Entre 0 et 26
Formation ou profession antérieure	Nombre de députés ayant une formation ou une profession antérieure en lien direct avec les finances (économiste, comptable, gestionnaire d'entreprise)	10	3	8	21
	Nombre de députés n'ayant pas une formation ou une profession antérieure en lien direct avec les finances (enseignant, avocat, médecin, artisan)	2	6	3	11
Genre	Nombre de députés de sexe masculin	10	7	10	27
	Nombre de députés de sexe féminin	2	2	1	5
Âge	Âge du député au moment de l'entretien	Entre 37 et 69	Entre 53 et 67	Entre 35 et 68	Entre 35 et 69

* Fonction politique élective : maire ou conseiller municipal.

Source : *Anthony M. Weber.*

Références

Andeweg, R. B. (2016). "Roles in legislatures." In *The Oxford Handbook of Legislative Studies*, edited by S. Martin, T. Saalfed, and K. Strom, 267–85, Oxford, Oxford University Press.

Aspinwall, M. et G. Schneider (2009). « Un menu commun pour des tables séparées. Le tournant institutionnaliste de la science politique et les études sur l'intégration européenne », 105. Dans *Le choix rationnel en science politique : débats critiques*, Rennes, Presses universitaires de Rennes.

Auel, K. et T. Christiansen (2015). "After Lisbon: National Parliaments in the European Union", *West European Politics* 38 no. 2 (special issue) : 282–304.

Bonsaint, M. (2012). *La procédure parlementaire du Québec*, Québec, Assemblée nationale du Québec.

Boudon, R. (2004). « Quelle théorie du comportement pour les sciences sociales ? » présenté à Conférence Eugène Fleischmann III, Nanterre, mai 26.

Brack, N. (2014). *L'euroscepticisme au sein du parlement européen. Stratégies d'une opposition anti-système au cœur des institutions*, Bruxelles, Larcier.

Demazière, D. (2013). « Typologie et description. A propos de l'intelligibilité des expériences vécues », *Sociologie* 4 (3): 333-47.

Döring, H. (1995a). "Is Government Control of the Agenda Likely to Keep Legislative Inflation at Bay?" In *Parliaments and Majority Rule in Western Europe*, edited by H. Döring. Frankfurt/M., Campus.

Döring, H. (1995b). "Time as a Scarce Resource: Government Control of the Agenda", In *Parliaments and Majority Rule in Western Europe*, edited by H. Döring, 223–46, Frankfurt/M., Campus.

Fish, M. S. et M. Kroenig (2009). *The Handbook of National Legislatures: A Global Survey*, Cambridge, Cambridge University Press.

Fölscher, A., A. Bartholomew et R. Carter (2008). *Utilisation et contrôle de l'appui budgétaire. Analyse comparative de l'examen de l'appui budgétaire octroyé par les parlements donateurs*, Parlement européen.

Geddes, M. (2019). "Performing Scrutiny along the Committee Corridor of the UK House of Commons", *Parliamentary Affairs*, 72: 821–840.

Geddes M. et R. A. W. Rhodes (2018). "Towards an Interpretive Parliamentary Studies", In *The Sociology of Parliaments*, edited by J. Brichzin, D. Krichewsky, L. Ringel, and J. Schank, Wiesbaden, Springer.

Griglio, E. et N. Lupo (2012). "Parliamentary Democracy and the Eurozone Crisis", *Law and Economics Yearly Review* 1 (2): 314–362.

Hamilton, A. (2010) [1774]. *A Full Vindication of the Measures of Congress*, Gale Ecco.

International Monetary Fund (2001). *Manual on Fiscal Transparency*, Washington D.C., International Monetary Fund.

Jefferson, T. (1943) [1774]. *Summer Review of the Rights of British America*, Scholars' Facsimiles and Reprints.

Jenny, M. et W. C. Müller (2012). "Parliamentary Roles of MPS in Sharp and Soft Focus. Interviews and Behavioural Record Compared", In *Parliamentary Roles in Modern Legislatures*, edited by M. Blomgren and O. Rozenberg, 145–61, Abingdon, Oxon, Routledge.

Kerrouche E. (2004). « Appréhender le rôle des parlementaires : études comparatives des recherches menées et perspectives ». Dans *Vers un renouveau du parlementarisme en Europe*, sous la dir. de O. Costa, E. Kerrouche, P. Magnette, 35-55, Bruxelles, Éditions de l'Université de Bruxelles.

Lauvaux, P. (2010). « Le contrôle, source du régime parlementaire, priorité du régime présidentiel », *Pouvoirs* 134 (3) : 23-36.

Loewenberg, G. (2011). *On Legislatures: The Puzzle of Representation*, Boulder, Paradigm Publishers.

March, J.G. et J. P. Olsen (1984). "The New Institutionalism: Organizational Factors in Political Life", *American Political Science Review* 78 (3): 742.

Monjou, C. (2007). « Question fiscale et révolution : l'exemple américain », *Regards croisés sur l'économie*, 1 (1) : 54–55.

National Democratic Institute for International Affairs (2000). *Strengthening Legislative Capacity in Legislative-Executive Relations*, Washington, D.C., National Democratic Institute for International Affairs.

Navarro, J. (2007). « Les députés européens et leur rôle. Analyse sociologique de la représentation parlementaire dans l'Union européenne », Thèse de doctorat en science politique, Bordeaux, IEP Bordeaux.

Navarro, J. (2009). *Les députés européens et leur rôle. Sociologie interprétative des pratiques parlementaires*, Bruxelles, Éditions de l'Université de Bruxelles.

OECD (2002). "OECD Best Practices for Budget Transparency", *OECD Journal on Budgeting* 1 (3): 7–14.

Paine, T. (1986) [1776]. *Common Sense*, New York, Penguin Classics.

Pelizzo, R. et R. Stapenhurst (2004). *Tools for Legislative Oversight. An Empirical Investigation*, Washington D.C., World Bank.

Pelizzo, R., R. Stapenhurst et D. Olson (2006). *Parliamentary Oversight for the Government Accountability*, Washington D.C., World Bank.

Rousseau, J-J. (2019) [1755]. *Discours sur l'économie politique*, Paris, Arvensa Éditions.

Rozenberg O. et Blomgren M. (2012). "Bringing Parliamentary Roles Back In", In *Parliamentary Roles in Modern Legislatures*, edited by O. Blomgren and M. Rozenberg, 211–30, Abingdon, Oxon, Routledge.

Rozenberg, O. (2005). « Le Parlement français et l'Union européenne (1993–2005) : l'Europe saisie par les rôles parlementaires », Thèse de doctorat en science politique, Paris, IEP de Paris.

Searing, D. (1994). *Westminster's World. Understanding Political Roles*, Cambridge, Harvard University Press.

Shepsle, K. A. (2002). "Assessing Comparative Legislative Research", In *Legislatures: Comparative Perspectives on Representative Assemblies*, edited by G. Loewenberg, P. Squire, and D.R. Kiewiet, 387–97. Ann Arbor, University of Michigan Press.

Sieberer, U. (2011). "The Institutional Power of Western European Parliaments: A Multidimensional Analysis", *West European Politics* 34 (4): 731-54.

Sinnassamy, C. (2008). « Contrôle ou évaluation : réalités et illusions du management public », *Pyramides*, 15.

Stapenhurst, R. (2004). *The Legislature and the Budget*, Washington D.C., World Bank.

Stapenhurst, R., D.M. Olson et L. Trapp (2008). *Legislative Oversight and Budgeting. A World Perspective*, Washington D.C., World Bank.

Stapenhurst, R. et R. Pelizzo (2002). "A Bigger Role for Legislatures", *Finance and Development* 39 (4): 46-48.

Strom, K. (1997). "Roles, Reasons and Routines: Legislative Roles in Parliamentary Democracies", *Journal of Legislative Studies* 3 (1): 155–74.

Strom, K. (2012). "Roles as Strategies: Towards a Logic of Legislative Behavior", In *Parliamentary Roles in Modern Legislatures*, edited by O. Blomgren and M. Rozenberg, 85-100, Abingdon, Oxon, Routledge.

Thelen, K. (1999.) "Historical Institutionalism in Comparative Politics", *Annual Review of Political Science* 2 (1): 369–404.

Thiers, É. (2010). « Le contrôle parlementaire et ses limites juridiques : un pouvoir presque sans entraves », *Pouvoirs* 134 (3): 71-81.

Tsebelis, G. (2002). *Veto Players: How Political Institutions Work*, Princeton, Princeton University Press.

Tsebelis, G. (2009). "Agenda Setting and Executive Dominance in Politics." In *Parlamente, Agendasetzung und Vetospieler. Festschrift für Herbert Döring*, edited by S. Ganghof, C. Hönnige, and C. Stecker, 13–24, Wiesbaden, VS Verlag für Sozialwissenschaften.

Türk, P. (2011). *Le contrôle parlementaire en France*, Paris, L.G.D.J, Lextenso éditions.

Wahlke J. C., H. Eulau H., W. Buchanan W. et L.C. Fergusson (1962). *The Legislative System. Explorations in Legislative Behaviour*, New York, John Wiley and Sons.

Wehner (2004). *Back from the Sidelines? Redefining the Contribution of Legislatures to the Budget Cycle*, Washington D.C., World Bank.

Wehner, J. (2006). "Assessing the Power for the Purse: An Index of Legislative Budget Institutions", *Political Studies* 54 (4): 767–85.

West, W. F. et J. Cooper. (1989). "Legislative Influence v. Presidential Dominance: Competing Models of Bureaucratic Control", *Political Science Quarterly* 104 (4): 581–606.

White H. (2015). *Parliamentary Scrutiny of Government*, London, Institute for Government.

Wildavsky, A. (1975). *Budgeting: A Comparative Theory of Budgeting Processes*, Boston: Little, Brown and Company.

Wood, D. M. et J.-B. Yoon (1998). "Role Orientations of Junior MPs: A Test of Searing's Categories with Emphasis on Constituency Activities", *Journal of Legislative Studies* 4 (3): 51–71.

Yamamoto, H. (2007). *Les outils du contrôle parlementaire. Étude comparative portant sur 88 parlements nationaux*, Genève, Union interparlementaire.

Zittel, T. (2012). "Legislators and their Representational Roles. Strategic Choices or Habits of the Heart", In *Parliamentary Roles in Modern Legislatures*, edited by O. Blomgren and M. Rozenberg, 101–20, Abingdon, Oxon, Routledge.

Zittel, T. et T. Gschwend (2008). "Individualised Constituency Campaigns in Mixed-Member Electoral Systems: Candidates in the 2005 German Elections", *West European Politics* 31 (5): 978–1003.

CHAPTER 5

Change and Prayers: An Analysis of Prayers in the Legislative Assembly of British Columbia, 2003–2020

Teale N. Phelps Bondaroff, Katie E. Marshall, Ian Bushfield, Ranil Prasad, Noah Laurence, and Adriana Thom[1]*

Abstract

This chapter investigates the practice of opening sittings of the Legislative Assembly of British Columbia (B.C. Legislature) with prayer. It examines prayers delivered in the Legislature from 2 October 2003 to 14 August 2020. In late 2019, the B.C. Legislature significantly reformed its practices and changed the name of this element of routine business from "prayers" to "prayers and reflections." It also updated and expanded the list of sample prayers from which members can read. Particular attention is given in the chapter to participation in prayer and how the religiosity, content, structure, and length of prayers delivered in the B.C. Legislature have varied since these recent changes were implemented.

1 The authors are indebted for the assistance of the 55 people who volunteered to help transcribe the prayers analyzed in this study, including Mark Taylor, Lynda Worth, and Dylan Carter. We are grateful for support and funding from the members of the BC Humanist Association and the Canada Summer Jobs Program and for editorial and research assistance from Alexandre Darveau-Morin, Stan Phelps, and Felix Morrow. This chapter was produced on the traditional territories of the W̱SÁNEĆ- and Lkwungen-speaking Peoples and on the traditional and unceded territories of the hənq̓əminəm̓- and Sḵwx̱wú 7mesh-speaking Peoples and the Kanien'kehá:ka Nation.

Résumé

Ce chapitre examine la pratique consistant à ouvrir les séances de l'Assemblée législative de la Colombie-Britannique par une prière. Il examine les prières prononcées à l'Assemblée législative entre 2003 et 2020. En 2019, l'Assemblée législative de la Colombie-Britannique a adopté d'importants changements dans ses procédures, ce qui a notamment amené le changement de nom de cette activité de « prières » à « prières et réflexions ». Cette réforme a aussi mis à jour et élargi la liste d'exemples de prières que les députés peuvent lire. Une attention particulière est portée aux changements des prières prononcées à l'Assemblée législative et à qui les prononce, ainsi qu'à leur religiosité, leur contenu, leur structure et leur longueur depuis la mise en place de ces récents changements.

After entering the chamber with all the pomp and circumstance of the Westminster system, the Speaker of the Legislative Assembly of British Columbia (B.C. Legislature) rings a bell summoning Members of the Legislative Assembly (MLAs) to their seats (Legislative Assembly of British Columbia 2017). Before these elected officials can begin the complex process of debating and passing legislation that will affect the lives of a diverse population of five million British Columbians, the Speaker calls on one member to lead the chamber in prayer. An MLA rises and either reads a prayer from a list of sample prayers or delivers one of their own devising.

This was the procedure that was followed in the B.C. Legislature up until the end of 2019, when two changes were made: B.C. MLAs voted unanimously to change procedures so that daily sittings were to begin with "prayers and reflections" rather than simply "prayers." The list of sample prayers provided to MLAs was revised and expanded by the Clerk to include sample prayers from a number of faith traditions.

In 2018, we set about investigating legislative prayer in B.C., seeking to better understand the nature of these prayers and determine the extent to which the prayers delivered in the B.C. represented the beliefs of British Columbians. In September 2019, we released *House of Prayers*, a report that analyzed prayers delivered in the B.C. Legislature from 2 October 2003 to 12 February 2019 (Phelps Bondaroff et al. 2019). This report found that "fewer MLAs are delivering prayers, and that prayers are getting longer and more religious" and that, comparing demographic data with the types of prayers delivered in the legislature, the prayers did "not reflect the diversity of beliefs in the province" (Phelps Bondaroff et al. 2019, 10).

Having previously studied prayer in the B.C. Legislature, we were interested in how these two changes would impact the religiosity, content, and length of the prayers delivered at the start of each day. To that end, this chapter investigates prayers delivered in the Legislature from 2 October 2003 to 14 August 2020, analyzing the religiosity, content, and length of these prayers and exploring how these factors vary by party and have changed following the shift in procedure in late 2019.

Legislative Prayer in British Columbia: Procedures and Recent Changes

Up until late 2019, procedures surrounding prayer in the B.C. Legislature were outlined in Standing Order 25, which states that "prayers are held in the House with both officers and strangers present. Prayers are generally interdenominational and are delivered by Members, visiting clergy or the Speaker" (MacMinn 2008, 56). Prayers are delivered by an MLA at the start of each daily sitting of the Legislature when the Speaker calls upon an MLA to "lead us in prayer" or to "lead this house in prayer." The MLA delivering the prayer is selected by their caucus and can choose to deliver a prayer of their own devising or read one of five prayers from a list of sample prayers, either directly or with modifications as they see fit (see Appendix 1). On days featuring a Speech from the Throne, a member of the public would typically be invited to deliver the prayer; this has historically been a member of the clergy of an established religion or an Elder representing one of the First Nations in the province.

There is no set limit for the duration of the prayer or any guidelines as to its content, and it could take the form of anything from a recitation of the Lord's Prayer, an abridged sermon, the reading of poetry, references to current events or significant holidays, offers of condolences or well wishes to members of the House or community experiencing hardship, all the way across the spectrum to partisan swipes.

Towards the end of 2019, two changes were made to the procedures and practices around prayer in the B.C. Legislature. First, on

7 October 2019, the Clerk released a revised list of sample prayers (see Appendix 2), which included both changes to the existing prayers and the addition of a number of prayers broadly representing different faith traditions. These changes were made "to ensure that prepared prayers provide a breadth of non-religious reflections, as well as prayers from major religious groups" (K. Ryan-Lloyd Acting Clerk of the House, correspondence with authors, 21 August 2019; and see Bushfield and Phelps Bondaroff 2020). The changes included the removal of the first sample prayer—one of the more traditional and religious of the sample prayers. The remaining four prayers had the "Amen" dropped from their endings, and the fifth prayer was reworded and had references to God removed. An additional generic sample prayer was added, along with a traditional land acknowledgement and prayers representing the Buddhist, Christian, Hindu, Jewish, Muslim, and Sikh faith traditions (see Appendix 2). For ease of reference, we have sequentially numbered all prayers across both sample lists. For clarity, we refer to this change as "list change" throughout the chapter.

The second change came on 25 November 2019, when a unanimous vote amended Standing Order 25 so that the daily routine business of the B.C. Legislature begins with an MLA, "the Speaker or invited faith leaders or Indigenous leaders or Elders" delivering "prayers and reflections" (Ryan-Lloyd et al. 2020, 97; and see Legislative Assembly of British Columbia 2019). As a result, the opening sitting on 11 February 2020 featured the Speaker asking a member "to lead this house in prayer or reflection" (Legislative Assembly of British Columbia 2020). Additionally, *Hansard* began including the name of the MLA who delivered the prayer in the Hansard Blues and Official Transcripts.[2] Prior to this, the verbatim record of the Legislature had only indicated that a prayer had been delivered (Legislative Assembly of British Columbia 2020). However, the content of the prayers remains "the only proceedings not transcribed verbatim for publication in the Hansard transcript" (Ryan-Lloyd et al. 2020, 97). For clarity, we refer to this change as "procedure change" or "change of procedures" throughout the chapter.

---

2   Hansard Blues are the first draft of Assembly transcripts and are typically released as unofficial transcripts shortly after the words are spoken in the Chamber. The Official Hansard Transcripts are later released after they are properly edited.

Legislative Prayer in Canada: Practice and Controversies

Practices with respect to legislative prayer vary considerably across Canada. British Columbia is one of only a few jurisdictions where MLAs are invited to deliver a prayer of their own devising—the others being Nunavut and the Northwest Territories, which will sometimes also feature drumming/drum prayers. In Alberta, the Speaker reads a prayer of their own devising, while in Saskatchewan and Manitoba, the Speaker reads a standard non-denominational prayer, and in the Yukon, the Speaker reads one of four standard prayers. In New Brunswick, an MLA reads prayers to God and Jesus for the well-being of the Queen, Lieutenant-Governor General, and the Legislature, followed by the Lord's Prayer, in a blend of French and English. In Prince Edward Island, the Speaker reads prayers to God and Jesus for the well-being of the Queen, and Lieutenant Governor General, followed by the Lord's Prayer (the public is excluded from the chamber for the prayers). In Ontario, the Speaker reads the Lord's Prayer, followed by the reading of a prayer from a rotating schedule that includes prayers from Indigenous, Buddhist, Muslim, Jewish, Baha'i, and Sikh faith traditions. The Nova Scotia Legislature opens with a moment of quiet reflection, a practice which was adopted in October 2021. Previously the Speaker had read an extended version of the Lord's Prayer. Sittings of the National Assembly of Quebec open with a "moment of reflection," after the practice of opening them with prayer was abandoned in 1976, and Newfoundland and Labrador has never included prayer in its legislature. At the federal level, both the House of Commons and Senate begin with the Speaker reading a non-denominational prayer, which is then followed by time for silent reflection (see Phelps Bondaroff, Prasad et al. 2020; and see Fizet 2010, 2; Bueckert et al. 2017, 25; and Lanouette 2009, 6).

The inclusion of prayer in Canadian legislative assemblies is not without controversy, and over the years elected officials, individuals, and civil society organizations have criticized and challenged the practice. Member of Provincial Parliament (MPP) Elmer Sopha raised objections to the Lord's Prayer opening daily sittings of the Ontario Legislature in 1969 (Fizet 2010, 3), and the controversy following Premier Dalton McGuinty's attempt to abolish the practice resulted in the current amended version being adopted in 2008 (Fizet 2010, 1; and see Boissinot 2015; Lanouette 2009, 5). Objections have been unsuccessfully raised by MLAs in Nova Scotia

(2001) (CBC News 2001b) and New Brunswick (2019) (Poitras 2019). Civil society organizations have also campaigned against the practice, including the Centre for Inquiry Regina, which has circulated petitions calling for the end of the practice in Saskatchewan in both 2016 and 2018 (White-Crummey 2018). The BC Humanist Association launched a campaign against the practice in 2018, led by several of the authors of this chapter (BC Humanist Association 2018; and see BC Humanist Association 2019).

While attempts to remove legislative prayer from provincial and federal legislative bodies have thus far encountered only limited success, the inclusion of prayer in municipal councils was found to be unconstitutional by the Supreme Court. The 2015 *Saguenay* decision found the practice of opening municipal council meetings with prayer to constitute a violation of the state's duty of religious neutrality. In this case, which concerned the practice of beginning municipal council meetings of the City of Saguenay, Quebec, with prayer, the Court found that the state has a duty to remain neutral on issues relating to religion (*Mouvement laïque québécois v. Saguenay* 2015, para. 76) and that the state has a "democratic imperative" to ensure that every citizen can participate equally in "public life regardless of their beliefs" (*Mouvement laïque québécois v. Saguenay* 2015, para. 75). *Saguenay* did not directly address the question of prayer in the legislative chambers of higher levels of government, but in the ruling, Justice Gascon did note that the circumstances in these chambers were potentially different and that the practice could be shielded by parliamentary privilege (*Mouvement laïque québécois v. Saguenay* 2015, para. 142). The question of the constitutionality of prayer in provincial and federal legislative chambers in Canada remains a live issue. Understanding the nature of prayer in the B.C. Legislature and how it has been affected by recent changes contributes valuable insight to this ongoing discussion.

Studying Prayer in the B.C. Legislature

There is limited literature on the subject of legislative prayer in Canada—and only one quantitative study: Bueckert et al. examined 31 prayers delivered between 1992 and 2016 before Speeches from the Throne, which we refer to as "Throne Prayers" (Bueckert et al. 2017). This study identified the religion of the prayers using the affiliation of the guest delivering them. Prayers were found to be predominantly

"Christian" (67.7%), followed by "non-denominational" (12.9%), "Indigenous" (9.7%), "Jewish" (6.5%), and "Muslim" (3.2%) (Bueckert et al. 2017, 26). A comparison of these results with the religious affiliation of British Columbians in the 2011 National Household Survey led the authors to conclude that "the faiths represented […] do not directly correlate to the percentage of British Columbians that identify with each respective faith group" (Bueckert et al. 2017, 28).

Our first examination of the subject, the *House of Prayers* study, analyzed all the prayers delivered in the B.C. Legislature, from 6 October 2003, when video recordings became available, to 12 February 2019, the end of the 3rd Session of the 41st Parliament (Phelps Bondaroff et al. 2019). The *House of Prayers* report sought to provide a better understanding of the content and practices surrounding daily prayer in the B.C. Legislature. Here, we build on this report and expanded our existing data with prayers delivered from 12 February 2019 to 14 August 2020, creating a sample of 974 prayers delivered by 143 people between 6 October 2003 and 14 August 2020.

Coding Process and Protocols

The content of prayers delivered in the B.C. Legislature are not recorded in *Hansard*, but are available on *Hansard*'s video archive from 6 October 2003 onwards (Legislative Assembly of British Columbia, n.d.). A team of over 50 volunteers were recruited to assist with transcription; 89 prayers were transcribed twice, to verify transcription and accuracy, and random spot checks were also conducted. We were unable to access the videos for and, hence, to transcribe six prayers. Once transcribed, prayers were manually coded in a number of categories by two coders (see details below). To avoid potential bias, coders were only provided with the text of the prayer and the date it was delivered. Intercoder reliability was verified by a third coder. We chose to have prayers manually coded to avoid the problem of polysemy—where words like "father" could refer to a deity or to a parent—and to best capture the nuance, and therefore the religiosity, of the prayers. A note on language usage: while not all the statements could be considered prayers (or reflections), we refer to them all as "prayers" for brevity's sake.

Coding Categories

Prayers were manually coded in a number of categories using a detailed rubric (Phelps Bondaroff et al. 2019, 95–105). While most are relatively straightforward, the category of "religiosity" requires elaboration. We developed four categories for religiosity and the following descriptions were used to code prayers appropriately:

- Not a Prayer: Anything that could not be classified as a prayer or invocation, such as reading a secular quote, reciting a poem, or a moment of silence. The content could not be part of a broader invocation, contain elements of a prayer, or be delivered in a prayer-like structure.
- Secular Invocation/Prayer: Any invocation or call of thanks not invoking or directed towards a deity or the transcendent. It could still end in Amen, but could not use any other religious language or include references to the supernatural or a deity/power.
- Non-Sectarian Prayer: Prayers that were religious in nature but could not easily be identified with a specific religious tradition. This category included any prayer that invoked the divine or transcendent, a deity, power, or supernatural entity, or relied on religious language. Building on the non-denominational category used in Bueckert et al., prayers would be coded in this category if they "did not contain words associated with a specific religion to the exclusion of others" (Bueckert et al. 2017, 26).
- Sectarian Prayer: Any prayer with religious content of a specific, identifiable faith tradition. Indices of religions might include the names of a deity exclusive to a religion; references to, or quotes from a religious text or figures; references to a specific religious holiday; reciting prayers specific to a religion; or employing language closely associated with a specific religion. To facilitate this process, glossaries of names of deities and religious language were constructed (Phelps Bondaroff et al. 2019, 98). Coders were instructed to only code a prayer as sectarian if they could identify the religion specific to that prayer. Prayers were categorized into major faith traditions: Christian (including Catholicism and all the various sects of Protestantism), Muslim (including

Sunni, Shia, and Salafi), Jewish (including Reform, Orthodox, and Hassidic), Buddhist (including all various sects), Sikh, Indigenous, and Other.

Coders were instructed to be very conservative in their coding and not to apply any specific personal knowledge of a particular faith tradition. We recognized that this would likely result in under-selecting prayers that seemed to be very Christian but that used terminology that could belong to a number of faith traditions—for example, a prayer delivered in the form of a personal dialogue, spoken directly to a god, with multiple references to "Lord." The structure and content of this prayer would likely point to it being a Christian prayer, however, this language is also common with other religions, and, as such, barring the inclusion of any words specific to Christianity, it would be coded as non-sectarian. The term "Father," when it referred to a deity, was considered sufficiently Christian for these prayers to be coded as sectarian-Christian. Discussions with the coders indicated a number of borderline cases, and where sufficient doubt existed, prayers were coded as non-sectarian.

With respect to coding prayers as sectarian-Indigenous, we recognized that describing Indigenous content as religious or even "spiritual" was problematic, inaccurate, and would likely result in the omission of prayers that had a specific Indigenous focus but that lacked elements that could be classified as a "conventional religion." For example, in a recent Supreme Court of British Columbia case, *Servatius v. Alberni School District*, involving a dispute over whether a smudging ceremony in a Port Alberni school violated the school's requirement to operate on "strictly secular and non-sectarian principles," the Nuu-chah-nulth Tribal Council argued that "smudging is a cultural practice, not a religious one" (2020; and see Beaman 2020). Despite the some-times blurry distinction between cultural and spiritual practice, we still wanted to know the extent to which Indigenous content, beyond individual words, was being included in prayers. Therefore, in order for a prayer to be coded as sectarian-Indigenous, it need not necessar-ily have religious/spiritual content, but rather use Indigenous content beyond a single word or include explicit Indigenous content in English—such as language exclusively used in First Nations invoca-tions, such as "Great Spirit" or "all my relations." The question of Indigenous language use in prayers is explored extensively in Phelps Bondaroff et al. (2019) and Bushfield et al. (2020).

Some discussion on the distinction between the sectarian and non-sectarian categories is pertinent. In critiquing the idea of distinguishing non-sectarian from sectarian prayers, Delahunty argued that the idea of a non-sectarian prayer "presupposes that some generic, 'non-sectarian' prayer language can be disengaged from the specific faith traditions and forms of worship that give prayer its vitality, power, and inner meaning. That presupposition is false" (Delahunty 2007, 539). These criticisms are linked to the debate surrounding the possibility of drafting, and the nature of, non-denominational prayer. Many commentators note that it is impossible to craft a prayer that is truly universal, because no common denominator exists (Stone 1983). This is because every individual word and structural choice is permeated with assumptions and meaning. As Delahunty elaborates, "*every* prayer, by its very nature, reflects and conveys a particular system of beliefs about the nature of ultimate reality and is thus 'sectarian.' However inclusionary or ecumenical a prayer is intended to be, it necessarily incorporates a particular theological viewpoint or belief" (2007, 522).

Many of the prayers coded as non-sectarian employ subtle language and structural cues that, upon further analysis, would likely serve to identify them with a specific faith tradition. However, this level of analysis falls beyond the scope of this project. The conservative approach adopted dictated that where there was uncertainty, a prayer would be coded as non-sectarian. Because of the overall religious nature of both non-sectarian and sectarian prayer, however, these are often grouped together in the analysis under the category of religious prayers.

Analytical Methods

Analysis was conducted in R, using the "plyr" package for data reorganization when required (R Core Team 2018 ; Wickham 2011). Prayer length, in words, was calculated from transcripts using the str_count command in the "stringr" package to search for spaces between words (Wickham 2019). When differences among groups were tested with a continuous response (e.g., prayer length or total prayers given per MLA), general linear models were used (ANOVA, ANCOVA, and regression) to test for statistical differences among predictors. We examined the distribution of both continuous predictors and responses by generating histograms, and a natural logarithm transformed these variables to improve normality if necessary. When we tested differences among groups with a binary response (e.g., whether the prayer was secular or not), we used logistic regression implemented as a generalized linear model with binomial distribution. Alpha was set to 0.05 in all tests, however, for $0.05 < p > 0.10$ we report the effect size and p-value for interpretation of trends.[3]

Results and Analysis

Here we examine the overall religiosity of prayers, religious content within prayer, sample prayer use, the number of MLAs delivering prayers, and the length of prayers. For each of these elements we provide an overview of our findings, and then explore how these elements have changed over time and vary between parties. When tracking changes over time, we typically plot time on a yearly basis, unless otherwise specified. To examine the effect of party affiliation on the types of prayer each MLA delivered, we began by removing all Throne Prayers. Over the period examined, the B.C. Legislature has been dominated by two parties, the Liberal Party and the New Democratic Party (NDP). MLAs will occasionally sit as independents, and the Green Party has also won a number of seats. However, only one Green Party MLA has delivered prayers (on two occasions), and no prayers were delivered by an independent; as a result, they have been excluded from the analysis.

Descriptive Statistics

Between 2 October 2003 and 14 August 2020, 974 prayers were delivered in the B.C. Legislature by 143 people. Of these, 3 were inaudible (and were dropped from further analysis) and 27 were Throne Prayers, which were excluded from analysis along party lines. A total of 938 of these prayers were given before, and 36 were given after the change from "prayer" to "prayers and reflections" (procedural change). And 919 prayers were delivered before, and 55 prayers delivered after the list of sample prayers was updated (list change).

---

3   The generated R script showing analysis steps, along with the fully coded dataset is available at DOI 10.17605/OSF.IO/9DJBW or https://osf.io/9djbw/.

Prayer Religiosity

We found that 70.4 percent of prayers (678 prayers) could be classified as religious (combining the prayers coded as non-sectarian and sectarian), and the majority of these (468 prayers) could not be specified to a particular religion (non-sectarian). Among religious prayers, where religion could be determined, the overwhelming majority were classified as Christian (94.1%), with Indigenous prayers the next most common (2.9%) (Table 5.1). Six prayers were delivered in non-English languages and could not be classified by religion and were, therefore, dropped from the analysis. One prayer was delivered honouring Vaisakhi, which is both a Sikh and Hindu religious holiday; as such, it was counted in both columns.

TABLE 5.1.
Identified Religion in Sectarian Prayers Delivered in the B.C. Legislature, October 2, 2003–August 14, 2020 (n = 965)

Religion	Number of Prayers	Proportion of Total Prayers	Proportion of Sectarian Prayers
Buddhist	1	0.001	0.005
Christian	192	0.199	0.941
Indigenous	6	0.006	0.029
Gaian	1	0.001	0.005
Hindu	2	0.002	0.010
Jewish	4	0.004	0.020
Muslim	3	0.003	0.014
Sikh	2	0.002	0.01
Non-sectarian	468	0.482	N/A

Source: Katie Marshall.

Change in Religiosity Over Time

Prior to the procedural change, the most common prayer type was non-sectarian, which accounted for a total of 48.7 percent of all prayers. After the procedural change, we found this proportion significantly decreased to 30.6 percent of prayers (logistic regression; deviance explained = 4.72, df = 972, p = 0.030) (Table 5.2). Similarly, the representation of "not a prayer" (e.g., poems) significantly increased from 1.6 percent of all delivered prayers to 11.1 percent of all prayers (logistic regression; deviance explained = 8.29, df = 972, p = 0.004) (Table 5.2). Major contributors to this change were Sheila Malcolmson (NDP MLA for Nanaimo) and Claire Trevena (NDP MLA for North Island), who adopted the practice of reading poems on regular occasions (see, e.g., prayers delivered by Malcolmson, 27 February 2020, and Trevana, 15 July 2020). Overall, 287 non-religious prayers (not a prayer and secular combined) were delivered in the B.C. Legislature, representing 29.6 percent of all prayers, but the proportion of non-religious prayers changed significantly after the procedure change, from 28.8 percent to 47.2 percent.

The full breakdown of the types of prayers delivered in the Legislature can be found in Table 5.2. Here "unknown" indicates a prayer that was delivered entirely in a non-English language and, therefore, could not be coded. The asterisk in the post-procedural change column indicates a significant difference in the proportion of prayers that belong to a particular category in a logistic regression following the procedure change. The number of non-religious prayers changed significantly after the procedure change.

TABLE 5.2.
Types of Prayer Given in the B.C. Legislature, October 2, 2003–August 14, 2020 (n = 971)

Prayer Type	Total	Total Proportion	Proportion Pre-procedural Change	Proportion Post-procedural Change
Unknown	6	0.006	0.006	0
Not a prayer	19	0.020	0.016	0.111*
Secular	268	0.276	0.287	0.361
Non-sectarian	468	0.482	0.487	0.306*
Sectarian	210	0.216	0.215	0.222

Source: Katie Marshall.

While the occurrence of secular and sectarian prayers did not change, the shifts in the delivery of content that was not a prayer and non-sectarian prayer use resulted in an overall reduction of religious prayer usage from 71.2 percent of all prayers to 52.8 percent of all prayers following the procedure change (logistic regression; deviance explained = 5.23, df = 972, p = 0.022).

Change in Religiosity Over Time, by Party

Looking at religiosity over time by party, we found that while overall religious prayer use did not change over time (F = 0.848, df = 1, 29, p = 0.848), sectarian religious prayer use significantly increased over time (F = 6.044, df = 1, 29, p = 0.020). Liberal MLAs generally delivered many more sectarian prayers than NDP MLAs, and this difference has been increasing over time (Figure 5.1). In Figure 5.1, the vertical dashed line indicates the date of procedure change, and solid lines indicate a locally weighted regression fit separately for each party. As we can see, the general trends continue after the procedure change.

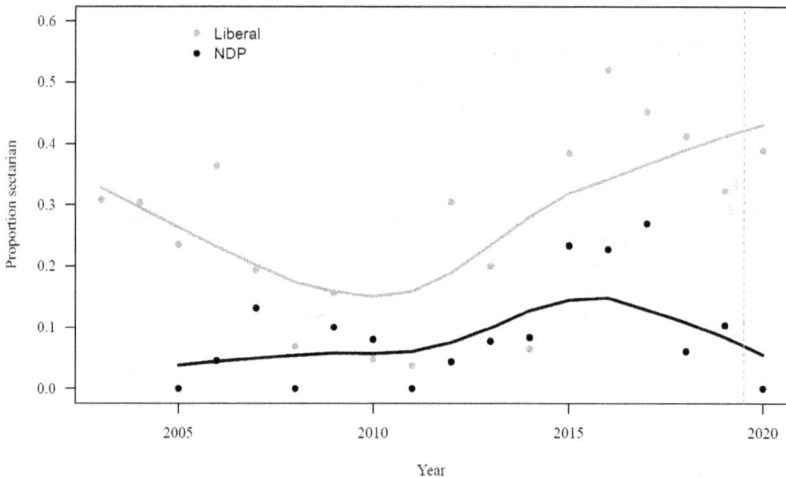

FIGURE 5.1. Proportion of Sectarian Prayers Delivered in the B.C. Legislature, October 2, 2003–August 14, 2020, by MLA Party.

Source: Katie Marshall.

There is no effect of year on the proportion of religious prayer over time, but Liberal MLAs generally gave more religious prayers (Figure 5.2). In Figure 5.2, the vertical dashed line indicates the date of procedure change, and the solid lines indicate a locally weighted regression fit separately for each party.

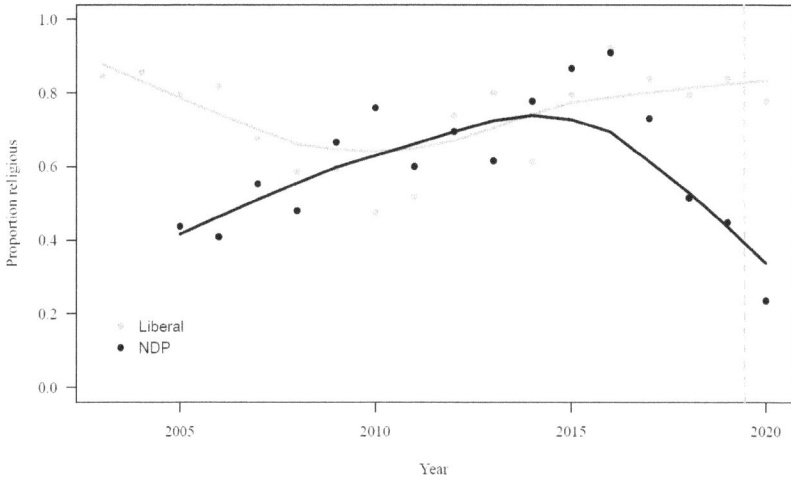

FIGURE 5.2. Proportion of Religious Prayers (Non-sectarian and Sectarian) Delivered in the B.C. Legislature, October 2, 2003–August 14, 2020.

Source: Katie Marshall.

Religious Content

Religious content was very common in prayers delivered in the B.C. Legislature. We coded for three classes of religious content: direct references to a deity (using a glossary of names of deities, see Phelps Bondaroff et al. 2019, 98), the inclusion of the word "Amen," and the inclusion of other religious language (using a glossary of other religious language, see Phelps Bondaroff et al. 2019, 98).

Of a total of 974 prayers, only 53 (5.4%) contained zero religious language. These were either not prayers (12 total) or secular prayers (41). Prayers that we classified as secular therefore almost always contained religious language (84.7% of the time)—very often the word "Amen." On average, 87.2 percent of all prayers ended in the word "Amen," including 80.9 percent of prayers classified as secular (Table 5.3). Additional findings are outlined in Table 5.3., with the asterisk indicating a significant difference in the proportion of prayers with that language after the procedure change, in a logistic regression.

TABLE 5.3.
Religious Content in Prayers in the B.C. legislature, October 2, 2003–
August 14, 2020

Religious Language	Total	Total Proportion	Proportion Pre-procedure Change	Proportion Post-procedure Change
Reference to Deity	505	0.520	0.528	0.306*
Ends in "Amen"	856	0.872	0.906	0.444*
Other Religious Language	628	0.645	0.647	0.583

Source: Katie Marshall.

Our coders used "references to a deity" and "other religious language" as key elements in assisting them in coding the religiosity of prayers (see above). Over half (52%) of all prayers delivered in the B.C. Legislature referred to some deity directly, and an even greater percentage (64.5%) included some kind of religious language other than the word "Amen" (Table 5.3).

Change in Religious Content Over Time

We noticed a number of changes in the use of religious language over time. Before the list change, 90.5 percent of prayers ended in "Amen" and 3.3 percent ended in "thank you," while after the list was adopted, 49.1 percent of prayers ended in "Amen" (logistic regression; deviance explained = 53.13, df = 1,933, $p < 0.001$) and 18.9 percent ended in "thank you." After the procedure change, the use of "Amen" declined significantly to only 44.4 percent of all prayers (logistic regression; deviance explained = 41.65, df = 972, $p < 0.001$) (Table 5.3). Prior to this change, only 4.2 percent of prayers ended in "thank you" and, following the procedure change, this increased to 16.7 percent of prayers (logistic regression; deviance explained = 7.55, df = 972, $p = 0.006$).

There was also a significant change in the recording of prayers containing a direct reference to a deity. Prior to the procedure change, 52.8 percent of prayers referred to a deity directly, while only 30.6 percent did so afterwards. There was no significant change in the use of other religious language.

Change in Religious Content Over Time, By Party

The use of "Amen" to close a prayer was initially common in both parties, but generally more common among Liberal MLAs (logistic regression; deviance explained = 108.58, df = 1, 931, p < 0.001). However, over time, this practice has declined significantly in both parties (logistic regression; deviance explained = 1, 932, p < 0.001 on non-linear year predictor). We can see this trend in Figure 5.3, where the vertical dashed line indicates the date of procedure change, and the solid lines indicate a locally weighted regression fit separately for each party.

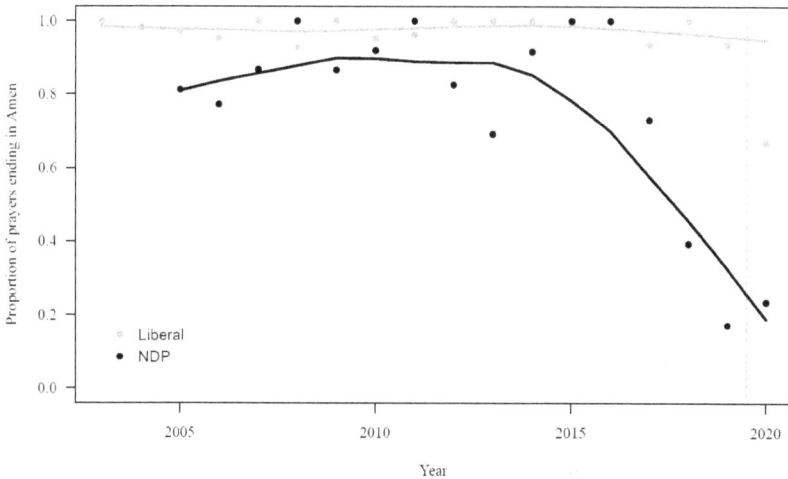

FIGURE 5.3. Use of "Amen" to End Prayers Delivered in the B.C. Legislature, by Party, October 2, 2003–August 14, 2020.

Source: Katie Marshall.

There was only weak evidence that the use of other types of religious language (reference to a deity or other religious language) has declined over time in either party (logistic regression; deviance explained = 3.03 ; df = 1, 933, p = 0.082), but in general, NDP MLAs deliver a lower proportion of prayers with other religious content (logistic regression; deviance explained = 7.34, df = 1, 931, p = 0.007) (Figure 5.4). This is illustrated by Figure 5.4, where the vertical dashed line indicates the date of procedure change, and the solid lines indicate a locally weighted regression fit separately for each party.

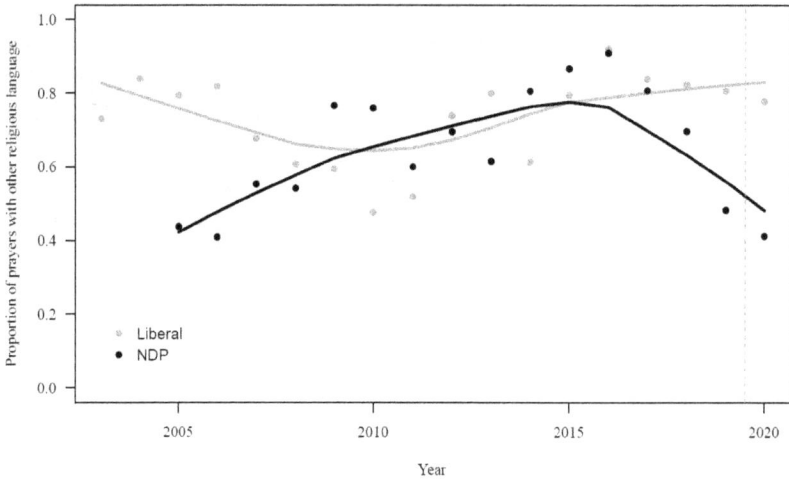

FIGURE 5.4. Proportion of Prayers with Other Religious Language (Reference to a Deity, or Other Religious Language) in the B.C. Legislature, by Party, October 2, 2003–August 14, 2020.

Source: Katie Marshall.

Sample Prayer Use

In the B.C. Legislature, MLAs are given the choice of delivering a prayer of their own devising or reading a sample prayer from a list provided by the Clerk. While most MLAs who read a sample prayer would typically read an individual prayer unaltered, coders did note minor and major alterations and instances where two or more sample prayers were read in combination. Minor alterations constituted variations in delivery such as the removal of the prefix "as we commence proceedings" or the transposition of words, where major variations included changes that would alter the coding of the prayers' religiosity (the removal of the word "God" for example) or adding additional content to the sample prayer or embedding it in a longer prayer. A total of 47.5 percent of prayers used the sample prayer list, in some combination (461/971). Prior to the list change, MLAs preferred sample prayers 2, 4, and 3 (see Appendix 1) and were more likely to combine sample prayers 4 and 5 than to deliver sample prayer 1 (see Table 5.4).

Change in Sample Prayer Use Over Time

Following the procedure change, the use of sample prayers declined significantly to only 27.7 percent of all prayers (logistic regression; deviance explained = 5.97, df = 972, p = 0.015). Similarly, prior to the list change, 48.1 percent of prayers were sample prayers, while after the list change, only 34.5 percent were sample prayers (logistic regression; deviance explained = 3.90, df = 1, 972, p = 0.048).

TABLE 5.4.
Sample Prayer Use in the B.C. Legislature, October 2, 2003–August 14, 2020

Prayer	Total Usage	Number Pre-list Change	Number Post-list Change
1	27	27	0
2	124	124	0
2 + 3	1	1	0
3	76	76	0
3 + 4	1	1	0
3 + 4 + 5	2	2	0
3 + 5	3	3	0
4	122	122	0
4 + 5	36	36	0
5	50	50	0
New sample list disseminated by Clerk, October 7, 2019			
6	5	0	5
7	2	0	2
7 + 8	1	0	1
8	5	0	5
8 + 9	1	0	1
10	1	0	1
11 + 13	1	0	1
12	1	0	1
13	2	0	2

Source: Katie Marshall.

Due to relatively few sample prayers being used after procedure change and the list change, we did not test the relative usage of each sample prayer. It is also worth noting that the new list of sample prayers (see Appendix 2) did not represent entirely newly drafted sample prayers. While sample prayer 1 was dropped, the remaining sample prayers were retained, with "Amen" dropped from their endings. As such, sample prayer 2 became 6, 3 became 7, 4 became 8, and 5 became 9, with the latter also having the word "God" removed. The relative preference of sample prayers 6, 8, and 7 is consistent with pre-list change practices.

Change in Sample Prayer Use Over Time, by Party

Sample prayer use has declined in both parties significantly over time ($F = 33.27$, $df = 1$, 30, $p < 0.001$) and was also significantly lower in the NDP overall ($F = 44.27$, $df = 1$, 30, $p < 0.001$) (Figure 5.5). In Figure 5.5., the dashed vertical line indicates the date when the sample prayer list changed.

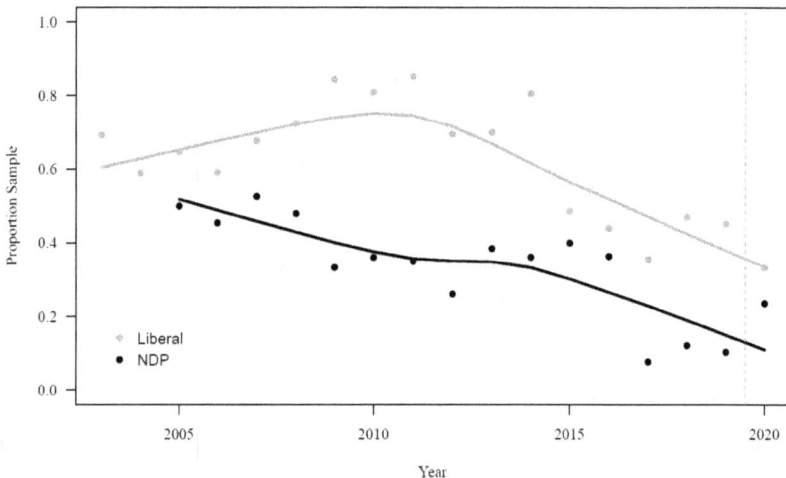

FIGURE 5.5. Proportion of Sample Prayer Use by Party in the B.C. Legislature, October 2, 2003–August 14, 2020.

Source: Katie Marshall.

MLA Participation in Delivering Prayers

We created league tables comprising all the MLAs who delivered prayers and the number of prayers they delivered, per Parliament. When we did this, we found that the number of prayers delivered by individual MLAs varied considerably, from zero to 96 prayers

(Figure 5.6), and the number of MLAs offering prayers or reflections has been on the decline. By far the most prolific MLA, when it comes to delivering prayer, was Leonard Krog, NDP MLA for Nanaimo from 21 September 2005 to 15 May 2018.

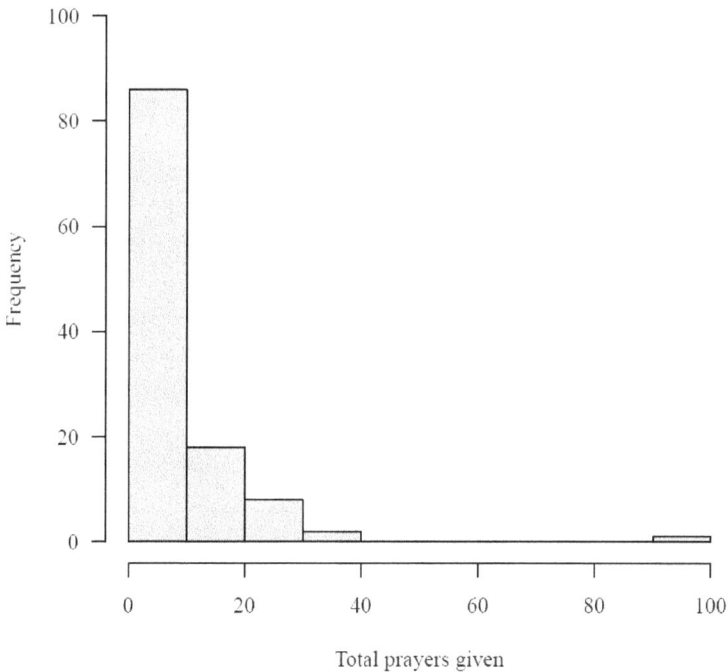

FIGURE 5.6. Frequency of Individual MLA Participation in Delivering Prayers in the B.C. Legislature, October 2, 2003–August 14, 2020.
Source: Katie Marshall.

Change in MLA Participation Over Time

The number of MLAs offering prayers has been on a steady decline, such that in the most recent parliament, only 27 percent of MLAs delivered prayers (Table 5.5). To control for the variable number of prayers delivered per parliamentary session, the number of MLAs per prayer is calculated as the number of unique MLAs who delivered prayers in a particular session of parliament divided by the total prayers delivered in that session. This significantly declined over time such that while an average of 21.8 individual MLAs were delivering an average of 30.4 prayers per session in the first five years of our dataset (0.717 unique MLAs per prayer), by the last five years, 18.8 MLAs were delivering an average of 41.4 prayers per session (0.454 unique MLAs per prayer). Because who delivers the prayer is determined by caucus whips (Ryan-Lloyd et al. 2020, 97), we chose not to examine prayer participation by parties or changes in the same.

TABLE 5.5.
Percentage of MLAs Delivering Prayers, per Parliament, B.C. Legislature, October 2, 2003–August 14, 2020

Parliament	# MLAs Total	# MLAs Delivering Prayers	% MLAs Delivering Prayers
41	88	24	27%
40	88	28	32%
39	88	36	41%
38	77	42	55%
37	78	34	44%

Source: Katie Marshall.

On average, prayers delivered in the B.C. Legislature are 92.7 words long. There was significant variation in length, however, with standard deviation being 64.62 (Figure 5.7). The longest prayer, which was delivered twice as part of Throne Speeches by Rev. Steve Bailey, was 591 words long (October 3, 2011 and February 12, 2013). The longest prayer delivered by an MLA (i.e., non-Throne Prayer) was a non-sectarian religious prayer of 324 words delivered by NDP MLA Anne Kang (Burnaby-Deer Lake) on February 14, 2019. The shortest prayer was 23 words long and was delivered by NDP MLA Jenn McGinn (Vancouver-Fairview) on November 2, 2005; it was a non-sectarian prayer that read, "So many words are spoken in this House, join me in silent prayer for peace throughout the world and happiness for all humanity."

It is worth noting a potential source of error with respect to prayer length; as we were unable to transcribe content delivered in non-English languages, we could not determine the length of this content. In these instances, transcribers would include a note within the prayer, flagging non-English language, and while we have endeavoured to exclude these notes from word counts, some may have been counted.

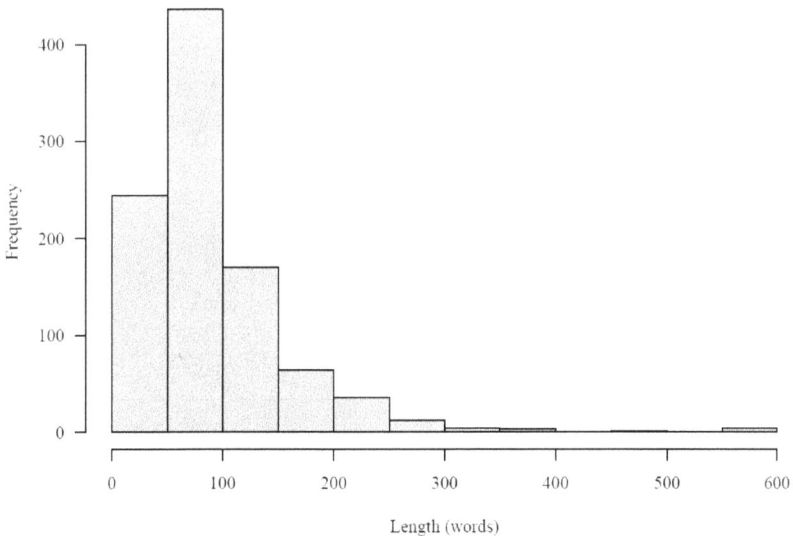

FIGURE 5.7. Frequency of Prayer Length in the B.C. Legislature, October 2, 2003–August 14, 2020.

Source: Katie Marshall.

Prayer Length Over Time and by Prayer Type

Prayers in the B.C. Legislature have been getting significantly longer over time (F = 72.39, df = 1, 930, p < 0.001). The drivers of this effect are complex, with the party affiliation of the MLA interacting with the religiosity of the prayer to drive length changes over time (F = 8.08, df = 1, 916, p = 0.004).

Looking first at the length of prayers based on their religiosity, we see that non-religious prayers (not a prayer and secular prayers [1]) are generally shorter than religious prayers (non-sectarian and sectarian prayers [0]), but that, generally, the length of both types of prayer has been increasing over time (Figure 5.8).

Next, we were interested in the interaction between prayer length and religiosity. There were significant differences in length among prayer types (F = 115.5, df = 3, 961, p < 0.001). Generally, sectarian and non-prayers (not a prayer) were the longest (averaging 140.0 and

125.5 words respectively), while secular prayers were the shortest (averaging 60.4 words) (Figure 5.9). We can see this effect in Figure 5.9, where prayer length was log base 10 transformed to improve visualization.

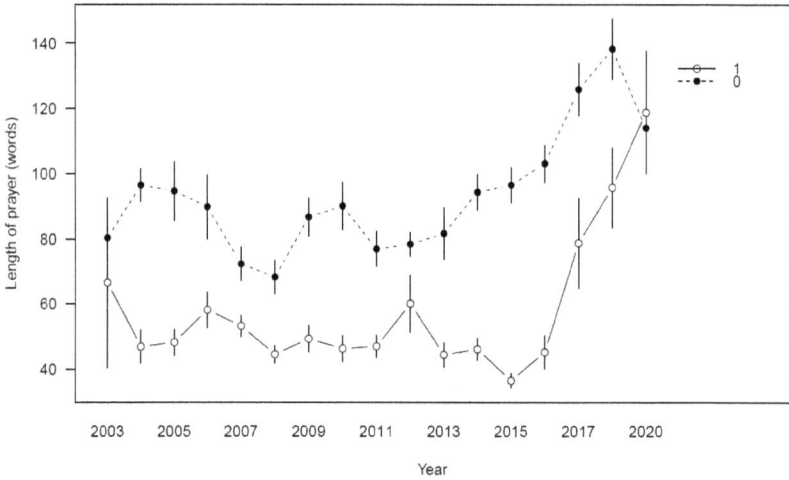

FIGURE 5.8. Length of Religious (0) and Non-religious (1) Prayers in the B.C. Legislature, October 2, 2003–August 14, 2020.

Source: Katie Marshall.

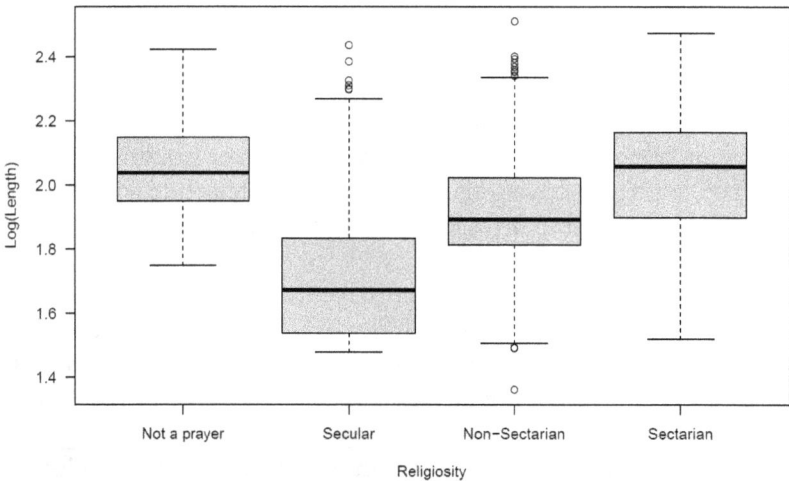

FIGURE 5.9. Differences in Length of Prayer Based on Type of Prayer Delivered in the B.C. Legislature.

Source: Katie Marshall.

Prayer Length Over Time, by Party and Religiosity

As noted, the factors affecting prayer length are complex, and there were a number of interactions between prayer length, party, and religiosity. Overall, we see that prayer length has increased for both parties, with this being particularly the case for NDP MLAs (Figure 5.10). In Figure 5.10, the dashed vertical line indicates the date when the sample prayer list changed; as can be observed, the general trends continue.

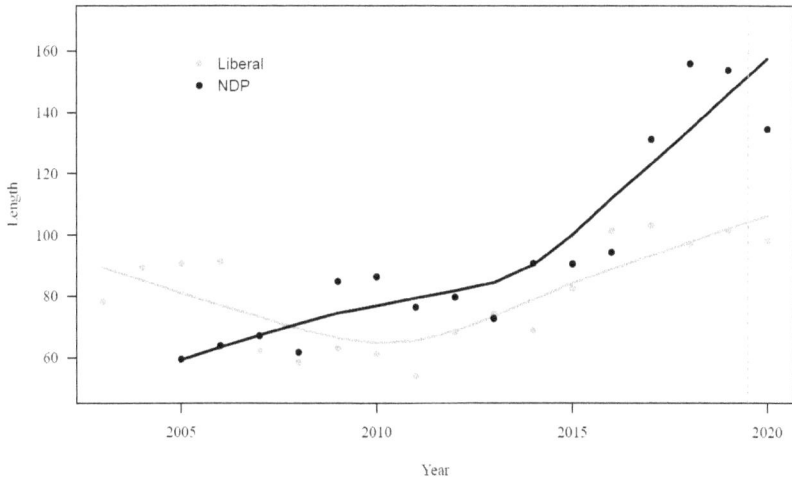

FIGURE 5.10. Prayer Length by Party in the B.C. Legislature, October 2, 2003–August 14, 2020.

Source: Katie Marshall.

When we look at the interaction between party, length, and religiosity (Figure 5.11), there was a significant interaction between party affiliation and religiosity of the prayer ($F = 13.30$, $df = 3$, 926, $p < 0.001$) such that prayers given by Liberal MLAs were significantly shorter if they were non-religious (either secular or not a prayer), while prayers given by NDP MLAs changed relatively little as a function of religiosity (Figure 5.11).

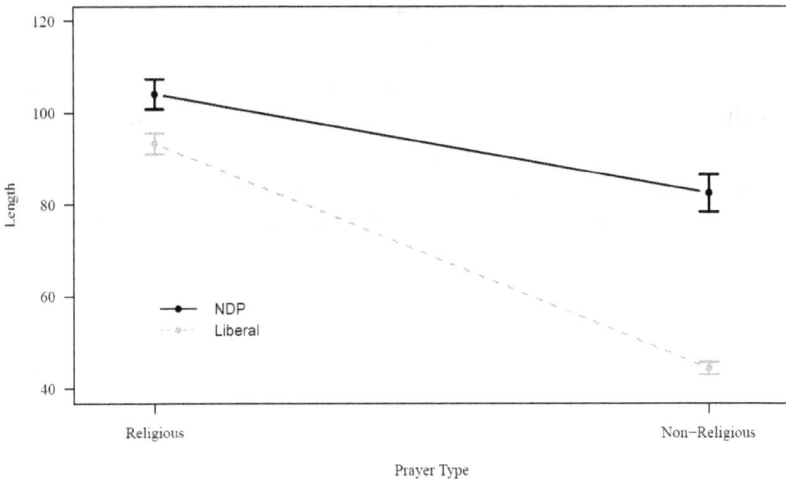

FIGURE 5.11. The Effects of Prayer Religiosity and Party Affiliation of the MLA on Prayer Length in the B.C. Legislature.

Source: Katie Marshall.

Discussion

Overall, a strong majority (70.4%) of prayers and reflections delivered in the B.C. Legislature over the period studied were religious, and where the religion could be identified, were overwhelmingly (94.1%) identified as Christian. Such numbers do not accurately reflect the diversity of religious beliefs in B.C.; the 2011 Household Survey found that 44.6 percent of British Columbians identified as Christian and 44.1 percent identified as having no religious affiliation (Statistics Canada 2011), not to mention a severe under-representation of other non-Christian faith traditions.

Given this disparity, it is appropriate that MLAs and the Clerk would seek to amend their procedures and sample prayer list, respectively. These efforts clearly sought to make the practice of opening sittings of the B.C. Legislature with prayers (and reflections) more inclusive. Our analysis reveals that the religiosity and content of prayers delivered after these changes did, indeed, change. Following both changes, we observe a decrease in the proportion of non-sectarian prayers and an increase in the proportion of content that was not a prayer. Long-term trends in the religiosity of prayers by party continued, with Liberal prayers becoming more religious and NDP prayers becoming less so.

The idea of starting a meeting with prayer, regardless of the content of that prayer, is in and of itself an exclusory practice: "the nomenclature, 'prayers,' reflects a specific conceptual framework and does not reflect the diversity of nomenclature used to describe religious and secular ritualistic activities" (Berry 2005, 631). There are many non-theistic religious traditions for which prayer is a foreign concept, or traditions for which the practice of prayer in a setting such as a legislative assembly would be unacceptable or even sacrilegious (Phelps Bondaroff et al. 2019, 25–26). And, furthermore, as Beaman explains, transmuting prayer into something that encapsulates "universal and inclusive shared values [...] contributes to exclusionary practices in diverse societies. It does this by fabricating an entrenched vision and version of a history that belongs only to a particular segment of society, which is in turn located at the apex of a hierarchy of citizenship and belonging" (2020).

Even though MLAs are given free rein to say anything as part of their prayer, the act of calling this agenda item "prayer" seems to influence how this time is used, reflecting one conceptual framework to the exclusion of others (see Phelps Bondaroff et al. 2019, 72). We can see this reflected by the fact that the number of prayers containing no religious language is still very low (5.4%), and even those delivering otherwise secular prayers still felt the need to end their statements in "Amen" (80.9% of the time overall).

As a result, renaming this agenda item from "prayer" to "prayers and reflections" should signal that faith traditions that may not include prayer are more welcome, as would be non-religious content. This effect was observed in our analysis. After the procedure change, we observe a significant reduction in the proportion of prayers making reference to a deity (from 52.8% to 30.6%). Furthermore, the ending of prayers changed following both the procedure and list changes (where a number of prayers had "Amen" dropped from their endings). Prior to the list change, 90.5 percent of all prayers ended in "Amen" and only 3.3 percent ended in "thank you." After the change, only 49.1 percent ended in "Amen" while 18.9 percent ended in "thank you." Likewise, after the procedure change, only 44.4 percent of prayers ended in "Amen," and the use of "thank you" increased from 4.2 percent of prayers to 16.7 percent. With respect to parties, this trend holds for both parties, though the effect is more pronounced with NDP MLAs.

Amendments to the sample prayer list to make it more inclusive are only effective at producing more inclusive results if the list is consistently used and if the prayers on the list are used at similar frequencies. Unfortunately, the changes to the sample list seem to have resulted in fewer MLAs reciting prayers from the list. While MLAs reach for the sample prayer list about half of the time (47.5%) overall, their use of this list declined significantly after it was updated. Prior to the list change, 48.1 percent of prayers were prayers from the sample prayer list, whereas only 34.5 percent of MLAs read sample prayers afterwards. Similarly, only 27.7 percent of MLAs read sample prayers after the procedure change. It is worth noting that the use of sample prayers was on a gradual decline prior to both changes, and Liberal MLAs continue to read sample prayers more often than NDP MLAs.

If, indeed, the practice of beginning sittings of the B.C. Legislature is an inclusive practice, we might expect to see widespread participation. While there is considerable variation of participation, with some MLAs choosing to deliver a considerable number of prayers, our analysis reveals that most MLAs are not participating and that there has been a steady decline in participation over time, such that only 27 percent chose to deliver prayers in the most recent parliament. This is a trend that pre-dates the changes to the sample prayer list and procedures.

One final observation is that prayers delivered in the B.C. Legislature are getting steadily longer, with a number of factors driving prayer length. Our analysis found that non-religious prayers are generally shorter than religious prayers, but the length of both has been increasing. The longest prayers were sectarian prayers, followed by content that we classified as not a prayer. This suggests that the more religious are more comfortable delivering overtly religious public prayer. As a result, despite the change in nomenclature, time allocated for prayers and reflections in the B.C. Legislature represents only a mild opening of this agenda item for non-religious content. This is reinforced in the term itself, whereby "prayers" is put before "reflections." The space is still allocated for prayer, with reflection added as an afterthought; otherwise, the agenda item would simply be "reflections," or "time for reflection" as is the practice in the Scottish Parliament (Scottish Parliament 2019). Prayer length has been increasing for both parties, especially prayers delivered by NDP MLAs. And we noted a significant interaction between party affiliation and prayer religiosity; Liberal prayers were significantly shorter if they were non-religious (secular or not a prayer).

Sources of Error, Limitations, and Future Research

We recognize a number of potential sources of error and limitations on this study, and have flagged potential issues with the data and coding process above. A number of external factors could have also influenced prayers in the B.C. Legislature. As a result of the COVID-19 pandemic, sittings of the B.C. Legislature were disrupted, and when sittings recommenced, procedures, practices, and the number of MLAs present in the chamber changed significantly (see Sajan 2020; Legislative Assembly of British Columbia 2020c). It is likely that safety protocols, such as the reduction of the number of MLAs present in the chambers, had some influence on who delivered prayers and reflections, as well as their content, religiosity, and length. Another external influence was the BC Humanist Association's campaign for the abolition of legislative prayer, led by a number of authors of this chapter. This campaign resulted in members of the public sending 580 letters to their MLAs and the premier. It is possible that these letters may have influenced MLAs in their choice of language when delivering prayers.

While this chapter explores the impact of such factors as time, party affiliation, and procedural and list changes on prayers delivered in the B.C. Legislature, we recognize that there is a wide range of other factors that could influence prayer religiosity, content, structure, and who is delivering the prayers. Additional research into the influence of such factors as age, age at election, gender, time in office, position (minister/critic vs. backbencher), and the demographics of the MLA's constituency may yield further insight into factors influencing prayers in the B.C. Legislature.

Conclusion

Unlike in the Ontario Legislature, where prayers from various faith traditions are read on a rotating basis after the Lord's Prayer (Phelps Bondaroff, Prasad et al. 2020), B.C.'s practice of MLA choice in prayer content makes the sample prayer list an unreliable way of increasing the representation of various faith traditions. Use of the amended sample list is considerably lower than for the previous list, and its use continues to decline. The amended list continues to suffer from a lack of invocations that accurately represent non-believers (Phelps Bondaroff et al. 2019, 85–86, 106). Assuming it were possible to draft such an invocation, the practice of beginning sittings with prayer would continue to exclude non-believers. As Justice Gascon noted in *Saguenay*, "even if a religious practice engaged in by the state is 'inclusive,' it may nevertheless exclude non-believers" (*Mouvement laïque québécois v. Saguenay* 2015, para. 137 and see 92).

The B.C. Legislature's expansion of its sample prayer list and change of procedures is a tacit admission that the previous practice was discriminatory. While the amendment renaming the Standing Order "prayer" to "prayers and reflections" appears to have reduced the amount of religious content and increased the number of presentations that could be classified as not a prayer, this change does little to rectify the core problem, as it is the inclusion of prayer itself that is discriminatory, not the content of the prayer. While these amendments demonstrate the good intentions of B.C. legislators, the problem will persist until legislative prayer is abolished.

Appendix 1:
Sample Prayers Provided to B.C. MLAs until 7 October 2019

Darryl Plecas, Office of the Speaker, Legislative Assembly of British Columbia, correspondence with authors, 16 January 2019. Numbers added for ease of reference.

A member may deliver reflections of his or her own choice or read one of the following:

1) Most gracious God, we humbly beseech Thee to behold with Thy blessing our country and the peoples of the Commonwealth. We pray especially for this Province, for the Lieutenant Governor, and for the Legislative Assembly at this time assembled, that all things may be so ordered and settled by their endeavours, upon the best and surest foundations, that peace and happiness, truth and justice, religion and piety may be established among us for all generations. Amen.

2) As we commence proceedings today in this Assembly, we ask for divine guidance so that our words and deeds may bring to all people of this great Province hope, prosperity and a vision for the future. May the deliberations in this chamber be characterized by temperance, understanding and reason to the end that we may better serve those who have made the Members of this House guardians of, and trustees for, all the citizens of British Columbia. Amen.

3) We give thanks for the bounty of our Province—our people, our land and our resources. We pledge ourselves to tend with care our heritage on behalf of all British Columbians. Amen.

4) As Canadians and British Columbians, we give thanks for the precious gifts of freedom and peace which we enjoy. As Members of this Legislative Assembly, we rededicate ourselves to the values and traditions of parliamentary democracy as a means of serving our Province and our country. Amen.

5) We pray to God to keep us mindful of the special and unique opportunity we have to work for our constituents and our Province, and in that work give us strength and wisdom. Amen.

Appendix 2:
Sample Prayers Provided to B.C. MLAs from 7 October 2019

Kate Ryan-Lloyd, Clerk of the Legislative Assembly, Legislative Assembly of British Columbia, correspondence with authors, 18 August 2020. Numbers added for ease of reference, otherwise formatting has been maintained.

A selection of Prayers and Reflections that may be read at the first daily sitting of the House. A Member may deliver reflections of their own choice, or read one of the following:

1) As we commence proceedings today in this Assembly, we ask for divine guidance so that our words and deeds may bring to all people of this great Province hope, prosperity and a vision for the future.

   May the deliberations in this Chamber be characterized by temperance, understanding and reason to the end that we may better serve those who have made the Members of this House guardians of, and trustees for, all the citizens of British Columbia.

2) We give thanks for the bounty of our Province—our people, our land and our resources. We pledge ourselves to tend with care our heritage on behalf of all British Columbians.

3) As Canadians and British Columbians, we give thanks for the precious gifts of freedom and peace which we enjoy. As Members of this Legislative Assembly, we rededicate ourselves to the values and traditions of parliamentary democracy as a means of serving our Province and our Country.

4) We pray for mindfulness of the special and unique opportunity we have to work for our constituents and our Province, and for strength and wisdom as we undertake that work.

5) Grant us wisdom, knowledge and understanding to preserve the blessings of this Province. May our deliberations be respectful and may the laws we make be good and just for the benefit of all citizens of British Columbia.

6) [Traditional Land Acknowledgement] I would like to acknowledge the Lekwungen-speaking peoples, known today as the Songhees and Esquimalt First Nations, on whose traditional territories we gather today. We pay respect to the Elders, past and present, of all of British Columbia's Indigenous peoples. May our deliberations be mindful of their history, cultures and traditions, and may our decisions promote reconciliation in our Province.

7) [Buddhist Prayer] May all beings have happiness and the causes of happiness. May all be free from sorrow and the causes of sorrow. May all never be separated from the sacred happiness which is sorrowless. May all live in equanimity, without too much attachment and too much aversion. And may all live believing in the equality of all that lives.

8) [Christian Prayer] Heavenly Father, as the events of the day unfold, we seek Your guidance and Your peace. We know that You are with us, and we ask that You guide us in our deliberations today. May we be temperate and respectful of one another as we exchange ideas on how to make this blessed and rich land that we call home a better place for our fellow citizens. In Jesus' name I pray. Amen.

9) [Hindu Gayatri Mantra] Om Bhur Bhuvah Swah. Let us meditate on that excellent glory of the divine vivifying Sun. May he enlighten our understandings.

10) [Jewish Prayer] May it be Your will, our God and the God of my ancestors, that with Your abundant mercy You will bestow wisdom on all of us gathering here to ensure that the matters we deliberate and the decisions made here today bring justice and peace to our communities, to better the lives of our fellow citizens, whom are all created in the image of their Creator, and let us say: Amen.

11) [Muslim Prayer] In the name of Allah, the most merciful, the benevolent, peace be upon all the prophets and messengers.

Praise be to the Lord of the Universe for the opportunity we have to gather in this legislative body here today. I ask Allah the most high to grant us peace and understanding, to guide us all, and to keep us steadfast in our work. Amen.

12) [Sikh Prayer] Let us show kindness to each other and be mindful that God judges us according to our deeds. Truth is above everything, but higher still is truthful living. We know that we attain God when we love, and only that victory endures in consequence of which no one is defeated.

References

BC Humanist Association. 2018. "BC Humanists Launch Study of Legislature Prayers." December 17, 2018. https://www.bchumanist.ca/bc_humanists_launch_study_of_legislature_prayers.

BC Humanist Association. 2019. "Prayers Replaced by 'Prayers and Reflections' in B.C. Legislature." November 28, 2019. https://www.bchumanist.ca/prayers_and_reflections_to_begin_every_sitting_of_bc_legislature.

Beaman, Lori G. 2020. *The Transition of Religion to Culture in Law and Public Discourse.* London, UK: Routledge.

Berry, Devon. 2005. "Methodological Pitfalls in the Study of Religiosity and Spirituality." *Western Journal of Nursing Research* 27 (5): 628–647.

Boissinot, Jacques. 2015. "The End of Prayer in the Councils of the Nation." *Globe and Mail*, April 17, 2015. https://www.theglobeandmail.com/opinion/editorials/the-end-of-prayer-in-the-councils-of-the-nation/article24010902/.

Bueckert, Chardaye, Robert Hill, Megan Parisotto, and Mikayla Roberts. 2017. "Religion, Faith and Spirituality in the Legislative Assembly of British Columbia." *Canadian Parliamentary Review* (Spring): 25–29.

Bushfield, Ian, and Teale N. Phelps Bondaroff. (2020). "Arbiters of Faith: Legislative Assembly of B.C. Entanglement with Religious Dogma Resulting from Legislative Prayer." *Secularism and Nonreligion* 9: 1–16.

CBC News. 2001. "Nova Scotia Reconsidering Lord's Prayer in Legislature." April 19, 2001. https://www.cbc.ca/news/canada/nova-scotia-reconsidering-lord-s-prayer-in-legislature-1.270636.

Delahunty, Robert J. 2007. "'Varied Carols' : Legislative Prayer in a Pluralist Polity." *Creighton Law Review* 40: 517–568.

Fizet, Christiana. 2010. "Reopening the Discussion on the Use of 'The Lord's Prayer' in the Ontario Legislature." Working paper presented at the Annual Meeting of the Canadian Political Science Association, Concordia University, Montréal, Canada, June 2, 2010. https://www.cpsa-acsp.ca/papers-2010/Fizet.pdf.

Lanouette, Martin. 2009. "Prayer in the Legislature: Tradition Meets Secularization." *Canadian Parliamentary Review* (Winter): 1–7.

Legislative Assembly of British Columbia. 2017. *Member's Guide to Policy and Resources.* May 11, 2017. https://members.leg.bc.ca/work-of-mla/routine -business.htm.

Legislative Assembly of British Columbia. 2019. *Official Report of Debates of the Legislative Assembly [Hansard].* 41st Parliament, 4th Session, No. 301 at 10870, November 28, Hon. M. Farnworth.

Legislative Assembly of British Columbia. 2020. *Official Report of Debates of the Legislative Assembly [Hansard].* 41st Parliament, 5th Session, No. 302 at 10883, February 11, Prayers and reflections.

Legislative Assembly of British Columbia. 2020. *Official Report of Debates of the Legislative Assembly [Hansard].* 41st Parliament, 5th Session, No. 326 at 11635, March 23, Prayers and reflections.

Legislative Assembly of British Columbia. 2020. *Legislative Assembly of British Columbia COVID-19 Safety Plan – July 10, 2020.* https://www.leg.bc.ca /Documents/LABC-COVID19-SafetyPlan.pdf.

Legislative Assembly of British Columbia. n.d. "Learn About Us: Hansard Services." https://www.leg.bc.ca/learn-about-us/hansard-services.

MacMinn, E. George. 2008. *Parliamentary Practice in British Columbia,* 4th ed. British Columbia, Canada: Government of British Columbia.

Mouvement laïque québécois v. Saguenay (City). 2015. S.C.C. 16 [2015] 2 S.C.R. 3.

Phelps Bondaroff, Teale N., Ian Bushfield, Katie E. Marshall, Ranil Prasad, and Noah Laurence. 2019. "House of Prayers: An Analysis of Prayer in the Legislative Assembly of British Columbia, 2003–2019." BC Humanist Association, September, 2019. https://www.bchumanist.ca /house_of_prayers_report.

———. 2020. "Decolonizing Legislative Prayers: A House of Prayers Supplementary Report." BC Humanist Association, May, 2020. https:// www.bchumanist.ca/decolonizing_legislative_prayers.

Phelps Bondaroff, Teale N., Ranil Prasad, Noah Laurence, Alexandre Darveau-Morin, Ian Bushfield and Adriana Thom. 2020. "Legislative Prayer Across Canada." BC Humanist Association, August, 2020. https://www. bchumanist.ca/prayer-across-canada.

Poitras, Jacques. 2019. "Green MLA's Motion Aims to Do Away with Daily Lord's Prayer." CBC News, April 2, 2019. https://www.cbc.ca/news /canada/arseneau-higgs-austin-christian-prayer-legislature-1.5081671.

R Core Team. 2018. *R: A Language and Environment for Statistical Computing.* R Foundation for Statistical Computing, Vienna, Austria. https://www. R-project.org/.

Ryan-Lloyd, Kate, Artour Sogomonian, Susan Sourial, and Ron Wall, eds. 2020. *Parliamentary Practice in British Columbia,* 5th ed. Victoria, B.C., Canada: Legislative Assembly of British Columbia.

Sajan, Bhinder. 2020. "Plexiglas, Physical Distance and Politics: Session Returns at the B.C. Legislature." *CTV News*, June 22, 2020. https://bc.ctvnews.ca/plexiglas-physical-distance-and-politics-session-returns-at-the-b-c-legislature-1.4995578.

Scottish Parliament. 2019. "Scottish Parliament Fact Sheet: Contributors to Time for Reflections," sessions 5. June 27, 2019. https://www.parliament.scot/ResearchBriefingsAndFactsheets/Factsheets/Contributors_to_Time_for_Reflection_Session_5.pdf

Servatius v. Alberni School District No. 70. 2020. B.C.S.C. 15.

Statistics Canada. 2011. *National Household Survey (NHS), Profile 2011.* https://www.12.statcan.gc.ca/nhs-enm/2011/dp-pd/prof/index.cfm?Lang=E.

Stone, Geoffrey R. 1983. "In Opposition to the School Prayer Amendment." *University of Chicago Law Review* 50: 823–848.

White-Crummey, Arthur. 2018. "To Pray or Not to Pray? The Place of God in the Sask. Legislature." *Regina Leader-Post*, November 2, 2018. https://leaderpost.com/news/saskatchewan/to-pray-or-not-to-pray-the-place-of-god-in-the-legislature.

Wickham, H. 2011. "The Split-Apply-Combine Strategy for Data Analysis." *Journal of Statistical Software* 40 (1): 1–29.

———. 2019. *Stringr: Simple, Consistent Wrappers for Common String Operations* R package version 1.4.0. https://CRAN.R-project.org/package=stringr.

CHAPTER 6

Passive Time Management and the Erosion of Scrutiny of Government Bills in the Yukon Legislative Assembly

Floyd McCormick

Abstract

Since 2000, the Yukon Legislative Assembly has fundamentally changed the way in which it manages its time. The Assembly's annual parliamentary calendar is now more transparent, predictable, and consistent than ever. However, the Assembly's shift in emphasis from active to passive time-management mechanisms has created a situation where government bills no longer routinely receive the scrutiny they should in order for the Assembly to truly fulfill its constitutional role. The chapter asserts that the situation can be addressed without sacrificing the organizational gains made over the years. However, doing so will require members to change their approach to rule modification from one that focuses on expediting the Assembly's business to one that prioritizes thorough scrutiny of government bills.

Résumé

Depuis l'an 2000, l'Assemblée législative du Yukon a fondamentalement changé la façon dont elle gère son temps. Le calendrier parlementaire annuel de l'Assemblée est maintenant plus transparent, plus prévisible et plus cohérent que jamais. Cependant, l'adoption de nouveaux mécanismes actifs de gestion du temps a eu pour effet que les projets de loi du gouvernement ne sont plus régulièrement examinés comme ils le devraient pour que l'Assemblée puisse véritablement remplir son rôle constitutionnel. Cette situation peut cependant être résolue sans renoncer aux avancées réalisées au fil des ans. Toutefois, il faudra pour cela que les députés changent leur approche en matière de modification des règles, en délaissant l'objectif d'accélérer les travaux de l'Assemblée pour mettre en place des mécanismes qui mettent l'accent sur l'examen approfondi des projets de loi du gouvernement.

The Yukon Legislative Assembly (the Assembly), like all parliamentary bodies, has rules and procedures to manage the use of its sitting time when the Assembly is in session. Since 2000, amendments to the Assembly's Standing Orders (rules of procedure) have fundamentally changed how the Assembly manages its time. The changes have been a success in making the organization of the Assembly's proceedings (though not Yukon politics itself) more predictable, transparent, and consistent. However, the new rules (and how they have been used) have also eroded the effectiveness of the Assembly's ability to scrutinize government bills.

To demonstrate how and why this has happened, this chapter examines: (1) how specific Standing Order changes have increased organizational transparency, consistency, and predictability; and (2) how and why these changes eroded the Assembly's ability to scrutinize government bills. Finally, we suggest procedural changes the Assembly should adopt to improve its ability to scrutinize government bills while retaining organizational predictability.

Why is this important? Across Canada, Parliament and the provincial and territorial legislative assemblies have adopted, and continue to adopt, rules and practices designed to make these institutions more organizationally predictable and more efficient in their use of the limited time available for formal sittings. This effort is often discussed in terms of making assemblies more businesslike, matched to a growing desire to make legislative bodies more family-friendly and assisting members (and staff) in achieving a better work-life balance. This chapter illustrates that while these are necessary goals for modern legislatures, they should not be done—and do not have to be done—at the expense of the legislative body's core functions.

Time Management

In order to function effectively, a parliamentary body needs rules and practices that establish how it will manage the limited time it spends in formal sessions. The purpose of time-management procedures is to ensure that the parliamentary body can deal with the business placed before it in a manner that allows that body to fulfill its core functions efficiently and effectively. Time management is also increasingly viewed in relation to the effect that the general conduct of parliamentary business has on the work-life balance of elected members and parliamentary, caucus, and cabinet staff and their families.

This chapter analyzes the rules and practices the Yukon Legislative Assembly uses in terms of active and passive time-management procedures.

Both active and passive procedures originate in an assembly's Standing Orders. Active time management involves deliberate actions taken by the members of the parliamentary body to manage time in specific circumstances, to limit or expedite proceedings. This includes requests for unanimous consent to bypass established rules and procedures and motions for time allocation, closure, to adjourn a debate or to adjourn the House, the extension of sitting hours or general programming motions that set out the way the assembly will conduct its affairs over a specified period of time in a way that is different than what is specified in the Standing Orders.

Passive time management refers to actions that do not require deliberate action by the assembly in order to be applied in specific circumstances. This would include Standing Orders that specify the months of the year or days of the week when the assembly will meet, the hours it will sit when in session, and time limits imposed on certain procedures (e.g., debates, Question Period) or the length of questions, responses, comments, and speeches. These rules and procedures are applied by the presiding officer according to the Standing Orders.

All assemblies have both active and passive procedures at their disposal. What varies, from one assembly to the next or over time, is the degree to which an assembly relies on one type of procedure as opposed to another. Since 2000, the Yukon Legislative Assembly has moved from a heavy reliance on active time management to an almost exclusive reliance on passive time management, particularly with regard to how spring and fall sittings are concluded.

Motion No. 47 and the 1996 Memorandum of Understanding

Prior to 1996, the Standing Orders of the Yukon Legislative Assembly contained comparatively few passive time-management procedures. The rules, for example, stipulated the days of the week the House would sit when in session and its sitting hours; they also specified an overall time limit on the length of the oral Question Period and the length of certain speeches. By practice, the government determined when a spring or fall sitting would begin. However, ending a sitting often required active time management, such as a motion to extend sitting hours until government business was dealt with or a programming motion that would specify how the House would deal with government business over the last few sitting days.

This situation began to change on 12 February 1996 when the three party leaders—the Government Leader (Premier), Hon. John Ostashek (Yukon Party), the Leader of the Official Opposition, Piers MacDonald (NDP), and the Leader of the Third Party, Jack Cable (Liberal Party)—reached agreement on a memorandum of understanding (MOU) regarding the conduct of assembly proceedings.

The MOU's content illustrates the concerns the members had at the time about the House proceedings. For example, the MOU provided that there would be two legislative sittings per year, including a spring sitting to focus on the government's budget and a fall sitting to focus on other substantive legislation. "Housekeeping" legislation could be introduced in either sitting. There was a commitment to limit the Assembly to a maximum of 60 sitting days per calendar year, 35 in the spring and 25 in the fall. There was also a commitment that the government would introduce its bills early in a sitting to ensure that they could be adequately debated before the sitting ended.

Holding annual spring and fall sittings had been a generally observed practice. However, the pattern was broken in 1995. The 1994 Fall Sitting began on 1 December and adjourned on 15 December. It resumed on 4 January 1995 and concluded on 3 May 1995. The sitting encompassed 76 sitting days—by far the most days ever in a sitting for the Yukon Legislative Assembly. The Assembly did not sit again after that until February 1996. The MOU addressed this situation by requiring a separate spring and fall sitting and by capping the number of annual sitting days.

In order to illustrate the leaders' commitment to the MOU, on 21 February 1996 Ostashek moved Motion No. 47, which the Assembly adopted. The motion provided for several Standing Order changes, including modification of existing passive time-management procedures, shortening Question Period, and reducing speaking times for individual members during debates. The motion also appended the MOU to the Standing Orders. This elevated the status of the MOU and ensured it would not be forgotten by future assemblies. However, the changes contained in the MOU were not formal rule changes. As such, neither the Speaker nor the Assembly could enforce the MOU's provisions. The MOU created a different set of norms and expectations rather than a different set of rules.

The MOU successfully secured at least two sittings per year from 1996 to 2001. It was less successful in having the Assembly adhere strictly to the 60-sitting-day limit. The Assembly sat for 45 days in 1996, 53 days in 1997, 63 days in 1998, 59 days in 1999, 63 days in 2000, and 64 days in 2001.[1] One could argue that the MOU had a pretty good, though not perfect, track record in ensuring the 60-sitting-day maximum. However, as an unenforceable norm, it left open the possibility of many more sitting days.

Motion No. 1

The 30th Legislative Assembly convened for its second session on 23 October 2000. The first motion for which notice was given was a government motion to change the Assembly's daily sitting schedule. At the time, the House sat from 1:30 p.m. to 5:30 p.m. Monday through Thursday. The House would then reconvene for evening sittings on Monday and Wednesday from 7:30 p.m. to 9:30 p.m. Motion No. 1 proposed changing the Assembly's sitting hours to 1:00 p.m. to 6:00 p.m. on each sitting day. The number of sitting hours per week would remain the same, and the sitting hours would be the same every sitting day.

Evening sittings allowed the public to attend sittings two evenings a week. This, some argued, made the business of the Assembly more accessible to the public and the members, therefore, more accountable to the public. Whatever the merits of evening sittings, however, by 2000 some members regarded a split sitting day as

---

1   Statistics on annual sitting days are found on the Yukon Legislative Assembly website at https://yukonassembly.ca/sites/default/files/inline-files/history-sitting-days-by-year-2020-03-31.pdf.

counterproductive. The Assembly's Standing Committee on Rules, Elections and Privileges (SCREP) could not successfully deal with this matter. In response, the government brought Motion No. 1 to the House.

Debate on Motion No. 1 was acrimonious. The government argued that changing the sitting hours was a routine matter that made the Assembly's schedule consistent. The Opposition argued that the government wanted to eliminate night sittings in order to avoid public scrutiny. The Opposition also objected to the government bringing the issue directly to the Assembly rather than relying on SCREP, which was due to meet within days to consider this matter and others. The government countered that it was the Opposition members who had subverted SCREP by making it difficult to convene meetings. The sitting day ended without a decision on Motion No. 1. The debate continued on the following day and the motion eventually carried 9–6 with all government members voting in favour of the motion and all Opposition members voting against it (Yukon Legislative Assembly 2000).

Changing the sitting hours did not affect the balance between active and passive time management in the Assembly. The sitting hours were still set by the rules and passively applied. Only the hours changed. Still, the change was significant in that it eliminated split sittings twice a week, making the sitting schedule uniform for each sitting day.

Motion No. 169

The most profound change to the Standing Orders, and the one that firmly established passive time management as the dominant approach in the Assembly, occurred on 19 November 2001 when the Assembly adopted Motion No. 169. This date marks the dividing line between the "old days," when active time management dominated the end-of-sitting procedures, and the current era, when passive time management rules.

One of the reasons for the profundity of the changes contained in Motion No. 169 is their comprehensive nature. Rather than introducing one new rule or modifying an existing rule, the changes added an entire chapter—Chapter 14—to the Standing Orders (Yukon Legislative Assembly 2020, 57–63). The changes codified some existing practices but also added new features. Overall, these changes added to the arsenal of passive time-management procedures and more pre-dictably organized Assembly proceedings.

The first feature of these new Standing Orders is a procedure for reconvening the Assembly when it stands adjourned at the end of a spring or fall sitting. Standing Order 73 requires that when the pre-mier wishes to see the Assembly recalled the Speaker must be advised "in sufficient time to allow the Speaker opportunity to give a mini-mum of two weeks' notice of the date on which the House shall meet" (Yukon Legislative Assembly 2020, 57). This codified a practice that had evolved over time. However, codification was significant, as it reduced the discretion available to the premier in calling the Assembly into session—though not in regard to determining a sitting's start date.

A second feature of the new Standing Orders, was that once the Assembly is in session "the government shall introduce all legislation, including appropriation bills, to be dealt with during that Sitting by the fifth sitting day" (Yukon Legislative Assembly 2020, 57). Unanimous consent of the House would be required if the government wanted to introduce a bill after Day 5. The 1996 MOU included a commitment that the government would introduce its bills early in a sitting, though there was no definition of what constituted early. The requirement is now defined and enforceable by the Speaker.

The third feature codifies the goal articulated in the 1996 MOU of having the Assembly sit for a maximum of 60 days each calendar year, with the sitting days divided between a spring sitting and a fall sitting. However, in order to function as a rule, the goal had to be more detailed. Standing Order 75 stipulates that once the government has presented the bills to be dealt with during a given sitting, the House leaders are to negotiate the number of sitting days required to deal with anticipated House business. The rules do not stipulate the 35/25 split set out in the MOU. Instead, the Standing Order says that the House leaders are to agree upon a sitting of between 20 and 40 sitting days. If the House leaders cannot reach agreement, the Speaker would declare that both the spring and fall sittings for that year will last a maximum of 30 days each (Yukon Legislative Assembly 2020, 58).

Establishing a maximum number of sitting days for a spring or fall sitting is one thing on paper. The challenge is in making the rule work. What would the Assembly do with government bills that had yet to proceed through all enactment stages once the maximum num-ber of sitting days had been exhausted? Would they simply remain on the Order Paper until the next sitting, or would there be a process by which the bills could be expedited through the Assembly? The resolution of this issue would obviously have important implications regarding the leverage available to the government or Opposition as a sitting drew to a close.

Relying on the adage that "the minority shall have its say and the majority shall have its way," a procedure was developed whereby the Assembly could vote on the government bills remaining on the Order Paper at the end of the final designated sitting day, as long as the bill had received at minimum some debate at second reading. This procedure, contained in Standing Order 76, is the fourth feature of the Standing Orders adopted on 19 November 2001. It is also the feature that most directly limits the Assembly's ability to scrutinize government bills.

Standing Order 76 is applied, if necessary, at 5:00 p.m. on the final designated sitting day of a sitting. It provides for a number of scenarios for concluding a sitting of the Assembly. Typically, however, the Assembly is in Committee of the Whole and is considering estimates in a main or supplementary appropriation bill at that time. Standing Order 76 specifies that once 5:00 p.m. is reached on the final sitting day, the chair of the Committee of the Whole shall interrupt the proceedings and invoke this Standing Order ending committee proceedings. The chair then asks the government House leader which of the government bills then remaining before the committee should be put to a vote. The government House leader will then identify those bills. Typically, all government bills remaining before the committee are identified.[2] Members then vote on whether the bill(s) then before the committee should be reported to the House with, or without,

---

2   There have, so far, been two exceptions. During the 2010 Spring Sitting, the government introduced Bill No. 82, *Civil Forfeiture Act*. The bill received second reading and was considered in Committee of the Whole. However, the bill proved controversial and on 28 April 2010, the House unanimously adopted Motion No. 1031 moved by Steve Cardiff (Mount Lorne, NDP) urging the government to delay further consideration of the bill until meaningful public consultation occurred. On 20 May 2010, the Minister of Justice, Hon. Marian Horne, delivered an oral response to a petition regarding the bill (Petition No. 12, presented by Mr. Cardiff on 6 May). In this response, the Minister stated that Bill No. 82 would not be further proceeded with. During the 2021 Fall Sitting, the government introduced Bill No. 3, *Act to Amend the Assessment and Taxation Act and the Municipal Act (2021)*. The bill received second reading on 1 December 2021, and as of the end of the 2021 Fall Sitting, still stands referred to Committee of the Whole (where, as of this writing, the bill has not yet received any consideration by the committee).

amendment as the case may be. Importantly, once Standing Order 76 is invoked, no further debate is permitted and no amendments may be moved. Since this Standing Order became operative, the Committee of the Whole has voted, in all instances, to report the government bills to the Assembly.

Once the Committee of the Whole has made its decisions, the committee adopts a motion that the Speaker be recalled to the chair. The chair of Committee of the Whole then reports to the Assembly the committee's decision(s) on the bill(s) that were before it. The Assembly then votes on whether to adopt the committee's report. Once the House adopts the committee's report (which so far it always has) the bill(s) then proceed to third reading.

The typical procedure at third reading mirrors that in Committee of the Whole. First, the Speaker informs the Assembly of the requirements of Standing Order 76 as they apply at third reading. The Speaker then asks the government House leader to identify the government bill(s) now awaiting third reading that the government wishes to see put to a vote (this often includes bills that have reached third reading prior to the application of Standing Order 76).[3] The Speaker then puts the question on motions for third reading and passage of the government bills identified by the government House leader. Once the House has voted on all these government bills (no government bill has ever been defeated at third reading) the commissioner of Yukon is summoned to the chamber to grant assent to those bills.[4] Once the commissioner departs, the Assembly proceeds with any required or routine business associated with the end of a sitting. Once this business is concluded, the Speaker declares the sitting adjourned. The normal time of adjournment does not apply once Standing Order 76 is invoked (Yukon Legislative Assembly 2020, 59–62).[5]

To deal with unforeseen circumstances, Chapter 14 includes procedures for calling the Assembly into session on less than two weeks' notice, extending the length of a sitting, and calling additional sittings in addition to those in the spring and fall. The Standing Orders also

3   There was one occasion when Standing Order 76 was applied to a government bill that stood on the Order Paper at second reading. This example will be discussed later in greater detail.

4   In the absence of the commissioner, the territorial administrator or the chief justice of the Yukon Supreme Court may grant assent to bills.

5   However, once Standing Order 76 is invoked, the Assembly typically adjourns earlier than the normal hour of adjournment (5:30 p.m.).

allow the Assembly to adjust its calendar of sittings during a year in which a general election takes place.

Like the 1996 MOU, the rule changes proposed in Motion No. 169 were not the product of deliberations by SCREP. During the fall of 2001, the Premier, Hon. Pat Duncan (Liberal Party), the Leader of the Official Opposition, Eric Fairclough (NDP), and the Leader of the Third Party, Peter Jenkins (Yukon Party), met informally to negotiate time-management rules. The Speaker, Hon. Dennis Schneider, chaired these informal, in camera, meetings in his office. Also in attendance were the Clerk of the Legislative Assembly, Patrick L. Michael, and the Deputy Clerk of the Legislative Assembly, the author of this chapter.

The party leaders reached agreement on 8 November 2001. As their meetings were informal, there are no official records of their discussions. The text of Motion No. 169 attests to what they agreed to. On 15 November 2001, Premier Duncan gave written notice of Motion No. 169. The following sitting day, 19 November 2001, pursuant to an agreement among the house leaders, the government House leader, Jim McLachlan, requested the unanimous consent of the Assembly for Motion No. 169 to be called for debate, without the notice requirement having been met. Mr. McLachlan also requested the unanimous consent of the House "in recognition of the length of the motion for the motion to be taken as having been read from the Chair and for it to appear in *Hansard* as having been read" (Yukon Legislative Assembly 2001, 2720). Unanimous consent was granted for both requests. Motion No. 169 was then agreed to on a voice vote without debate.

Motion No. 689

Three women, Hon. Elaine Taylor (Yukon Party), Pat Duncan (Liberal Party), and Lorraine Peter (NDP) were elected to the 31st Legislative Assembly (2002–2006). These members formed an informal women's caucus. One product of the work of the women's caucus was Motion No. 689, moved by Hon. Ms. Taylor on 11 May 2006. The motion proposed changing the Assembly's normal hour of adjournment from 6:00 p.m. to 5:30 p.m. The reasons for the proposed change are discussed later in this chapter.

Based on a maximum of 60 sitting days per calendar year, the change would reduce the maximum annual sitting hours from 300 to 270. This meant 30 fewer hours devoted to Orders of the Day, that part of the sitting day when government bills would be debated. The proposed change was not accompanied by a proposal to add additional sitting days to make up for the lost sitting hours or any other active or passive time-management procedures that would have made for more efficient use of the Assembly's remaining time. For that reason, some members expressed reservations during debate. Taylor argued members would have to adjust their approach to House business. The motion was adopted by 15 votes to 1 (Yukon Legislative Assembly 2006, 465–466).

Motion No. 127 (Motion Respecting Committee Reports No. 1)

On 5 October 2017, Paolo Gallina (Liberal), Chair of SCREP, moved Motion No. 127 (Motion Respecting Committee Reports No. 1). The purpose of the motion was to have the Assembly concur in the recommendations contained in the committee's first report, which Mr. Gallina had tabled on 3 October 2017. One of the recommendations was a change to Standing Order 75. The change further refined the mandating of annual spring and fall sittings by stipulating that the spring sitting would begin during the first week of March and the fall sitting would begin during the first week of October. The Assembly adopted the motion on a voice vote (Yukon Legislative Assembly 2017, 996–998).

This Standing Order change added to organizational predictability and reduced the premier's discretion in determining the start date for the spring and fall sittings.

Eliminating Extended Sitting Hours and Programming Motions

While the Assembly has amended its Standing Orders in regard to time management, it has also, indirectly, rendered redundant two active time-management procedures (extended sitting hours, and programming motions) and one scheduling practice (split sittings) that were used occasionally.

Standing Order 2(5) authorizes the government House leader, or designate, up to 30 minutes prior to the normal hour of adjournment, to move, without notice, a motion to extend the sitting day. The motion must indicate the business to be dealt with during the extended sitting hours. The Assembly must adopt the motion before the normal hour of adjournment, or the sitting day ends at its usual time (Yukon Legislative Assembly 2020, 2).

Since the formal adoption of party politics in 1978, 40 sitting days have been extended in this way. Such motions were commonly moved on the agreed-upon final sitting day of a spring or fall sitting to conclude business. Seventeen of those extensions occurred after the adoption of the MOU in 1996 and prior the adoption of Motion No. 169 in 2001.[6] In some cases, the sitting day was extended by only a few minutes. In the most extreme case, the Assembly sitting that began at 1:30 p.m. on Monday, 15 December 1997 ended at 6:27 a.m. the following morning (Yukon Legislative Assembly 1997, 168–170).

Also, prior to 2002, the government would on occasion introduce a programming motion that laid out a schedule for a series of sitting days. These motions included, among other features, extended sitting hours for certain sitting days and identifying the government business to be dealt with on those days.

Though these procedures are still available to the Assembly, Standing Order 76 rendered them obsolete (with one exception, see note 15). Since Standing Order 76 ensures that government bills will be put to a vote by the end of the final designated day of a sitting, it is no longer necessary for the government to seek extra time or specifically program the Assembly's schedule. Using passive time-management procedures, the government no longer faces any political costs associated with employing active time-management motions that could be deemed heavy-handed. Now it is the rules of the Assembly itself not the government that passively brings a spring or fall sitting to an end and has, thus far, ensured the passage of government bills that have not been debated at all enactment stages.[7]

And just as the Assembly has done away with split sitting days, it has also abandoned split sittings. In 1981, 1986, 1987, 1989, 1993, and 1994, the Assembly began its fall sitting in November or December. The Assembly then adjourned prior to Christmas before reconvening in January. The Assembly then resumed sitting for days, weeks, or even months. As mentioned above, the 1994–1995 split sitting carried on until May 1995 and provided part of the motivation for the 1996

6   Statistics compiled using the Journals of the Yukon Legislative Assembly.

7   The 35th Legislative Assembly (elected on 12 April 2021) resulted in a minority government. A confidence and supply agreement between the government (Liberal) and the third party (NDP) has, so far, prevented the defeat of government bills.

MOU. The codification of spring and fall sittings in 2001 and the specification of March and October start dates for those sittings in 2017 illustrate the Assembly's preference for more compact sittings.

Reasons for Change

Over the years, members have provided a variety of reasons to support, or oppose, proposed changes to the Standing Orders. By far the most common reason to support change is the desire to achieve greater efficiency in the use of the Assembly's time and the conduct of its business.

For example, during debate on Motion No. 47, Government Leader Ostashek explained that the party leaders who negotiated the rule changes and the MOU "are trying to expedite the business of this House. [...]"[8] Mr. MacDonald concurred saying that the discussions among the party leaders focused on "how the rules of the Legislature might be improved to increase its effectiveness and efficiency." A heightened level of organization of the proceedings would, he said, avoid "legislative action through exhaustion." Mr. Cable said,

> I think it is all agreed that these rule changes will make for greater efficiency and that is one of the main driving forces behind the rule change. [...] The agreement is not perfect, but we have to recognize that it is not written in stone or on a tablet; it is simply a rule, a change made in the House. If it does not work, we are free to amend it. (Yukon Legislative Assembly 1996)

In describing his willingness to accept the changes, MacDonald, a member since 1982, said,

> For those of us who have been in the Legislature for a very long time, it is a change. Change is difficult for some of us to accommodate. I could very easily operate under the old rules as opposed to the new rules, but I am willing as one Member—even one who has been around for a while—to try new things if people feel that is a wise or reasonable innovation. (Yukon Legislative Assembly 1996)

---

8   The quotes from the debate on Motion No. 47 are taken from the Yukon Legislative Assembly *Hansard* (Yukon Legislative Assembly 1996).

Arguments about the Assembly being more family-friendly and working towards a better work-life balance for members were used during the debates on Motion No. 1 and Motion No. 689.

During the debate on Motion No. 689, for example, Hon. Ms. Taylor spoke of how she, Ms. Duncan, and Mrs. Peter "[a]lmost immediately [...] recognized there was common ground" among them in their roles as "caregiver, parent and grandparent" and that they shared a frustration "with the sitting hours, specifically the 6:00 p.m. adjournment." Motion No. 689, she said, "speaks to the recognition of the importance of family and making accommodation for family while serving the people of the Yukon" (Yukon Legislative Assembly 2006). Duncan said,

> This motion is about women, women politicians, and fundamentally about women politicians making a difference in our ways of work. [...] Some of us in this Assembly are grandparents. Some of us have grown children. Some have babies. Some have tweens, and some of us are yet to be blessed with the greatest of teachers. All of us are part of a family unit of some kind.

The challenge she said, was to figure out how to "balance our role, being part of a family, and [...] walk the talk of balancing our hours of work" (Yukon Legislative Assembly 2006).

Peter said the greatest challenge "for women in politics is to find a balance between making accommodations for family with dignity and pride while serving the people who elected us. We care about our families, Mr. Speaker; we care about their future; we care about their health." Yet she admitted to hearing "concerns about the hours we keep, that they are not family-friendly, and the reality of the atmosphere we work in does not appeal to women" (Yukon Legislative Assembly 2006).

As mentioned above, Taylor, Duncan, and Peter were the only women to serve in the 18-member 31st Legislative Assembly. Three women also served in the 32nd Legislative Assembly, while the number of female MLAs increased to six in the 33rd Legislative Assembly.[9] The 34th Legislative Assembly included seven women. Women now

---

9   Elaine Taylor and Marian Horne were elected in the general election on October 20, 2006. Elizabeth Hanson was elected in a by-election on December 13, 2010 (Yukon Legislative Assembly Office 2021).

occupy 8 of the 19 seats in the 35th Assembly. It is impossible to draw a causal connection between the Standing Order changes described in this chapter and the increase in women MLAs. However, in debating these motions, the members made clear their belief that a more predictable calendar of sittings is more likely to attract persons with family responsibilities than the more unpredictable arrangements that prevailed prior to 2000.

Effects of Standing Order Changes

From an organizational perspective, then, the effects of the Standing Order changes are clear: the annual schedule of Assembly sittings is now more predictable, transparent, and consistent than it was prior to 2002. Barring extraordinary circumstances (such as the COVID-19 pandemic) or a general election, the Assembly will sit during March, April, October, and November. Other than on statutory holidays as defined by the *Interpretation Act*, the Assembly will sit from Monday to Thursday during those months from 1:00 p.m. to 5:30 p.m. Members will not be subject to split sitting days, extended sitting hours, or split sittings. The Assembly will sit for a maximum of 60 sitting days per calendar year. Overall, the Assembly has developed a sitting schedule that is as predictable as can be expected in the frequently unpredictable world of politics.[10]

This evolution also illustrates the preference members have shown, over time, for passive time-management procedures as opposed to active ones. Prior to 2002, there were few rules that constrained the government in terms of controlling when sittings would begin. At the same time, there were no rules the government could passively rely on to ensure when a sitting would end. Without them, a government could use its majority to pass a programming motion or a motion to extend sitting hours. However, even these devices were of limited utility without the agreement of the Opposition. Ultimately, the parties—through their house leaders—relied on their powers of persuasion and coercion to negotiate an end to a sitting. This made for a situation that was both more unpredictable and more flexible in responding to circumstances. Among other things, the reliance on

---

10 Of course, the Assembly's sitting schedule is only one aspect of the lifestyle of an MLA.

passive time-management procedures eliminates the need for inter-party negotiation to end a sitting.

Effects on the Scrutiny of Government Bills

While the Standing Order changes have provided organizational advantages, the price of predictability, transparency, and consistency has been an erosion of the Assembly's ability to perform a core func-tion—scrutinize government bills.

A system that passively relies on established rules, rules that are known in advance by the participants, appears to make for a fairer process than one that is situationally specific and relies on persuasion, coercion, and negotiation. But the reality is that the government can easily use the new time-management rules to shield government bills, or parts of government bills, from the Assembly's scrutiny. This is the effect even where it is not the intent.

The problem, simply put, is this: Prior to 2002, all government bills had to be presented to the Assembly for debate at all enactment stages to become law. The only way a bill could proceed through one or more stages without debate was through the use of the active time-management procedure of requesting, and receiving, the unanimous consent of the House. That is no longer the case.

Another important factor is Standing Order 12(2). This Standing Order says, "When government business has precedence, that busi-ness may be called in such sequence as the government chooses" (Yukon Legislative Assembly 2020, 10). Combined with Standing Order 76, this means that it is the government, not the House, that decides which bills and which votes will, and will not, be put before the Assembly for scrutiny.

Standing Order 76 did not come into use as soon as it was avail-able to the Assembly. It was initially regarded as a procedure of last resort and was not used in the 2002 Spring Sitting and the 2003 Spring Sitting.[11] It was first used to end the 2003 Fall Sitting and then again to end the 2004 Spring Sitting. However, it was not used to end the 2004 Fall Sitting—but was again applied in the 2005 Spring Sitting and has since become the standard way of ending a spring or fall sitting.

---

11 There was no 2002 Fall Sitting, due to a general election, which resulted in a change in the governing party.

As mentioned above, legislating is one of the core functions of a legislative assembly. However, the Assembly is not merely a "bill mill." To be of value, the act of legislating must consist of more than just passing government bills. Proper scrutiny of those bills is required. Proper scrutiny not only tests the government during proceedings but also legitimizes its proposals should they pass the Assembly.

From the 2002 Spring Sitting through to the 2021 Fall Sitting (inclusive), the Yukon Legislative Assembly passed 285 government bills in sittings in which Standing Order 76 was used. Of that number, 94 passed third reading without debate due to the application of Standing Order 76. Eighteen of those 94 bills also received no consideration in Committee of the Whole for the same reason.[12] Reporting a bill to the House without consideration at the committee stage has a significant negative effect on parliamentary scrutiny, because this is the stage at which members examine bills and appropriations in detail and may propose amendments to them.

During the 2012 Fall Sitting, one bill, Bill No. 48, *Act to Amend the Access to Information and Protection of Privacy Act*, was on the Order Paper at second reading on the final sitting day. The bill had been debated at second reading but had yet to pass that stage. Nonetheless, the bill was eligible to be expedited via Standing Order 76. After 5:00 pm on 13 December 2012, the bill passed second reading without further debate. Having passed second reading, the bill bypassed the committee stage and proceeded to third reading where it was again voted on without debate. Having passed the House, it was assented to on that day (Yukon Legislative Assembly 2012, 249–252). This is hardly a model of proper legislative scrutiny and accountability, particularly for a bill that drew substantive and procedural objections from the Opposition and raised concerns from Yukon's information and privacy commissioner (Ronson 2012).

This is the only bill, so far, to receive second reading after the application of Standing Order 76. However, pursuant to this Standing Order, 17 other bills have been expedited through Committee of the

---

12 In the Yukon Legislative Assembly, Standing Order 57(4) says, "Unless otherwise ordered by the Assembly, when a Government Bill or a Private Member's Bill is read the second time, it stands ordered for consideration by Committee of the Whole." The motion for second reading would have to be amended to refer a bill to a standing, select, or special committee for consideration. This happens very rarely.

Whole and third reading without debate after receiving second reading.

Forty-three of the 94 bills that passed third reading without debate due to Standing Order 76 were appropriation bills (main or supplementary). While Bill No. 19, *Fourth Appropriation Act, 2014-15* is the only appropriation bill to be reported by Committee of the Whole without debate, it is common for individual votes within appropriation bills to receive no scrutiny due to the application of Standing Order 76.[13] From the 2003 Fall Sitting (when Standing Order 76 was first applied to an appropriation bill) to the 2021 Fall Sitting, 226 votes (out of a total of 662) passed through Committee of the Whole in this way. The appropriations in these votes total $2,294, 957,000—10.45 percent of the overall appropriations contained in these 42 bills.

The number of votes and percentage of appropriations carried without debate varies from year to year. An analysis of main appropriation acts from 2004 to 2021 shows that the amount of appropriations that were not considered by Committee of the Whole ranged from $5.36 million in 2004 (0.75% of total appropriations) to $495.909 million in 2010 (45.9%). The passive time-management procedures contain no provision that limits the number of votes or the amount of appropriations that can be carried without debate in Committee of the Whole.

The above statistics only refer to those bills that received no scrutiny from Committee of the Whole and / or at third reading and those appropriations that received no scrutiny in Committee of the Whole. Other bills and votes receive scrutiny that can range from a few minutes to multiple hours but are still formally before the Assembly or committee when Standing Order 76 is applied. So, these bills and votes have received some scrutiny, but the process is incomplete.

Opposition members have, on occasion, criticized the end-of-sitting procedures. In 2008, former NDP leader Todd Hardy called them "one of the worst things that ever happened to democracy in the legislative assembly" and called for their repeal (Thompson 2008). Governments, however, have shown little interest in reforming a procedure that serves their interests so well. Criticism of the end-of-sitting process has become less frequent over time. This may be due to the

---

13 A "vote" in this context is the appropriation for individual government departments, corporations, and other entities such as the Legislative Assembly and Officers of the Legislative Assembly (the Office of the Ombudsman, the Child and Youth Advocate Office, and Elections Yukon).

large turnover of MLAs since 2002. Seventeen of the 19 members elected to the current (35th) Assembly were first elected in 2011 or later. By that time, the use of Standing Order 76 had become the standard end-of-sitting procedure. Because the rules are applied passively, they do not draw as much attention as a motion moved by a minister or government caucus member.

However, on 13 October 2021, the Assembly debated Motion No. 113 moved by Currie Dixon, Leader of the Official Opposition (Yukon Party). The motion proposed amending Standing Order 76 so that it only applied to appropriation bills. Debate adjourned without a decision being taken on the motion or on an amendment proposed by the Minister of Community Services, Hon. Richard Mostyn (Liberal) to refer the matter to SCREP.[14] Perhaps SCREP and the Assembly will address this issue in the near future.

Reforming Time Management

Before addressing ways of improving the scrutiny of government bills, it should be said that the situation that preceded the current end-of-sitting procedure was not ideal. It is true, for example, that (barring unanimous consent) all votes in an appropriation bill needed to be considered by Committee of the Whole before the bill could be reported back to the House. However, this requirement could not guarantee that such scrutiny was effective, particularly if it was taking place late at night or in the wee hours of the morning, due to extended sitting hours. This—what MacDonald called "legislation by exhaustion"—was something the Assembly sought to eliminate in 1996. As mentioned, Standing Order 76 has essentially done away with extended sitting hours.[15] Procedurally, there is no going back. The Assembly must find a better route forward.

It is neither necessary nor advisable to discard the organizational improvements made since 1996 to improve the Assembly's ability to scrutinize government bills. However, the Assembly has to rearrange its procedural priorities. As it stands, ending a sitting on a

14 The amendment to the motion was removed from the Order Paper on 15 November 2021 as the amendment became outdated.

15 Extended sitting hours were used on 19 March 2020 to prematurely end the 2020 Spring Sitting due to the COVID-19 pandemic.

predetermined date takes precedence over ensuring that government bills are thoroughly scrutinized. That has to change.

For change to occur, two things must happen. First, the members of the Legislative Assembly must recognize that the current end-of-sitting procedure undermines their ability to perform a core function. Second, the members must commit themselves to the proposition that to better perform this core function, the Assembly must consider all government bills at all enactment stages for the bill to become law. This, obviously, presents a challenge.

The deficiencies of the current procedure are rooted in the Assembly's almost complete reliance on Standing Order 76 to manage the conclusion of a sitting. The fundamental problem with the Standing Order is that once it is applied, there is no more opportunity for debate or amendment.

What can be done? The Assembly does not need new rules or more rules. One option is to employ existing active time-management procedures prior to 5:00 p.m. on the final sitting day so that Standing Order 76 is not required. The Standing Orders do not provide for time-allocation or closure motions. However, the Assembly still has active time-management options, such as programming motions, that it could use to manage time prior to the application of Standing Order 76.

If the members prefer to rely on passive time management, they will have to modify the end-of-sitting procedure to one where all government bills must be presented to the House at all enactment stages before becoming law. Similarly, all appropriation votes must be presented to Committee of the Whole for its consideration. It should be up to the House, not the government, to decide if a bill or vote will proceed through a stage without debate.

Standing Order 76 could be modified so that rather than signalling the end of all debate, its application would signal the start of a different end-of-sitting process.

For example, after a specified number of sitting days have elapsed, the Assembly could adopt a modified Order Paper—one that would specify that the only matters to be taken up under Orders of the Day, from that day forward, would be the outstanding government bills. No government motions, no private members bills or motions, or other matters. Since departmental votes are considered individually in Committee of the Whole, there would have to be time limits on the consideration of each individual vote, not just an overall time limit for the committee stage of an appropriation bill.

The Assembly would also have to develop a process for determining the order in which Committee of the Whole considers votes. As mentioned, the government currently has complete discretion when it comes to the scheduling of government business. This can mean that certain appropriations do not get considered at all. In order to prevent the government from taking advantage of a modified Standing Order 76, larger appropriations would have to be dealt with before time limits are imposed.

Supporters of the current procedures might argue that this would undermine organizational efficiency, because the Assembly could not, in advance, identify a date on which a spring or fall sitting would end. This is true, but the number of additional sitting days needed to end a sitting under a modified Standing Order 76 would depend on how many government bills remained on the Order Paper and how much members wished to debate those bills.

Imposing strict time limits on additional sitting days would ensure that the Assembly would not face the prospect of a sitting with no end in sight—or the prospect of vastly extended sitting hours, which is the situation that gave rise to the MOU in 1996 and to the Standing Order changes that the Assembly has adopted since 2000.

Conclusion

During procedural debates since 1996, members expressed a desire for procedures that used limited sitting time more efficiently and effectively and where the organization of sittings was more conducive to a life that better balances the duties of public office with members' family life. They did not intend to create procedures that would impair the Assembly's ability to scrutinize government bills and hold the government accountable. Yet that is what these procedures have become.

The problem is that over time, scheduling has taken priority over scrutiny. As a result, government bills regularly do not receive the scrutiny they should for the Assembly to fully carry out its core functions of representation, legislating, and holding the government accountable. The situation can, however, be resolved without sacrificing the organizational gains made over the years. But doing so will require members to change their behaviour or change the Standing Orders in order to prioritize the thorough scrutiny of government bills and de-emphasize ending Assembly sittings on a predetermined date.

Postscript

On 13 October 2021, the Assembly debated Motion No. 113 moved by Currie Dixon, Leader of the Official Opposition (Yukon Party). The motion proposed amending Standing Order 76 so that it applied only to appropriation bills. Debate adjourned without a decision being taken on the motion or on an amendment proposed by the Minister of Community Services, Hon. Richard Mostyn (Liberal), to refer the matter to SCREP.[16]

On 8 March 2022, the Assembly adopted a similar motion, Motion No. 282, moved by the Government House Leader, Hon. John Streicker (Liberal). Motion No. 282 provides that: (1) Standing Order 76 will only apply to appropriation bills for the 2022 Spring Sitting, and (2) following that sitting, and prior to the 2022 Fall Sitting, SCREP will meet to examine the Standing Order.[17]

This rule change means that for the 2022 Spring Sitting (and perhaps permanently) government bills, other than appropriations bills, will have to be presented to the Assembly for consideration at all debate stages. While that is a good measure it is, ultimately, a half measure. The effect will be to transfer the entire weight of Standing Order 76 on to appropriation bills. The rule change does nothing to ensure that all votes in an appropriation bill will be presented to Committee of the Whole prior to the bill being reported to the House. Given the fact that Spring and Fall sittings will continue to be of a set duration, time devoted to debate on government bills other than appropriation bills will come at the expense of debate on appropriation bills. As a result, this rule change may lead to more votes being adopted without consideration in Committee of the Whole.

References

Canada, *Yukon Act*, S.C. 2002, c. 7.

Ronson, Jacqueline. 2012. "NDP Calls for Istchenko's Resignation." *Yukon News*, December 14, 2012. https://www.yukon-news.com/news/ndp-calls-for-istchenkos-resignation/.

---

16 Yukon Legislative Assembly, *Hansard*, 13 October 2021, pages 379–393. The amendment to the motion was removed from the Order Paper on 15 November 2021 as the amendment became outdated.

17 Yukon Legislative Assembly, *Hansard*, 8 March 2022, pages 1271–1273.

Thompson, John. 2008. "Guillotine Clause Severs Debate." *Yukon News*, October 30, 2008. https://www.yukon-news.com/news/guillotine-clause -severs-debate/.

Yukon Legislative Assembly. 1996. *Hansard*, 28th Legislature, 2nd Session, February 21, 1996. https://yukonassembly.ca/sites/default/files/hansard /28-2-080.html.

Yukon Legislative Assembly. 1997. *Journals*, 29th Legislature, 1st Session, December 15–16, 1997. https://yukonassembly.ca/sites/default/files/inline -files/Journals-29-1-1997-10-30-1997-12-16.pdf

Yukon Legislative Assembly. 2000. *Journals*, 30th Legislature, 2nd Session, Monday, October 31, 2000. https://yukonassembly.ca/sites/default/files /inline-files/Journals-30-2-2000-10-23-2000-12-14.pdf

Yukon Legislative Assembly. 2001. *Hansard*, 30th Legislature, 2nd Session, November 19, 2001. https://yukonassembly.ca/sites/default/files/hansard /30-2-87.html.

Yukon Legislative Assembly. 2006. *Journals*, 31st Legislature, 1st Session, May 11, 2006. https://yukonassembly.ca/sites/default/files/inline-files /Journals-31-1-2006-03-30-2006-05-24.pdf

Yukon Legislative Assembly. 2012. *Journals*, 33rd Legislature, 1st Session, December 13, 2012. https://yukonassembly.ca/sites/default/files/inline -files/Journals-33-1-2012-10-25-2012-12-13.pdf

Yukon Legislative Assembly. 2017. *Hansard*, 34th Legislature, 2nd Session, October 5, 2017. https://yukonassembly.ca/sites/default/files/hansard /34-2-033.pdf

Yukon Legislative Assembly. 2020. *Standing Orders of the Yukon Legislative Assembly*. November 19, 2020. https://yukonassembly.ca/sites/default /files/inline-files/Standing-Orders-2020-11-19-Indexed_1.pdf

Yukon Legislative Assembly Office. 2020. "Sitting Days by Calendar Year 1953–2020." https://yukonassembly.ca/sites/default/files/inline -files/history-sitting-days-by-year-2020-03-31.pdf

Yukon Legislative Assembly Office. 2021. "Women Elected to the Yukon Legislative Assembly." https://yukonassembly.ca/sites/default/files/inline -files/history-women-elected-to-legislative-assembly-2021-06-30.pdf

CONCLUSION

Les législatures en transformation

Geneviève Tellier et Marie-Ève Belzile

Résumé

Est-ce que les institutions parlementaires canadiennes tra-
versent une ère de réformes perpétuelles ? Cette hypothèse
avait été émise par C.E.S. Franks, il y a près de 50 ans, alors
qu'il notait l'apparition de changements législatifs importants
durant les années 1960 et 1970. À la lumière des réformes qui
ont été faites depuis, dont certaines très récentes font l'objet
d'analyses détaillées publiées dans cet ouvrage collectif, on
peut dire que cette affirmation est encore valide de nos jours.
Les institutions législatives sont le reflet de la société dans
laquelle elles évoluent. Par conséquent, elles cherchent à
s'adapter à un environnement qui change constamment.
Cependant, la plupart de ses réformes sont graduelles et
imparfaites. Faut-il donc une crise majeure pour instaurer des
changements importants et durables ? C'est très certainement
une question qui se pose dans un contexte de grave crise sanitaire, tel que celui de la pandémie de la COVID-19.

Abstract

Are Canadian parliamentary institutions in a state of perpet-
ual reform? C.E.S. Franks advanced this hypothesis some
50 years ago, when he noted the emergence of significant legislative institution reforms during the 1960s and 1970s. This
chapter provides a detailed analysis of some of the changes
that followed—including recent modifications to practices and
procedures—and finds that the hypothesis remains valid

today. Legislative institutions reflect the society in which they evolve and, thus, seek to adapt to a constantly changing environment. Yet most of these reforms are incremental and imperfect. Does it, in fact, take a major crisis to bring about significant and lasting change? This is certainly a question that can arise in the context of a serious health crisis, such as that caused by COVID-19.

Une ère de réformes ?

Lorsqu'il publia son livre sur le parlementarisme canadien en 1987, C.E.S Franks notait que le Canada et ses institutions démocratiques traversaient une « ère de réformes » (*An Age of Reforms*) sans précédent. Des modifications importantes, avançait-il, avaient profondément modifié le travail et les responsabilités des parlementaires au cours des vingt dernières années. Par exemple, les comités parlementaires s'étaient vus confier de nouvelles responsabilités pour faire l'étude des crédits budgétaires, lors de la réforme de 1968 ; le vérificateur général du Canada avait reçu le mandat d'effectuer des audits de performance, comme le recommandait la Commission Lambert en 1976 ; et les comités législatifs avaient obtenu de nouvelles ressources et aussi de nouvelles responsabilités notamment à la suite des rapports Lefebvre de 1982 et McGrath de 1984-1985. Les changements aux règles, procédures et institutions se sont poursuivis après les années quatre-vingt. Ainsi, le processus régissant l'étude des crédits budgétaires était encore une fois modifié, à la fin des années 1990, cette fois-ci pour améliorer la qualité de l'information transmise aux parlementaires ; de nouveaux postes d'agent du Parlement ont été créés, dont le plus populaire est sans doute celui du directeur parlementaire du budget (Tellier, 2014), établi en 2007 ; et de nouveaux mécanismes ont été mis sur pied pour accroître la participation du public, comme les consultations prébudgétaires annuelles, instaurées en 1994, et les pétitions électroniques, offertes depuis 2015[1]. Ces nombreux changements semblent indiquer que l'ère des réformes identifiée par Franks se poursuit encore de nos jours.

---

1   On trouvera une liste plus détaillée des principales réformes dans Chenier et coll. (2005). Pour une analyse des réformes de la procédure budgétaire parlementaire du gouvernement fédéral et des gouvernements provinciaux, consultez Tellier (2018).

À première vue, l'adoption de plusieurs réformes peut être interprétée comme étant un signe de vitalité du parlementarisme canadien. Les enjeux de société évoluant sans cesse, il semble normal que l'on tente d'adapter les institutions parlementaires à leur environnement qui ne cesse de changer. Le parlement doit être le reflet de la société. Par contre, plusieurs observateurs de la scène canadienne dressent un constat moins favorable. Franks émettait déjà plusieurs réserves en observant que les changements qui avaient été faits jusqu'alors n'avaient pas réussi à atténuer la partisanerie excessive, la domination du gouvernement (le pouvoir exécutif) dans les affaires parlementaires, pas plus qu'ils avaient permis de valoriser le travail et l'influence des députés d'arrière-ban et des comités et plus largement les fonctions de reddition de compte (Franks, 1987, 3). Malgré l'adoption de réformes subséquentes, les critiques initiales formulées par Franks ont été reprises par la suite par plusieurs autres observateurs de la scène parlementaire canadienne (voir, par exemple, Chenier et coll., 2005 ; J. Smith, 2003 ; D.E. Smith, 2013 ; Aucoin et coll., 2011 ; Savoie, 2010). Des parlementaires ont aussi exprimé leur insatisfaction vis-à-vis de l'état actuel de leurs institutions comme en font foi notamment plusieurs rapports de comités[2].

Il existe donc un danger à mettre en place des réformes qui ne donnent pas les résultats recherchés. Par contre, il ne faudrait pas non plus que le cynisme l'emporte et empêche tout progrès dans ce domaine. Par conséquent, les réformes sont nécessaires, mais elles doivent se faire en tenant compte de la nature même des institutions parlementaires et des responsabilités qui leur ont été octroyées : « Les réformes qui ne sont pas solidement ancrées dans la réalité n'ont pas de grandes chances de succès » (Franks, 1987, 3 ; notre traduction).

Quelles sont donc ces responsabilités parlementaires ? Le système parlementaire canadien s'inspire de la tradition britannique qui met à l'avant-plan le principe de la reddition de compte. Ainsi, le gouvernement (le pouvoir exécutif), élu démocratiquement, obtient de larges pouvoirs (dont celui de présenter les projets de loi à caractère financier), mais doit se soumettre à un examen des législateurs. Autrement dit, le gouvernement a l'obligation d'expliquer ses décisions aux représentants élus de la population, alors que ces derniers

---

2   Voir notamment les rapports de la bibliothèque du Parlement (2003) et du Comité permanent des opérations gouvernementales et des prévisions budgétaires (2003, 2019, 2012).

ont l'obligation d'examiner et de débattre les choix du gouvernement et même de proposer des solutions de remplacement[3]. Nous pouvons tirer deux grandes observations à partir de ce principe de reddition de compte. D'une part, les parlementaires ne gouvernent pas et donc ne peuvent pas participer directement à la gestion des affaires de l'État[4]. C'est le gouvernement qui a la responsabilité de formuler et de mettre en œuvre les politiques publiques. D'autre part, la reddition de compte exige que le gouvernement se soumette à un examen rigoureux de la part des parlementaires et tout particulièrement des membres des partis de l'opposition. Par ailleurs, ceux-ci peuvent aussi espérer devenir une solution de rechange au gouvernement en place, s'ils remportent les prochaines élections. Par conséquent, l'opposition a la légitimité de critiquer les décisions du gouvernement. C'est donc dire que les luttes partisanes font partie de la vie parlementaire. Ces deux observations expliquent plusieurs des constats présentés par les études réunies dans cet ouvrage.

La distinction entre les pouvoirs respectifs des parlementaires et la Couronne (le gouvernement) amène Chaplin à réfléchir sur le rôle des législateurs canadiens en matière de consultations publiques (voir le chapitre 4). Dans la cause opposant la Mikisew Cree First Nation au gouvernement canadien, la Cour suprême a statué qu'il revenait aux législateurs eux-mêmes de déterminer comment ils entendaient protéger les droits des populations autochtones à être consultées lorsque des propositions législatives sont présentées au Parlement. Selon Chaplin, le Parlement canadien devrait modifier ses procédures afin de s'assurer que les droits des peuples autochtones sont respectés, mais sans chercher toutefois à se substituer à la Couronne. L'obligation de consultation tombe sous la responsabilité du gouvernement. Le Parlement, pour sa part, a le devoir de s'assurer que le gouvernement remplit ses obligations. Par conséquent, les parlementaires devraient mettre en place des mécanismes et avoir des ressources qui leur permettent d'examiner les consultations menées par gouvernement auprès des peuples autochtones. Les

---

3   Selon Franks, les parlementaires canadiens remplissent quatre fonctions essentielles : choisir un gouvernement ; donner au gouvernement les ressources nécessaires (notamment financières) pour qu'il puisse gouverner ; surveiller le gouvernement ; offrir une solution de rechange au gouvernement actuellement en place (1987, 5).

4   À l'exception des parlementaires qui sont membres du cabinet.

suggestions formulées par Chaplin offrent un bon exemple de la séparation des pouvoirs et responsabilités entre les pouvoirs exécutifs et législatifs.

Cette séparation des pouvoirs et des responsabilités entre le législatif et l'exécutif ne semble cependant pas saisie par tous les législateurs. L'étude menée par Weber illustre bien cette situation (chapitre 5). Cette étude examine comment les parlementaires perçoivent leur rôle dans le processus budgétaire parlementaire. Selon Weber, on peut identifier trois types de représentants élus, en fonction de leur attitude face aux questions budgétaires : l'enquêteur, lequel demande des comptes au gouvernement, puisqu'il considère que cela fait partie de ses responsabilités ; le représentant, lequel tente d'influencer la politique budgétaire dans le but de servir les intérêts de ses propres électeurs ; et l'absent, lequel se désengage complètement du processus budgétaire jugé trop complexe ou encore inutile dans l'exercice de ses fonctions. Si l'étude de Weber montre que l'absent demeure assez marginal (seulement 5 des 32 députés interrogés ont été classés dans cette catégorie), les enquêteurs (15 députés) et les représentants (12 députés) ont une présence relativement similaire. Cette distribution explique bien la grande confusion qui semble encore exister quant au rôle des parlementaires. Même s'ils peuvent difficilement participer à la formulation de la politique budgétaire du gouvernement, plusieurs (les représentants) estiment qu'ils doivent le faire. Cette variété de points de vue sur le rôle du député peut sans doute expliquer pourquoi les réformes menées jusqu'à présent demeurent insatisfaisantes pour plusieurs. Les parlementaires ne partageant pas tous une définition commune de leur rôle et leurs responsabilités, il devient difficile de mettre en place des réformes qui font consensus.

Outre le partage des responsabilités entre le pouvoir exécutif et le Parlement, les réformes parlementaires doivent aussi tenir compte de la présence inévitable de débats partisans. La partisanerie a mauvaise presse et plusieurs, à commencer par de nombreux parlementaires, dénoncent les débats acrimonieux qui se déroulent fréquemment en chambre (Morden et coll., 2018 ; Docherty, 2005 ; Dobell, 2000 ; Chong, 2010). Mais la partisanerie a toujours fait partie et fera encore partie du paysage politique pour longtemps. Ceci s'explique notamment par le fait que la discipline de parti (c'est-à-dire le principe selon lequel on s'attend à ce que les députés appuient les positions prises par leur parti et surtout par leur chef de parti) joue un rôle important dans le régime parlementaire canadien. Plusieurs considèrent que la discipline de parti a trop d'influence, puisqu'elle force les députés à appuyer des prises de position qui peuvent être contraires aux intérêts de leurs propres électeurs, alors que d'autres dénoncent la trop grande emprise des chefs de parti sur les membres de leur caucus (Rathgeber, 2014 ; Venne, 2003 ; Strahl, 2001 ; Chong, 2019). Certaines réformes ont même été entreprises pour permettre plus de votes libres à la chambre, mais sans résultats (Lecomte, 2018). L'analyse menée par de Clercy et Marland (chapitre 2) permet d'expliquer cependant pourquoi la discipline de parti prévaut encore dans notre système politique. À partir d'entretiens menés auprès des députés de la Chambre des communes, les auteurs constatent que les parlementaires accordent beaucoup d'importance à la loyauté à leur caucus. Comme l'expliquait une députée : « Que vous l'aimiez ou non, vous faites partie d'une équipe. » Parallèlement à cette loyauté envers ses collègues, peu de députés semblent valoriser la collaboration entre les partis, et ce, même chez les députés ayant plus d'expérience parlementaire et donc ayant eu davantage l'occasion de travailler avec les membres d'autres formations. Cette loyauté au caucus s'explique en grande partie par l'obligation qu'a le parti au pouvoir d'obtenir la confiance de la chambre pour demeurer au pouvoir. La dissension pouvant mener à la défaite du gouvernement, on comprend mieux le rôle que joue la discipline de parti.

La partisanerie a aussi pour effet de favoriser le parti au pouvoir surtout lorsque ce dernier détient une majorité à la chambre (Russell, 2008). En effet, lorsqu'un gouvernement est majoritaire, la distinction entre le pouvoir législatif et le pouvoir exécutif devient parfois difficile à distinguer. Le premier ministre sait que, dans ces circonstances, il peut compter sur l'appui de ses députés (grâce à la discipline de parti) pour faire adopter ses propres initiatives. Par conséquent, les parlementaires peuvent parfois adopter des initiatives qui sont plus favorables au gouvernement qu'à leurs propres intérêts. La réforme examinée par McCormick (chapitre 6) illustre bien cette situation. Dans le but de favoriser la conciliation famille-travail, plusieurs changements ont été apportés au règlement de l'Assemblée législative du Yukon au cours des vingt dernières années. Ces changements ont mené à la mise en place d'un calendrier parlementaire plus prévisible, mais aussi plus rigide. À première vue, on pourrait penser que ces nouvelles règles procurent un avantage aux parlementaires en venant limiter la capacité du gouvernement (surtout s'il est majoritaire) à contrôler le calendrier parlementaire. Dans les faits, cependant, on constate que c'est le contraire qui s'est produit : le gouvernement a su tirer parti de ces nouvelles règles pour faire adopter rapidement ses projets de loi. Les nouvelles règles mises en place ont donc affaibli le pouvoir de surveillance des parlementaires.

L'analyse présentée par Phelps Bondaroff et ses collaborateurs (chapitre 6) offre un autre exemple d'une réforme qui n'a pas eu les résultats escomptés. Les auteurs se sont intéressés à l'usage de la prière à l'Assemblée législative de la Colombie-Britannique et plus particulièrement à la réforme adoptée en 2019. Cette réforme avait pour but de susciter la présentation de prières plus variées et plus inclusives afin de mieux représenter les diverses confessions présentes dans la province ainsi que pour permettre aux non-croyants de participer à cette activité. La période de « prière » a été changée en période de « prières et de réflexions » et plusieurs nouveaux textes de prières et de réflexions ont été préparés à l'intention des parlementaires pour les aider à prendre part à cette activité (les parlementaires peuvent cependant présenter leurs propres prières et réflexions). Malgré ces « bonnes intentions », pour reprendre l'expression utilisée par les auteurs, les résultats sont décevants. Contrairement aux attentes, l'usage de la période de prières et de réflexions n'a pas augmenté. De plus, les prières sont nettement plus utilisées que les réflexions. Enfin, seul un petit nombre de députés participent à cette activité. Force est de constater que les prières et réflexions faites à la législature de la Colombie-Britannique ne représentent pas la diversité des croyances religieuses de la population de la province malgré la réforme de 2019. Selon Phelps Bondaroff et ses collaborateurs, la seule solution viable serait d'abolir tout simplement la période de prières et de réflexions. À première vue, cette suggestion semble s'harmoniser avec les changements que l'on observe dans la société, considérant que la religion n'occupe plus une place prépondérante dans la société. Toutefois, la religion n'a tout de même pas complètement disparu du paysage politique et les questions religieuses demeurent importantes pour un certain nombre d'électeurs (Rayside et coll., 2017). Plusieurs de ces électeurs n'hésitent pas à défendre une cause précise pour en faire un enjeu électoral (pensons à la question de l'avortement, des programmes d'éducation sexuelle à l'école, du mariage entre conjoints de même sexe, etc.). Dans ces circonstances, l'abolition de la prière réclamée par Phelps Bondaroff et ses collaborateurs pourrait être difficile à mettre en œuvre.

Enfin, certaines réformes doivent composer avec la nature exceptionnelle des institutions parlementaires. Ceci est démontré de façon convaincante par Feldman qui aborde la mise en œuvre d'une politique pour contrer le harcèlement et la violence dans les milieux de travail parlementaire (chapitre 3). Il explique qu'en raison de l'évolution rapide du mouvement *#MoiAussi*, de nombreuses assemblées législatives, dont plusieurs au Canada, ont pris des mesures visant à prévenir la violence, l'intimidation, le harcèlement sexuel et d'autres comportements préjudiciables. Ces initiatives, en général souhaitées et bien reçues, posent un certain nombre de défis en contexte parlementaire. En effet, les caractéristiques uniques du lieu de travail législatif font en sorte que l'approche de prévention ou les mécanismes d'enquêtes utilisés dans les institutions non législatives s'y appliquent difficilement. Une assemblée législative qui tente d'imposer ou de modifier une politique de prévention du harcèlement sexuel doit d'abord définir les relations contractuelles qui gouvernent les employés vu les multiples sources de droit qui couvrent les relations de travail en contexte parlementaire. Toute initiative de réforme pourrait donc être ralentie ou complexifiée en raison des différentes conditions particulières. Pour être applicable, la politique de prévention du harcèlement d'une législature doit être intégrée dans les conditions d'emploi de l'employé. Or, Feldman explique que la relation de travail entre un parlementaire et son personnel peut prendre diverses formes. Le même employeur peut avoir des employés couverts sous différents régimes, par exemple, le personnel d'un parlementaire à l'Assemblée législative par rapport à celui qui travaille au bureau de circonscription. Enfin, il introduit la notion « d'espaces partagés » pour évoquer les lieux de travail variés dans lesquels les parlementaires et leurs employés effectuent leurs tâches, multipliant ainsi les contextes dans lesquels le comportement répréhensible peut se produire. Certes, la complexité du milieu parlementaire a probablement pour conséquence de ralentir les mouvements de réforme, mais on constate néanmoins que le milieu législatif peut prendre acte de l'émergence de nouveaux phénomènes sociaux et tenter de s'y adapter en conséquence, en dépit des risques de disparités et des lacunes.

Puis la pandémie survint…

Le présent ouvrage fait état de l'évolution des corps législatifs et de récents mouvements de réforme. À première vue, on pourrait penser que les réformes surviennent graduellement, au terme d'un projet structuré et développé sur une période relativement longue et ayant pour but d'améliorer ou de modifier le fonctionnement d'une institution. Par contre, en regard de la pandémie de la COVID-19 qui a pris de nombreuses législatures par surprise, on peut se demander si des changements durables ne peuvent pas aussi se produire à la suite d'une situation imprévue et urgente.

La présence de conventions, de pratiques et de coutumes est l'un des traits distinctifs des assemblées législatives. Ces diverses règles écrites et non écrites sont généralement adoptées pour être à l'épreuve du temps et elles doivent être difficiles à manipuler afin d'éviter l'excès de partisanerie ou l'octroi d'avantages éphémères. Néanmoins, la pandémie de la COVID-19 a provoqué d'importants changements au Parlement du Canada et dans les Assemblées législatives provinciales et territoriales. Les parlementaires ont dû rapidement repenser et redéfinir leurs façons de fonctionner, dans un contexte sans précédent.

Les efforts visant à maintenir un équilibre entre les pouvoirs extraordinaires requis par tous les paliers gouvernementaux pour faire face à l'urgence sanitaire et à la crise économique, d'une part, et les contrôles adéquats en matière de santé publique, de reddition de comptes et d'obligations constitutionnelles, d'autre part, ont posé des défis historiques au bon fonctionnement de nos institutions démocratiques.

Dès le 16 mars 2020, les bureaux de santé publique de nombreuses provinces et territoires du pays ont émis différentes ordonnances, ou étaient sur le point de le faire, afin de limiter les déplacements, voire imposer un confinement, ce qui a eu un effet immédiat sur la mobilité des parlementaires. D'autres mesures visant à prévenir la propagation du virus, telles que le port du masque et la distanciation physique et sociale, ont aussi limité les activités du Parlement canadien et des assemblées législatives provinciales et territoriales, à un moment où leurs activités étaient essentielles, ne serait-ce que parce qu'ils devaient examiner des projets de loi de mesures d'urgence.

L'une des premières décisions prises en réaction à la pandémie a été la suspension des accès aux édifices parlementaires au grand public. Sur la base des recommandations des différents bureaux de la santé publique au pays, de nombreuses assemblées législatives, incluant le Parlement canadien, ont choisi de restreindre en tout ou en partie les accès aux comités, aux tribunes et aux édifices parlementaires normalement ouverts au public (Bureau de régie interne, 2020 ; Président du Sénat, 2020). Si la décision prise à l'époque peut sembler anodine et logique aujourd'hui, il s'agissait d'une action aux conséquences philosophiques non négligeables. Le Parlement est l'emblème de la démocratie, la propriété des citoyens et le lieu où la voix de ces derniers est entendue. La fermeture des portes au public représentait donc le début d'un long cycle de négociations entre les différents leaders parlementaires et le fruit d'un premier accord pour protéger la santé et la sécurité de la population canadienne.

Dans le cas particulier du Parlement canadien, alors que la majorité des fonctionnaires fédéraux ainsi que de nombreux membres du personnel parlementaire s'ajustaient au travail à domicile, le Sénat et la Chambre des communes apportaient des modifications considérables à leurs calendriers parlementaires, à leurs règles et usages procéduraux, à leurs réunions de comités, ainsi qu'aux diverses actions prises par leur administration respective. Les législatures ont aussi eu recours rapidement à des outils technologiques pour permettre la poursuite des délibérations parlementaires dans le respect des directives de santé publique. La poursuite des travaux s'est faite de façon virtuelle ou hybride sur une version de la plateforme de vidéoconférence Zoom pour abonnés, laquelle assure une sécurité accrue en plus de permettre l'interprétation simultanée. Le vote à distance avec une application sécurisée a de plus été introduit à la Chambre des communes afin de permettre aux parlementaires de s'acquitter de ce droit même en séance virtuelle ou hybride[5].

L'obligation légale pour le Parlement du Canada d'offrir l'interprétation simultanée lors des séances du Sénat, de la Chambre des communes et de leurs comités respectifs, considérée comme une tâche relativement simple et bien rodée dans les opérations quotidiennes du Parlement, démontre à quel point un changement imprévu peut soudainement devenir critique et excessivement compliquée à

---

5   Pour une liste des nombreux changements faits à la Chambre des communes en réponse à la pandémie, voir le discours du président de la Chambre intitulé « La création du parlement hybride », disponible à l'adresse suivante : https://www. noscommunes.ca/speaker/fr/discours/discours/13.

remédier. Les parlementaires disposant d'un droit constitutionnel d'être entendus et d'exercer leurs fonctions dans la langue officielle de leur choix, il était crucial de fournir une solution sécuritaire et adaptée pour assurer la continuité des travaux dans les deux langues officielles dans le cadre de séances virtuelles et hybrides (Forget et coll., 2020).

Toutes les délibérations du Sénat et de la Chambre des communes devaient également continuer d'être diffusées simultanément sur le site Web du Parlement. Un défi de taille alors que plusieurs parlementaires participaient à distance et disposaient d'une connexion Internet de qualité variable. Les réunions hybrides requéraient que certains membres du personnel soient présents sur place afin d'offrir un soutien. En général, du personnel technique supplémentaire était nécessaire pour réunir les participants virtuels aux participants présents en Chambre et voir au bon fonctionnement de la diffusion, de la transcription, du sous-titrage et de l'interprétation simultanée des débats. Dans le cas des réunions de comité, les parlementaires, et les témoins le cas échéant, se branchaient à la plateforme de vidéoconférence à partir de divers endroits à l'aide d'un ordinateur portable et d'un casque d'écoute. Le personnel de soutien gérait les réunions à partir des salles de comité, afin de fournir un soutien procédural et technique et d'autres services essentiels tels que l'interprétation simultanée et la transcription des débats.

Des adaptations technologiques ont également été requises pour le travail dans les circonscriptions. La pandémie a entraîné une hausse importante de demandes d'aide de la part des électeurs. Tout d'abord, pour rapatrier les ressortissants canadiens ou leurs proches coincés à l'étranger, puis pour s'y retrouver dans la myriade de nouveaux programmes et mesures d'aide. La plupart des députés et leur personnel de circonscription ont dû répondre à ces demandes depuis leur domicile sans accès immédiat aux ressources habituellement utilisées dans leur bureau.

Ailleurs au Canada, des mesures ont également été prises pour assurer la poursuite des activités législatives pendant la pandémie. Les leaders politiques et le personnel législatif ont dû déterminer ce qui pouvait être modifié, ce qui pouvait être adapté et ce qui était tout simplement immuable. Des changements à la procédure, au calcul du quorum et aux méthodes pour enregistrer les votes ont notamment été proposés pour permettre aux parlementaires de participer en ligne et en présentiel. À l'Assemblée législative de la

Colombie-Britannique, des comités permanents ont tenu des réunions virtuelles pour traiter de questions ne se limitant pas à la pandémie de la COVID-19. Des réunions de commissions virtuelles ont été tenues à l'Assemblée nationale du Québec afin de permettre aux députés de poser des questions au gouvernement concernant la COVID-19. Le Comité permanent de la responsabilité et de la surveillance de l'Assemblée législative des Territoires du Nord-Ouest a continué à se réunir plusieurs fois par semaine pour discuter de l'impact de la COVID-19 sur l'ensemble du territoire. L'Assemblée législative de l'Île-du-Prince-Édouard a réussi à accueillir tous les députés en modifiant son plan de salle. Au cours des séances d'urgence liées à la COVID-19 de l'Assemblée législative de l'Ontario, un nombre limité de députés étaient présents à la Chambre, et des mesures spéciales ont dû être prises afin de répartir les places assises.

La pandémie a aussi eu des conséquences importantes sur la capacité des parlementaires à examiner les décisions budgétaires du gouvernement. Le gouvernement fédéral a lancé un plan de soutien économique sans précédent depuis la Deuxième Guerre mondiale. La pièce maîtresse de ce plan, le projet de loi C-13, Loi sur les mesures d'urgence visant la COVID-19, qui contenait 18 sections et 61 articles, a été débattue en moins de trois heures à la Chambre des communes le 24 mars. En tenant compte des projets de loi subséquents (C-14, C-15 et C-4) le gouvernement s'est engagé à dépenser plus de 200 milliards de dollars pour aider l'ensemble de la population canadienne à faire face à la pandémie[6]. En échange, cependant, les parlementaires ont obtenu le droit de recevoir des mises à jour régulières de la part du gouvernement. Ainsi, le ministre des Finances a dû comparaître devant le Comité permanent des finances pour faire rapport de l'état d'avancement du plan d'aide toutes les deux semaines au cours de l'été 2020. Par ailleurs, plusieurs études et rapports ont été déposés et d'autres le seront dans les prochains mois par des comités permanents et des agents du Parlement. Soulignons aussi que le gouvernement n'a pas eu recours à l'utilisation de mandats spéciaux, bien que la loi ait été modifiée pour en permettre l'usage[7]. Par contre, il

---

6   Selon les données compilées par le Directeur parlementaire du budget, ce montant s'élève à 212,3 milliards de dollars. Consulté le 10 avril 2021. https://covid19 .pbo-dpb.ca/#/fr/costing-economic-response-plan--etablissement-des-couts-plan -intervention-economique.

7   Les mandats spéciaux permettent au gouvernement d'engager des fonds publics sans l'autorisation préalable des parlementaires lorsque le Parlement est dissous.

a décidé de ne pas présenter de plan budgétaire pour l'année 2020-2021, contrairement à tous les gouvernements provinciaux et territoriaux[8].

Durant la pandémie, le gouvernement a usé de pouvoirs considérables afin de répondre rapidement à l'urgence de la situation. Les parlementaires lui ont octroyé ces moyens d'action, mais ont obtenu en échange davantage de pouvoirs de reddition de comptes. La pandémie a ainsi démontré qu'il était possible de modifier les règles et procédures en temps de crise sans minimiser le rôle des parlementaires en matière de reddition de comptes. Il reste à confirmer que ces nouvelles façons de faire vont inciter les parlements à adopter des réformes durables.

Les perturbations provoquées par la pandémie ont constitué un tournant historique pour nos institutions parlementaires canadiennes. Le Parlement du Canada ainsi que plusieurs assemblées législatives canadiennes ont non seulement su s'adapter rapidement à la réalité temporaire, mais ils ont aussi su faire preuve d'innovation afin de continuer à soutenir les travaux parlementaires essentiels, et ce, malgré les changements constants et les défis inhérents au travail à distance. La disponibilité des ressources humaines, ainsi que la capacité technique et physique afin de maintenir le niveau d'activité prépandémique, ont parfois été affectées, voire diminuées pendant les mois de confinement. Le Parlement du Canada et les assemblées législatives provinciales et territoriales ont donc dû réduire certains services et soupeser les risques et les conséquences d'une éclosion de la maladie au sein de leur institution contre les avantages de se réunir et faire progresser les travaux. L'équilibre entre la sécurité et l'engagement parlementaire s'est parfois avéré difficile à concilier, mais le Parlement, aussi rigide et ancré dans la tradition, les pratiques et les coutumes, s'est montré résilient. Il s'est adapté à un rythme impressionnant.

Cette procédure est utile lorsque les circonstances non prévues forcent le gouvernement à utiliser des fonds publics alors qu'il lui est impossible d'obtenir l'approbation des parlementaires, par exemple, durant une campagne électorale. Pendant les premières semaines de la pandémie, le parlement ne siégeait pas, mais n'avait pas été dissous, ce qui ne permettait donc pas au gouvernement d'utiliser les mandats spéciaux. Une exception a été adoptée le 13 mars en raison de la pandémie (C-12).

8   Certains gouvernements provinciaux et territoriaux avaient déposé leur budget avant le début de la pandémie, alors que d'autres ont repoussé la date de présentation de quelques mois.

Quelles leçons pouvons-nous tirer des changements apportés aux procédures parlementaires durant la pandémie ? Partant du principe qu'un parlement ou une assemblée législative est un lieu où l'on échange des idées sur les politiques publiques et les propositions législatives et où l'on demande des comptes au gouvernement, il va de soi que toute proposition visant à en modifier les pratiques, les règles ou les usages sera accueillie à la fois par des louanges, mais aussi par des critiques. L'expérience démontre toutefois que les parlementaires peuvent instaurer des réformes significatives lorsqu'il existe une volonté politique. Tous les changements apportés au cours de la pandémie ont été adoptés par les parlementaires à la suite de consultations, de négociations et de motions débattues et adoptées dans l'enceinte du Parlement, dans le but de modifier des règles et des pratiques historiques pour le bien de tous. Ceci illustre l'autonomie des parlements et des assemblées législatives en tant qu'entités ayant le privilège inhérent de se gouverner elles-mêmes. On doit en conclure qu'elles sont organiques et malléables et qu'elles peuvent s'adapter aux besoins changeants, qu'ils soient urgents ou non. Bien que les institutions politiques soient des instruments de tradition, elles perdurent dans le temps, évoluant avec les réalités contemporaines pour maintenir le niveau approprié de confiance du public à la lumière des responsabilités qui leur ont été confiées.

Mais la question demeure. Le terme « réforme » est-il juste et adéquat pour qualifier des changements survenus subitement, par exemple dans un contexte de pandémie visant à garantir la continuité des travaux parlementaires ? Tel que le stipulait le professeur Franks, « les réformes qui ne sont pas solidement ancrées dans la réalité n'ont pas de grandes chances de succès » (Franks, 1987, 3 ; notre traduction). Les changements historiques et sans précédent adoptés à la suite de la pandémie survivront-ils à l'épreuve du temps ?

Références

Aucoin, Peter, Mark D. Jarvis et Lori Turnbull (2011). *Democratizing the Constitution. Reforming Responsible Government*, Toronto, Emond Montgomery Publications.

Bibliothèque du Parlement (2003). *Un Parlement selon nos vœux*, Ottawa, Parlement du Canada.

Bureau de régie interne (2020). *Mesures préventives à la Chambre des communes en réponse à la situation de la COVID-19*, Déclaration, 13 mars, Ottawa, Chambre des communes.

Chenier, John A., Michael Dewing et Jack Stillborn (2005). "Does Parliament Care? Parliament Committees and the Estimates", In *How Ottawa Spends, 2005–2006: Managing Minority*, edited by Bruce G. Doern, 200-221, Kingston and Montréal, McGill-Queen's University Press.

Chong, Michael (2010). "The Increasing Disconnect Between Canadians and their Parliament", *Policy Options/Options politiques* : 24-27.

Chong, Michael (2019). "PM's Caucus Expulsions Reveal Rot in Parliament", *Policy Options/Options politiques*. https://policyoptions.irpp.org/magazines /may-2019/pms-caucus-expulsions-reveal-rot-in-parliament/.

Comité permanent des opérations gouvernementales et des prévisions budgétaires (2003). *Pour un examen valable : améliorations à apporter au processus budgétaire*, Ottawa, Parlement du Canada.

Comité permanent des opérations gouvernementales et des prévisions budgétaires (2012). *Renforcer l'examen parlementaire des prévisions budgétaires et des crédits*, Ottawa, Parlement du Canada.

Comité permanent des opérations gouvernementales et des prévisions budgétaires (2019). *Améliorer la transparence et le contrôle parlementaire des plans de dépenses du gouvernement*, Ottawa, Parlement du Canada.

Dobell, Peter (2000). « La réforme de la procédure parlementaire : le point de vue des députés », *Enjeux publics/Policy Matters* 1 (9) : 1-42.

Docherty, David C. (2005). *Legislatures*, Vancouver, University of British Columbia Press.

Forget, Chloé, Marie-Ève Hudon et Élise Hurtubise-Loranger (2020). *Les langues officielles et le Parlement*, paru le 12 octobre 2015, révisé le 19 mars 2020, Ottawa, Bibliothèque du Parlement.

Franks, C.E.S. (1987). *The Parliament of Canada*, Toronto, University of Toronto Press.

Lecomte, Lucie (2018). *La discipline de parti et le vote libre*, Ottawa, Bibliothèque du Parlement.

Morden, Michael, Jane Hilderman et Kendall Anderson (2018). *Laisser tomber le scénario. La législature doit redynamiser la démocratie représentative*, 12 juin, Toronto, Le Centre Samara pour la démocratie.

Président du Sénat (2020). *Le Sénat du Canada adopte des mesures préventives concernant la COVID-19*, Communiqué, 12 mars, Ottawa, Sénat du Canada.

Rathgeber, Brent (2014). *Irresponsible Government*, Toronto, Dundurn Press.

Rayside, David Morton, Jerald Sabin et Paul E. J. Thomas, eds. (2017). *Religion and Canadian Party Politics*, Vancouver, University of British Columbia Press.

Russell, Peter H. (2008). *Two Cheers for Minority Government: The Evolution of Canadian Parliamentary Democracy*, Toronto, Emond Montgomery Publications.

Savoie, Donald J. (2010). *Power: Where Is It?* Kingston and Montréal, McGill-Queen's University Press.

Smith, David E. (2013). *Across the Aisle: Opposition in Canadian Politics*, Toronto, University of Toronto Press.

Smith, Jennifer (2003). "Debating the Reform of Canada's Parliament." In *Reforming Parliamentary Democracy*, edited by F. Leslie Seidle and David D. Docherty, 150-167, Kingston and Montréal, McGill-Queen's University Press.

Strahl, Chuck (2001). « Pour un Parlement plus à l'écoute des Canadiens », *Revue parlementaire canadienne* 24 (1) : 2-4.

Tellier, Geneviève (2014). « Le directeur parlementaire du budget : le nouveau chien de garde financier du gouvernement fédéral canadien ? » Dans *Les surveillants de l'État démocratique*, sous la dir. de Jean Crête, 19-54, Sainte-Foy, Presses de l'Université Laval.

Tellier, Geneviève (2018). « Reddition de compte, transparence financière et finances publiques : le point sur les pratiques des gouvernements canadiens », Dans *Éléments de la finance responsable : une perspective multidimensionnelle*, sous la dir. de Frank Coggins, Claudia Champagne et Lyne Latulippe, 517-539, Montréal, Éditions Yvon Blais.

Venne, Pierrette (2003). « Le rôle des députés fédéraux », *Revue parlementaire canadienne* 26 (1) : 2-3.

Contributors / Collaborateurs

Marie-Ève Belzile est gestionnaire au secteur législatif du Sénat du Canada. Elle est actuellement Greffière principale pour les Échanges parlementaires et le Protocole à la Direction des affaires internationales et interparlementaires. Elle était précédemment assignée à la Direction des comités du Sénat où elle était l'une des deux greffières principales responsables de la gestion des opérations.

Marie-Ève Belzile is a manager in the Legislative Sector of the Senate of Canada. She is currently the Principal Clerk for Parliamentary Exchanges and Protocol in the International and Interparliamentary Affairs Directorate. She was previously assigned to the Senate Committees Directorate, where she was one of the two principal clerks in charge of managing its operations.

Ian Bushfield is Executive Director of the BC Humanist Association. He earned a BSc in engineering physics from the University of Alberta and a MSc in physics from Simon Fraser University. He also holds an associate certificate in non-profit management from the British Columbia Institute of Technology (BCIT). He has been a coauthor on articles in a diverse variety of fields including optics, diversity at non-religious conferences, clinical trial transparency, and legislative prayers. He is also a member of the British Columbia Civil Liberties Association's Board of Directors.

Ian Bushfield est le directeur général de la Humanist Association de la Colombie-Britannique. Il est titulaire d'un baccalauréat en génie physique de l'Université de l'Alberta et d'une maîtrise en physique de l'Université Simon Fraser. Il détient également un certificat en gestion dans le secteur sans but lucratif de l'ITCB. Il a copublié des articles dans une variété de domaines, y compris l'optique, la diversité aux conférences non religieuses, la transparence des essais cliniques et les prières dans les assemblées législatives. Il est également membre du conseil d'administration de la BC Civil Liberties Association.

Steven Chaplin is a Fellow of the University of Ottawa Public Law Centre. From 2002 to 2017, he was Senior Legal Counsel for the House of Commons, during which time he advised and represented the House on various matters, including parliamentary privilege and the constitutional functions of Parliament. He was an active member of the Association of Parliamentary Counsel in Canada, acting as President in 2015. He continues to write, blog, and lecture on the law of Parliament.

Steven Chaplin est membre du Centre de droit public de l'Université d'Ottawa. De 2002 à 2017, il occupe le poste de conseiller juridique principal de la Chambre des communes. Pendant cette période, il conseille et représente la Chambre sur diverses questions, notamment le privilège parlementaire et les fonctions constitutionnelles du Parlement. Il a été un membre actif de l'Association des conseillers parlementaires du Canada, dont il a été le président en 2015. Il continue d'écrire des articles, de tenir un blogue et de donner des conférences sur le droit parlementaire.

Cristine de Clercy is Professor of Political Science at Western University. She specializes in studying political leaders, Parliament, election law, and women and politics. Her recent work includes an examination of how populist voters judge the character of political leaders in democratic states such as Canada and the USA and why Canadian federal parties recruit star candidates from outside the political process to run in federal elections. Recent publications include articles in the *Leadership Quarterly Yearly Review*, *Politics and Governance*, and the *American Review of Canadian Studies*.

Cristine de Clercy est professeure de science politique à l'Université Western. Elle se spécialise dans l'étude des dirigeants politiques, du Parlement, du droit électoral, et des femmes en politique. Ses travaux récents portent notamment sur la façon dont les électeurs populistes jugent la personnalité des dirigeants politiques dans des États démo-cratiques comme le Canada et les États-Unis et sur les raisons pour lesquelles les partis fédéraux canadiens recrutent des candidats vedettes en dehors du processus politique pour se présenter aux élections fédérales. Ses publications récentes sont parues dans *The Leadership Quarterly Yearly Review, Politics and Governance* et *The American Review of Canadian Studies.*

Charlie Feldman is President of the Canadian Study of Parliament Group. He has served as a Parliamentary Counsel at the Senate and House of Commons of Canada, having previously worked at the Library of Parliament and on Capitol Hill. He is a Member of the Law Society of Ontario, has an LLM from McGill University, and serves on the Editorial Board of the *Journal of Parliamentary and Political Law.*

Charlie Feldman est le président du Groupe canadien d'étude des parlements. Il a été conseiller parlementaire au Sénat et à la Chambre des communes du Canada, après avoir travaillé à la Bibliothèque du Parlement et au Capitole. Membre du Barreau de l'Ontario et titulaire d'une maîtrise en droit de l'Université McGill, M. Feldman fait partie du comité de rédaction de la *Revue de droit parlementaire et politique.*

David Groves is Legal Counsel with the Office of the Law Clerk and Parliamentary Counsel at the Senate of Canada. He is a graduate of McGill University's Faculty of Law and has worked at the Library of Parliament and the Federal Court of Canada. He currently serves as Secretary for the Board of Directors of the Canadian Study of Parliament Group.

David Groves est conseiller juridique au Bureau du légiste et conseiller parlementaire du Sénat du Canada. Il est diplômé de la Faculté de droit de l'Université McGill et a travaillé à la Bibliothèque du Parlement et à la Cour fédérale du Canada. Il est en ce moment le secrétaire du conseil d'administration du Groupe canadien d'étude des parlements.

Noah Laurence is a political scientist and general policy enthusiast who works as a policy analyst. Having previously occupied positions as a public servant, in the private sector, and with the BC Humanist Association, he is interested in engaging with the ways in which solid, equitable, and ethical policies become laws that work to the benefit of all.

Noah Laurence est politologue et passionné de politique en général. Il travaille à titre d'analyste de politiques. Ayant précédemment occupé des postes de fonctionnaire, travaillé dans le secteur privé et auprès de la Humanist Association de la Colombie-Britannique, il s'intéresse aux moyens par lesquels des politiques solides, équitables et éthiques deviendront des lois qui profiteront à tous.

Alex Marland is Professor and Head of the Department of Political Science at Memorial University. He is the author of *Brand Command: Canadian Politics and Democracy in the Age of Message Control* (UBC Press, 2016) and *Whipped: Party Discipline in Canada* (UBC Press, 2020).

Alex Marland est professeur et directeur du Département de science politique de l'Université Memorial. Il est l'auteur de *Brand Command: Canadian Politics and Democracy in the Age of Message Control* (UBC Press, 2016) et de *Whipped: Party Discipline in Canada* (UBC Press, 2020).

Katie E. Marshall completed her PhD in invertebrate physiology at Western University in 2013. Since that time, she has held postdoctoral fellowships at the University of British Columbia and Wilfrid Laurier University and a professorship at the University of Oklahoma. She is currently Assistant Professor of Comparative Physiology in the Department of Zoology at the University of British Columbia.

Katie E. Marshall a obtenu son doctorat en physiologie des invertébrés à l'Université Western Ontario en 2013. Depuis, elle a réalisé des stages postdoctoraux à l'Université de la Colombie-Britannique et à l'Université Sir Wilfrid Laurier, puis a occupé un poste de professeure à l'Université de l'Oklahoma. Elle occupe en ce moment les fonctions de professeure adjointe de physiologie comparative au département de zoologie de l'Université de la Colombie-Britannique.

Floyd McCormick served the Yukon Legislative Assembly as Clerk from 2007 to 2019 and as Deputy Clerk from 2001 to 2007. He has a PhD in political science from the University of Alberta and a BA and MA in political science from Western University. His current work focuses on the history of the Yukon Legislative Assembly and in proposing ways in which the Assembly can improve its ability to fulfill its constitutional role.

Floyd McCormick a servi l'Assemblée législative du Yukon à titre de greffier de 2007 à 2019 et de greffier adjoint de 2001 à 2007. Il est titulaire d'un doctorat en science politique de l'Université de l'Alberta et d'un baccalauréat et d'une maîtrise en science politique de l'Université Western Ontario. Ses travaux actuels portent sur l'histoire de l'Assemblée législative du Yukon et proposent des moyens, pour l'Assemblée, d'améliorer sa capacité à remplir son rôle constitutionnel.

Teale N. Phelps Bondaroff has a PhD in politics and international studies from the University of Cambridge and BAs in political science and international relations from the University of Calgary. He is the Research Coordinator for the BC Humanist Association and has published extensively on the subject of legislative prayer. He also serves as the Director of Research for OceansAsia, a Hong Kong–based marine conservation organization.

Teale N. Phelps Bondaroff est titulaire d'un doctorat en science politique et en études internationales de l'Université de Cambridge, et de baccalauréats en sciences politiques et en relations internationales de l'Université de Calgary. Il est le coordonnateur de la recherche pour la Humanist Association de la Colombie-Britannique et a publié de nombreuses études sur le sujet des prières récitées dans les assemblées législatives. Il est également directeur de la recherche pour OceansAsia, un organisme de conservation marine de Hong Kong.

Ranil Prasad is a non-profit administrator based in Vancouver, B.C. He worked as a research assistant on the original House of Prayers project with the BC Humanist Association. He holds a BA in political science from the University of British Columbia, where he focused his studies in Canadian politics.

Ranil Prasad est un administrateur dans le secteur sans but lucratif de Vancouver, en Colombie-Britannique. Il a aussi été assistant de recherche pour le projet original de *House of Prayers* avec la Humanist Association de la province. Il est titulaire d'un baccalauréat en science politique de l'Université de la Colombie-Britannique, et ses études portaient sur la politique canadienne.

Geneviève Tellier est professeure titulaire à l'École d'études politiques de l'Université d'Ottawa. Ses principales recherches portent sur les politiques budgétaires au Canada. Ses récents travaux traitent du rôle des institutions parlementaires dans le processus d'élaboration des budgets. Son dernier livre, *Canadian Public Finances. Explaining Budgetary Institutions and the Budget Process in Canada* a paru en 2019 (University of Toronto Press). Elle est actuellement la trésorière du conseil d'administration du Groupe canadien d'étude des parlements.

Geneviève Tellier is Full Professor at the School of Political Studies at the University of Ottawa. Her primary research focuses on budgetary practices in Canada. Her recent work examines the role of parliamentary institutions in budget development. Her last book, *Public Finances: Explaining Budgetary Institutions and the Budget Process in Canada,* was published in 2019 (University of Toronto Press). She currently serves as Treasurer for the Board of Directors of the Canadian Study of Parliament Group.

Adriana Thom is a policy researcher with the BC Humanist Association. She is currently in the final year of a double major in geography and political science at the University of Victoria. When she is not working on legislative prayer, permissive tax exemptions, or crisis pregnancy centres, you can see her on *The View*, looking into "Hot Topics," such as the "Real Housewives," and a One Direction reunion.

Adriana Thom est recherchiste en politiques à la Humanist Association de la Colombie-Britannique. Elle effectue actuellement sa dernière année d'un double programme de baccalauréat en géographie et en science politique à l'Université de Victoria. Lorsqu'elle n'est pas en train d'étudier les prières dans les assemblées législatives, les exemptions d'impôt permissives ou les centres d'aide à la grossesse, on peut la trouver sur *The View* en train de présenter « Hot Topics », un épisode de « Real Housewives » ou une réunion du groupe One Direction.

Anthony M. Weber is a doctoral candidate in political sciences at Laval University. He received a master's degree in philosophy from the Université de Lorraine as well as a master's degree in European governance from the Université du Luxembourg. His doctoral research examines parliamentary behaviour. With the goal of understanding the motivations of parliamentarians when engaging in scrutiny, his work explores both the institutional and psychological factors behind this practice.

Anthony M. Weber est candidat en doctorat de science politique à l'Université Laval. Diplômé d'une maîtrise en philosophie de l'Université de Lorraine et d'une maîtrise en gouvernance européenne de l'Université du Luxembourg, ses recherches doctorales portent sur le comportement parlementaire. Intéressé par les motivations des députés à s'impliquer dans leur fonction de contrôle, il cherche à démontrer l'importance des facteurs à la fois institutionnels et psychologiques dans la compréhension de ce phénomène.

Politics and Public Policy

Series Editor: Geneviève Tellier

There has been a resurgence of the study of politics, inspired by debates on globalization, renewed citizen engagement and demands, and transformations of the welfare state. In this context, the study of political regimes, ideas, and processes as well as that of public policy contribute to refreshing our understanding of the evolution of contemporary societies. Public policy is at the heart of political and state actions. It defines the course and the objectives adopted by governments and steering citizen initiatives and collective actions. Political analysis is increasingly complex and dynamic, embracing more diverse political, social, economic, cultural, and identity-related phenomena. The *Politics and Public Policy* series is an ideal forum in which to present titles that promote an exploration of these questions in Canada and around the world.

Recent titles in the *Politics and Public Policy Series*

Stéfanie Morris, Karina Juma, Meredith Terretta, and Patti Tamara Lenard, *Ordinary People, Extraordinary Actions: Refuge Through Activism at Ottawa's St. Joe's Parish*, 2022.

Victor Konrad and Melissa Kelly, eds., *Borders, Culture, and Globalization: A Canadian Perspective*, 2021.

Stéphanie Collin, *Lumière sur la réforme en santé au Nouveau-Brunswick : évolution, jeux d'acteurs et instruments*, 2021.

Diane Saint-Pierre and Monica Gattinger, eds., *Cultural Policy: Origins, Evolution, and Implementation in Canada's Provinces and Territories*, 2021.

Julien Landry, *Les think tanks et le discours expert sur les politiques publiques au Canada (1890-2015)*, 2020.

Sarah Todd and Sébastien Savard, eds., *Canadian Perspectives on Community Development*, 2020.

Frances Widdowson, *Separate but Unequal: How Parallelist Ideology Conceals Indigenous Dependency*, 2019.

Helaina Gaspard, *Canada's Official Languages: Policy versus Work Practice in the Federal Public Service*, 2019.

Marie Drolet, Pier Bouchard, and Jacinthe Savard, eds., *Accessibility and Active Offer: Health Care and Social Services in Linguistic Minority Communities*, 2017.

John Hilliker, *Le ministère des Affaires extérieures du Canada Volume I : les années de formation, 1909-1946*, 2017.

Monika Jezak, ed., *Language is the Key: The Canadian Language Benchmarks Model*, 2017.

Linda Cardinal and Sébastien Grammond, *Une tradition et un droit : le Sénat et la représentation de la francophonie canadienne*, 2017.

For a complete list of University of Ottawa Press titles, see:
www.press.uOttawa.ca

www.ingramcontent.com/pod-product-compliance
Lightning Source LLC
Chambersburg PA
CBHW070327270326
41926CB00017B/3791